english for international business

nick andon and
seamus o'riordan

For over 60 years, more than 40 million people have learnt over 750 subjects the **teach yourself** way, with impressive results.

be where you want to be
with **teach yourself**

For UK order enquiries: please contact Bookpoint Ltd, 130 Milton Park, Abingdon, Oxon OX14 4SB. Telephone: +44 (0) 1235 827720. Fax: +44 (0) 1235 400454. Lines are open 09.00–18.00, Monday to Saturday, with a 24-hour message answering service. Details about our titles and how to order are available at www.teachyourself.co.uk

For USA order enquiries: please contact McGraw-Hill Customer Services, PO Box 545, Blacklick, OH 43004-0545, USA. Telephone: 1-800-722-4726. Fax: 1-614-755-5645.

For Canada order enquiries: please contact McGraw-Hill Ryerson Ltd, 300 Water St, Whitby, Ontario L1N 9B6, Canada. Telephone: 905 430 5000. Fax: 905 430 5020.

Long renowned as the authoritative source for self-guided learning – with more than 40 million copies sold worldwide – the **teach yourself** series includes over 300 titles in the fields of languages, crafts, hobbies, business, computing and education.

British Library Cataloguing in Publication Data: a catalogue record for this title is available from the British Library.

Library of Congress Catalog Card Number: on file.

First published in UK 2002 by Hodder Education, 338 Euston Road, London, NW1 3BH.

First published in US 2002 by Contemporary Books, a Division of the McGraw-Hill Companies, 1 Prudential Plaza, 130 East Randolph Street, Chicago, IL 60601 USA.

This edition published 2004.

Typeset by Transet Limited, Coventry, England.
Printed in Great Britain for Hodder Education, a division of Hodder Headline, 338 Euston Road, London NW1 3BH, by Cox & Wyman Ltd, Reading, Berkshire.

Hodder Headline's policy is to use papers that are natural, renewable and recyclable products and made from wood grown in sustainable forests. The logging and manufacturing processes are expected to conform to the environmental regulations of the country of origin.

Impression number 10 9 8 7 6 5 4 3 2
Year 2010 2009 2008 2007 2006 2005

contents

acknowledgements

The authors and publishers are grateful to the following for permission to reproduce copyright material in this book:

Unilever.com: 'Unilever Our History' (p. 30–1); *BBC News Online*: (pp. 32–3) 'Unilever: A company history', 22 February 2000; *Forbes Inc.*: one extract (pp. 36–7) from 'The Super 100' Reprinted by Permission of Forbes Magazine © 2001 Forbes Inc.; *The Economist Newspaper Limited*: one extract (p. 89) from 'Big MacCurrencies' © The Economist Newspaper Limited, London (27 April 2000); *Rebecca Mowling and Associated London Metro Ltd*: (p. 93) 'Two zeros add up to £32 billion loss', *Metro*, 16 May 2001; *Fiona Joseph and EL Gazette*: for extracts (pp. 119–20) from 'A look at the most effective options available to online advertisers' by Fiona Joseph, June 2001; *BBC News Online*: (pp. 148–50) 'Q&A The Oil Business', 24 March 2000; *BBC News Online*: (pp. 152–3) 'Alternatives to oil', 8 September 2000; *Bill Saunders and the Guardian*: one extract (pp. 185–6) from 'Can an outsider do an insider's job?', 20 March 2000; *BBC News Online*: (p. 189) 'South Korea's top conglomerates present restructuring plans', 14 February 1998.

Every effort has been made to trace and acknowledge ownership of copyright. The publishers will be glad to make suitable arrangements with any copyright holders whom it has not been possible to contact.

introduction

Welcome to *Teach Yourself English for International Business!*

This course will give you practice in reading, listening, speaking and writing English in business contexts.

Who is this course for?

It is intended for people who:

- already speak some English but want to improve;
- are working in business and need English for their jobs;
- are studying business and preparing to look for jobs which require English language skills;
- have some knowledge of grammar and vocabulary but are not confident in using their English in real business situations;
- are unable to attend English language classes;
- are following a general English course but would like some extra work on business English.

Business is becoming more and more international, and English is an important language, not just to do business in the United States, Britain, Australia and other English-speaking countries, but also as an international language, used when Japanese business people talk to Russian business people, Indonesians to Spanish, Brazilians to Saudi Arabians. In your business career you may find yourself visiting or working in an English-speaking country, working in a company where English is widely spoken, or using English as a medium of communication with other business people from all over the world. You will need to be aware not only of language differences but also of cultural differences that affect the way you talk to people from other countries.

What does the course provide?

The book contains **18 units**, including three for checking your progress, plus an **answer key** and a **language reference** section.

The units consist of: **conversations** set in a business context for you to listen to and answer questions about; **articles and reading texts** about business topics; **activities that focus on the language** in the listening and reading texts; activities to practise **speaking** in specific business situations; activities to practise **writing** business letters, e-mails and CVs; **suggestions for further practice** that you can do on your own.

There are also **recordings** to enable you to get the maximum benefit from the course.

How to use the course

Some useful tips for teaching yourself

1 Think about why you are learning English and how you will use your English. Think about the areas you are good at and the things that you are not so good at.

2 Set yourself targets for the week and for the month. Decide how much you are going to study and what you want to achieve in this time. Set realistic targets that you know you will be able to achieve in the time available.

3 Try to set yourself regular times to study each day or each week. A little and often (half an hour a day) is best.

4 When you sit down to study, it is also a good idea to get everything ready. You will probably need a notebook to write answers in, pens and pencils, a small notebook to record new vocabulary, and your dictionary.

5 If at all possible, use the recording. The listening exercises should be done without reading the conversations. You can read them later.

6 After you have done the listening exercises, you can listen to the conversations again. Many people find it useful to listen in the car or when they are travelling on the bus or train.

7 Once you have studied the exercises in the unit, find ways to use them for further practice. Study the vocabulary in the reading texts and use your dictionary to check the words you do not know. Study the pronunciation in the conversations and record yourself speaking.

8 Think about buying a good dictionary and a grammar reference book.
9 Combine the exercises in this book with other ways to practise your English, for example reading newspapers and business journals, writing letters or keeping a diary in English, listening to the news on the TV, watching videos in English, and finding opportunities to speak to people in English. You will find suggestions for extra work at the end of each unit, and in **Taking it further** at the back of this book.

Using the recording

All the listening passages are recorded and are in grey in the book. If you are studying without these, you can read a written version of the conversations in the book. However, it is much more useful to listen to the conversation without reading the text.

Most listening activities follow this pattern:

1 A **pre-listening activity** to make you think about the topic and prepare you to listen. Sometimes you will be asked to make predictions about what you are going to listen to. In real life this is a good strategy to help you understand and you probably do it all the time without thinking.
2 A **general listening task**. The first task is usually just for general comprehension. The best way to do this is to read the questions before you listen and find the answers while you are listening. Don't worry if you don't understand every word. You don't need to. If you feel unsure about the answers, you can listen again or look in the answer key at the back of the book. However, if you are fairly confident about the answers, go on and do the next listening activity. You can check your answers later.
3 **Listen for the details**. The second listening task is usually more detailed, so you will need to listen again carefully. It is better if you try to do this without reading the written version.
4 **Language exercises** focusing on the vocabulary, grammar and functions in the listening, so that you can study these in the context of the whole conversation.

Here are some other ideas for making use of the recorded conversations:

- You don't need to learn the conversations word for word. However, you could repeat them to practise your pronunciation. It is a good idea to try to make similar conversations adapting the ideas to your own company or your own job.
- Record your own conversation.
- Look up any useful words and expressions that you do not know and make a note of them. (See notes on learning vocabulary below.)

Try to find other opportunities to listen to English, such as the news on the radio or on cable TV. You can also listen to the news via the internet on websites like BBC Business News. Other ideas include watching English language videos (with the subtitles covered up), attending lectures and talks in English, or taking part in conversations in English with visitors, tourists or just with friends who want to practise their English with you. Don't worry if you don't understand everything, but try to make predictions based on the context, and try to understand the overall meaning before you worry about the details.

Using the reading texts

1 As with listening, before you read, it is a good idea to **make predictions** about what you are going to read. Try to guess from the title what the article is about, and think what you already know about this topic. The pre-reading activities will help you to make predictions and use your background knowledge.

2 The first reading tasks usually expect you to get **a general idea of what the text is about**. This is called 'skimming' a text. When you read for the first time, don't worry if you don't understand every word. The important thing is to identify the topic and the main points.

3 When you understand the general idea of the text, you can go back and read again. The second reading task usually helps you to **understand the details** of the text.

4 Now that you understand what the text is about, you can look for new vocabulary and study the grammar that you will find in the reading text. If you don't understand a word, you can try to use the context to guess the meaning.

Some of the reading texts can also be heard on the recording. These texts will contain many new useful words. When you learn the meaning of a new word you should also learn its pronunciation. Remember that we do not always say a word the way it is written. English is not phonetic. Most dictionaries give advice on pronunciation. Listening to these texts may also help you to develop a feeling for the rhythm and music of the English language.

Find things to read outside class. Business newspapers in English contain plenty of interesting business texts. Many English-language newspapers contain a business section. You can also read advertisements, stories, company brochures and business websites.

Learning vocabulary

1 You will come across many new words in this book, and many more if you are finding opportunities to read and listen to English outside the book. It is a good idea to try to guess the meaning:
   - **a** from the context – what is the conversation or article about?
   - **b** from the shape of the word, by analysing its parts, and thinking about similar words you already know. For example, the word *unhelpful* can be recognized easily if you have come across the parts *un-* (meaning *not*), *help*, and *–ful* (meaning the word is an adjective);
   - **c** from what you can work out about its grammar: for example, can you tell if it is a noun, verb, adverb or adjective? If it is a verb, what tense, what is the subject? If it is an adverb, which verb does it tell you about?

2 Use a dictionary. You will probably find it helpful to buy a good dictionary. Very small pocket dictionaries are probably not good enough, as they don't give all the definitions of a word. There are bilingual dictionaries (English–French, English–Japanese, etc.), monolingual dictionaries (English–English with definitions in easy-to-understand language) and specialist business dictionaries. If you are used to working with a computer, there are online dictionaries that you can use on the internet or purchase on CD.

3 Keep a vocabulary notebook. Note down words with their definitions or translations and write an example sentence. Make sure you review your vocabulary notebook regularly so that you learn the words. Become a word collector and find ways to rearrange your collection to help you remember them.

4 Look for useful expressions as well as single words, and write these down in your notebook as well.

Grammar and functions

The grammar sections in this book only deal with a few key points. We assume that most learners using this book already know the basics of English grammar. However, knowing a rule is not the same as being able to use it consistently without making mistakes.

Try to make a note of grammar rules you are not sure about. The **Language reference** section at the end of this book will help you with some areas of grammar, but you might find it helpful to buy a grammar study book. You can also study grammar online. See recommended websites in **Taking it further**.

Don't worry too much about grammar mistakes. It is important to be able to understand and communicate. The more you practise, the less often you will make these mistakes.

It can be helpful to think about how you would say the same thing in your own language. If you are aware of the differences, you are more likely to remember the rule in English and less likely to translate word for word.

Writing and speaking

There are exercises in this book to practise writing and speaking. Sometimes you will just be writing sentences. Other times you will need to write letters or write whole conversations like the ones in the book. This is all valuable practice, so try to find the time to do these longer exercises, even though you may find they take a little time.

Record yourself speaking, if possible with a friend. Then listen to your own conversations and concentrate on areas to improve.

Look for opportunities to talk to or write to people in English. Some suggestions:

a Find a 'study buddy' – another person who wants to study English – and try to meet regularly to practise the conversations and situations in the book, as well as ordinary conversations about yourself.

b If you are working in an English-speaking environment, use English as much as possible. Don't worry about making mistakes, grammar will improve with practice.

c Write letters to companies, for example, enquiring about products and services.

d Find pen friends or key pals (e-mail pen friends) and write to them regularly.

Taking it further

See the suggestions at the end of this book for practising business English. If you have access to the internet, this provides many exciting opportunities and we have included a section with useful web addresses.

Good luck with teaching yourself *English for International Business!*

companies

In this unit you will practise
- **reading about companies and what they do**
- **understanding descriptions of a company**
- **asking and answering questions about companies**
- **describing the company you work for**

Language
- **business sectors and activities**
- **word families**

Introduction

1.1 Different kinds of companies

A Are you working at the moment? Are you looking for a job? Answer these questions about your present company or about the type of company you would like to work for.

- What kind of company is it? What sector is it in (e.g. insurance, shipping, engineering, finance, consultancy, IT)?
- How large is the company? How many employees does it have?
- How many branches (factories, offices) does it have in your country? Does it operate in more than one country? Is it a multinational company?
- How old is your company? When was it founded?
- What exactly does your company do? What services does it provide? If it is a manufacturing company, what does it produce?
- Who are the customers of the business? Who do you sell goods and services to? Other companies? Or do you deal directly with members of the general public?

B Think of some well-known businesses in your country. Which of these words would you use to describe their activities?

produces manufactures designs retails distributes
provides consultancy services manages organizes imports
exports supplies markets publishes trades (in)

Example: *Microsoft designs and manufactures computer software.*

C Check in a dictionary what these words mean.

Reading 1

1.2 Skim reading – Describing companies

When you read something in English, it is a good idea to **skim read** it first, to get a general idea. Then you can read again more carefully.

- Read quickly

- Don't worry if you don't understand every word
- Look for the key words
- Think about the topic and the main ideas

Now read these descriptions of three businesses quickly to find the answers to these questions.

1 Which company is in the manufacturing sector?
2 What sectors are the other two companies in?
3 Which company is the newest?
4 Which company has the largest number of employees?
5 Which company has offices in the greatest number of countries?

MULTIMEDIA SOLUTIONS INCORPORATED

At Multimedia Solutions Incorporated we have been designing and managing state-of-the-art commercial websites since 1993. We provide e-commerce solutions for large and small companies in a number of sectors, including business consultancy, travel and tourism and insurance services, from a simple web presence to complete e-commerce solutions.

At present we have over 200 full time internet consultants and web designers on our permanent staff. Specialist e-commerce teams have wide experience providing consultancy services and setting up and managing sites to meet the requirements of different sectors. We have specialist web design teams working in the following sectors:

- financial services
- insurance brokering and underwriting
- travel services
- computer retailing
- vehicle leasing.

Our head office is in Guildford, near London. We also have offices in Birmingham, Manchester and Edinburgh, as well as agencies in Dublin, Paris, Rome and Madrid.

BENTON INTERNATIONAL POWDERS

Peter Benton founded Benton International Powders Limited in 1979 to manufacture the epoxy resin powder paint he had invented. The powder, when sprayed onto metal and heated in an oven, provides a flexible and durable coating that protects the metal underneath from corrosion. It is used in metal shelving, lampshades, vehicle components, metal garden furniture and thousands of other products.

In the early years it was a very small but profitable business with only six employees working out of a small factory in Surrey. In 1987 International Paints bought shares in the company and invested in its expansion. It is now the largest manufacturer and distributor of industrial powder paints in Europe, and employs 480 staff in six plants in the UK. It exports to 23 countries and last year turnover exceeded £25 million with profits of £4.8 million. Since 1999 the company's head office is in Birmingham near the main factory. The original factory in Surrey is now the site of Benton International Powders' R & D division, one of the world's leading centres of expertise in metalwork paint finishes.

BUSINESS TRAVEL LIMITED

Business Travel Limited is a specialist travel agency providing travel services exclusively for corporate travel. BTL's main office is in London where the company first started up in 1989. It now has 26 offices throughout Europe and in New York and Los Angeles in the United States.

BTL has built up extensive partnerships with a wide range of airlines, hotels and other partners in over 50 countries, and can offer economical travel solutions to large and small businesses. In addition to travel and accommodation arrangements, the company provides a range of services including country briefings before departure and arrangement of meetings and seminars abroad. Major clients include Shell Petroleum, the House of Fraser retail group and IBM (UK) and the company has over 200 travel executives out of a total staff of 270. Last year sales reached £33 million with profits of £1.3 million.

1.3 Read for details – Company profiles

Read the information about the three companies again and fill in the company profile chart below.

Company name	*Business Travel Limited*		
Main area of business		*Website design*	
Products / Services			
Customers			
Location: Head office Subsidiaries		*Guildford*	
When did it start up?			*1979*
Number of employees			*480*
Other information			

Language focus

1.4 Word families

In English, when you add the suffix *-er* (or sometimes *-or*) to a verb, it usually refers to the person who does that activity, e.g.

to teach a teacher to grow a grower to act an actor

Sometimes adding *-er* changes the verb to a noun that describes a tool or machine used to carry out the action:

a cook

a cooker **(not the person but the machine used for cooking food)**

With certain verbs describing the activities of a company (e.g. *to manufacture, to export, to insure*) adding *-er* (or sometimes *-or*) makes a noun which describes the company rather than the people who work in it.

*Benton International Powders is a paint **manufacturer**.*
*Marks and Spencer is a British clothing **retailer** and **exporter**.*
*VNU, a Dutch company, is the **publisher** of many British magazines including* PC World, Computer Active *and* What PC.
*European Autos is the British **distributor** for BMW & Volkswagen spare parts.*

There are different ways to form the noun that describes an area of business:

to publish a publisher publishing
*Our main business is **publishing** but we are also involved in television and radio.*

to produce a producer production
*Ford has stopped **production** of cars in Britain after more than 90 years.*

to manufacture a manufacturer manufacture (no change from verb form)
*Ford's plant at Longbridge will in future be used for the **research, design** and **manufacture** of diesel engines.*

The table below shows some of the verbs that are used to describe company activities, and the nouns associated with each one.

Verb (describing an activity)	Noun (for the company that is involved in this activity)	Noun (for the activity or sector that a company is involved in)
to manufacture	a manufacturer	manufacture or manufacturing
to produce	a producer	production
to export	an exporter	export
to design	a designer*	design
to distribute	a distributor N.B. note spelling	distribution
to supply	a supplier	supply
to market	————	marketing
to provide	a provider	provision
to publish	a publisher	publication
to trade	a trader	trade
to organize	an organizer*	organization
to sell	————	sale / sales
to retail	a retailer	retail retailing
to export	an exporter	export

to manage	a manager*	management
to insure	an insurer	insurance
to operate	an operator*	operation

* some of these nouns could also be used to describe a person's job as well as a company's activities.

Practice

A Add some more words to this list.

B Match these well-known company names with their activities in the box below. Use these words in sentences to describe what different companies do.

1 American Express _banking_
2 Amtrak ____________________
3 AOL Time Warner ____________________
4 Granada ____________________
5 HSBC ____________________
6 IBM ____________________
7 International Insurers Incorporated ____________________
8 Microsoft ____________________
9 Nortel Networks ____________________
10 Petromin ____________________
11 Royal Dutch Shell ____________________
12 Saatchi & Saatchi ____________________
13 Sony ____________________
14 The *Economist* Group ____________________
15 Toyota ____________________
16 Unilever ____________________
17 Walmart ____________________

advertising	hotels and catering
information technology	manufacture of consumer electronics
television production and broadcasting	operation and management of the rail network
food and soap manufacture	broadcasting and internet
petroleum production	design of computer software
publishing	electrical and electronics retailer
banking	retailing foods and consumer products
computer hardware manufacture	
motor car manufacture	
insurance	

1.5 Vocabulary – Companies

The following nouns are useful to describe large companies and their parts:

agency	branch	business	company
parent company	department	distribution centre	division
enterprise	factory	firm	head office
headquarters	main office	office	sister company
plant	production facility	multinational	
subsidiary	warehouse	conglomerate	section
group of companies	chain	franchise	

Practice

Group together the words with similar meanings from the list above:

Example:

a company *a business* *a firm* *an enterprise*

1 a factory
2 a warehouse
3 a subsidiary
4 the head office
5 a department
6 a multinational

Reading 2

1.6 A group of companies – Kingfisher plc

Complete the description of Kingfisher plc, with one word for each space. You can look at the missing words in the box opposite, or you can try to complete the description without looking for these words.

Kingfisher plc was (1) __________ in 1983 under the name of Woolworth Holdings, and changed its name to Kingfisher in 1989. It is one of the largest retail (2) __________ in Europe, with over 1,300 stores and over 90,000 (3) __________. Although the Kingfisher group is not so well known, its (4) __________ companies in the UK include famous (5) __________ such as B&Q and Comet. It also (6) stores selling home improvement goods, furniture and tools and

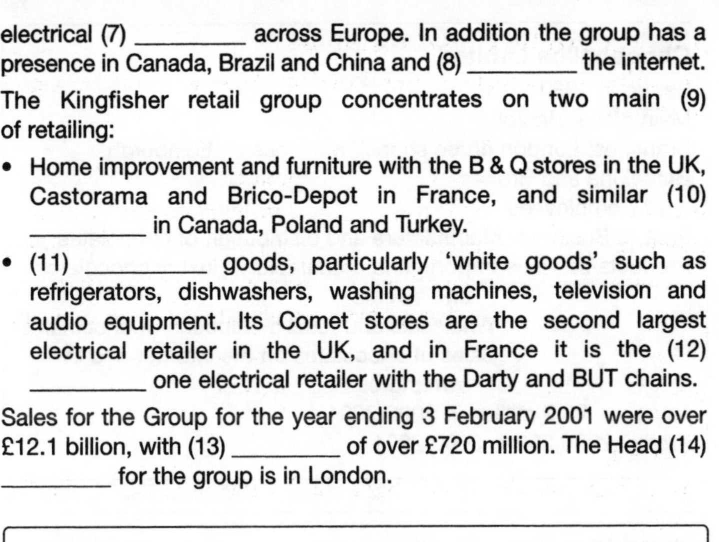

electrical (7) __________ across Europe. In addition the group has a presence in Canada, Brazil and China and (8) __________ the internet.

The Kingfisher retail group concentrates on two main (9) __________ of retailing:

- Home improvement and furniture with the B & Q stores in the UK, Castorama and Brico-Depot in France, and similar (10) __________ in Canada, Poland and Turkey.
- (11) __________ goods, particularly 'white goods' such as refrigerators, dishwashers, washing machines, television and audio equipment. Its Comet stores are the second largest electrical retailer in the UK, and in France it is the (12) __________ one electrical retailer with the Darty and BUT chains.

Sales for the Group for the year ending 3 February 2001 were over £12.1 billion, with (13) __________ of over £720 million. The Head (14) __________ for the group is in London.

established	on	groups	office	employees	profits	subsidiary
brands	owns	chains	number	electrical	areas	across	goods

1.7 Describing a company

Choose at least one of the following activities. If you like, you can do more than one, or all three.

A Look at the information about these companies. Write a short profile of one of them for a website, company brochure or newspaper article.

B Look at the information about these companies. Give a short talk about one of them to visitors who have come to find out about the company. If possible, record your talk and listen to it.

C Research your own company or a well-known company in your country. Write a short description about the company following the models in this unit.

When you have finished, read/listen to your description, and see if you can improve it.

Chocoholica Limited
Set up in 1990
Main office: Bristol
Branches: London (three shops), Manchester, Edinburgh, Barcelona and Bruges
217 employees
Area of Business: Manufacture and distribution of chocolates
Products/services: Imports and manufactures luxury chocolates and sweets
Wholesale and retail distribution of chocolates
Sales of chocolates on the internet and in own stores
Turnover: £3.7 million in 2000/2001
Profits: £920,000 in 2000/2001

Ryanair
Set up in 1985
Main office: London
Subsidiary offices: Dublin, Brussels
1,400 employees
Area of business: Low cost European airline
Products/services: Low cost flights between London, Ireland, Scotland, European and Scandinavian Airports. Internet booking services for over 90% of flight bookings
Turnover in 2000/2001: €487.4m
Profits in 2000/2001: €104.4m
Other information: Now UK's second largest airline, Europe's largest budget airline.
7 million passengers per year over 45 routes across 11 European countries served with a fleet of 31 aircraft.

Reading 3

1.8 Company organization

Read this description of the organization and structure of Benton International Powders, which is a subsidiary of International Paints, and find the answer to these questions:

1 How many divisions does the company consist of (in addition to Head Office)?
2 Which division is responsible for transportation?
3 Where are the company's production facilities located?
4 Which division is responsible for quality control?
5 Where is the European Distribution Centre?
6 What functions are carried out in the company's Guildford plant?

Benton International Powders consists of three divisions, Production, Research and Development, and Marketing, plus the Head Office division. Each division is under the overall management of a senior manager who reports directly to the Managing Director.

The Production Division is the largest in terms of numbers of staff, and also in terms of the space it occupies. The Production Manager is based in the Head Office in Birmingham and has overall responsibility for five manufacturing plants, in Birmingham, Leicester, Salford, Glasgow and South East London. In addition, the Logistics Department, which is also part of the Production Division, includes a number of distribution centres, the largest of which is the European Distribution Centre in Faversham, in Kent. The Logistics Department organizes deliveries, supplies of raw materials and stock maintenance.

The Marketing Division is also based in the company's Head Office in Birmingham and employs about 35 staff. The Marketing Division is responsible for advertising and marketing the firm's products, dealing with orders and customer relations and handling customer payments and accounts. These roles involve close co-ordination with the Production Division and the Logistics Department, as well as the Finance Department which is part of Head Office.

The Research and Development Division is based at the company's plant in Guildford in Surrey. That is actually where the firm's original factory was when the business started up in 1979, but now the site is only used for R&D. As well as the development of new products, the Research and Development Division has a quality control function, for example testing samples of paints produced in all the manufacturing plants. The R&D division also provides technical assistance to customers, for example advising on types of paints to use for different purposes, and advising customers about the processes they need to use.

The Company's Head Office, under the Managing Director, has overall control of the company and co-ordinates the other divisions, to make sure that they all work together smoothly. In addition the Finance and Personnel Departments are attached to Head Office and come under the direct control of the Managing Director.

Language focus

1.9 The organization of a company

A Look at this organization chart for Benton International Powders.

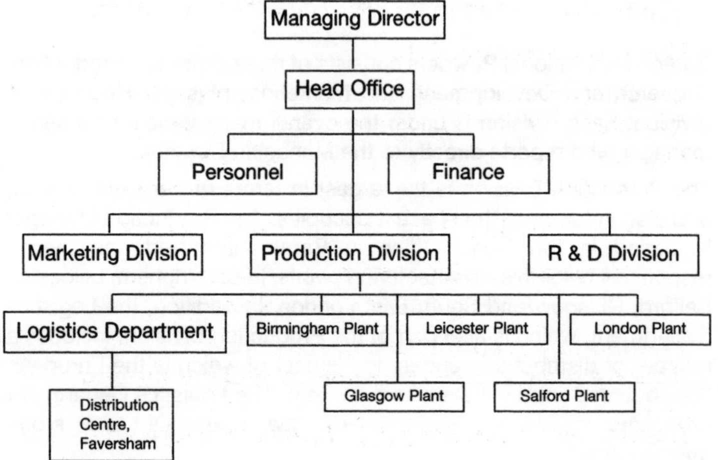

B Now talk/write about the organization of the company using these expressions:

The company ***is divided into*** *three divisions.*
consists of
is made up of
is organized into
has (got)
There are *three divisions in the company.*

The personnel department ***is part of*** *the company's Head Office.*
comes under
is under the control of
is the responsibility of

The company ***owns*** *five factories in Great Britain.*
has got
has

C Find the organization chart for your own company, or another company, and write about it in a similar way.

Lesson summary

Here are some of the things you practised in this lesson:

- Vocabulary related to a company's activities:

  produces manufactures designs retails distributes
  provides consultancy services manages organizes imports
  exports supplies markets publishes trades (in)

- Nouns and verbs (see **1.4**):

to produce	a producer	production
to export	an exporter	export
to design	a designer	design
to distribute	a distributor	distribution

- Vocabulary for describing large companies (see **1.9**):

  head office a department an agency a plant
  a distribution centre sister company

The company ***is divided into*** *three divisions.*
Business Travel Limited ***is organized into*** *five regional groups.*
International Paints ***has got*** *17 factories throughout the EU.*

The personnel department ***is part of*** *the company's Head Office.*
Accounts, sales and payroll are all ***under the control of*** *the finance director.*

Suggestions for further practice

1 Find out more about Kingfisher plc by looking at the company's website: http://www.kingfisher.com

2 Pick a company you have heard of and try to find out the key facts about it. Collect company brochures or find the information in the newspaper, in journals or on the internet.

3 Look at company profiles (in English if possible) and compare them to the information that you have read in this unit. Do they provide the same kinds of information? How are they different? What else do they tell you? What information do they leave out?

4 Copy the word families from **1.4** into a vocabulary notebook. See if you can add more examples of words that describe

business activities. Then think of some more topics for word families (e.g. *jobs* and *occupations*, *travel*, *money* and *finance*) and build up similar tables in your notebook.

5 Choose another exercise from **1.7** or do the same exercise again. It is helpful to repeat tasks and try to do them better each time.

6 Do exercise C from **1.9** or one of the exercises from **1.7**, this time using information from a different company.

7 Go through company profiles and look for words you are not familiar with. Try to find groups of words, for example make a list of all the words relating to the different parts of a company (*branch, subsidiary, parent company, head office*) or all the words relating to places and buildings (*site, factory, plant, regional office, distribution centre*) or money and finance (*profit, turnover, income, investment, loan*). Record these groups of words in a vocabulary notebook and learn how to use them.

02 jobs and introductions

In this unit you will practise

- **introducing yourself and other people you work with**
- **meeting people who work in a company**
- **asking and answering questions about jobs**

Language

- **job titles and job descriptions**
- **duties and responsibilities**
- **forms of address**
- **present simple tense**

Introduction

2.1 Job titles

Do you have a job at the moment? What is your job title in English? What job would you like to have in the future?

What other job titles do you know in English? How many can you think of? Write a list.

Do activity **A** or **B**.

A Look in an English-language newspaper that has job advertisements, or find a website on the internet that has job advertisements. (See **Suggestions for further practice** at the end of this unit.) Make a list of job titles. Use a dictionary of business English to find out what they all mean.

B Make a list of business job titles in your own language. You can just do this from memory, or you can look in a newspaper or website in your own language. Then try to translate all the job titles into English. Use a business dictionary to help you.

2.2 Pre-listening vocabulary

Match the business cards on the left with the job descriptions on the right.

1 JB Computers Ltd
Mary Black
Personnel Manager

2 Watermans Books plc
Andrew Neill
Finance Director

3 ABC Systems
John Smith
Managing Director

a Works closely with a senior executive. Manages the executive's diary, arranges travel and meetings, provides secretarial support such as typing, filing, answering the telephone.

b Is in charge of the arrangements for recruiting new staff, handling employees' problems, managing appraisal and personnel training, dealing with employment problems.

c Takes overall responsibility for the company's accounts, and controls money coming into and going out of the company. Advises the managing director on decisions related to finance.

4

Asia Tours
Dewi Sutanto
PA to the Head of Marketing

d Helps develop the IT skills of employees. Teaches basic PC skills and shows people how to use different software packages.

5

MRS Industrial Machinery
Noriko Kensuke
Technical Sales Executive

e The head of a company. Makes all the day-to-day decisions about how the company is run.

6

King's Consultancy Ltd
Mohan Singh
IT Trainer

f Talks to customers on the phone, arranges sales and delivery of a company's products and services, meets customers to discuss their needs.

Example: 1 b

Notice that job titles may be different in Britain and the USA. For example the top executive in a British company is usually called the Managing Director (or MD). In a large US company the equivalent title is Chief Executive Officer (usually shortened to CEO).

Different companies may have different names for the same job, and there are differences between large and small companies and companies in different sectors.

Listening 1

2.3 Introductions

Jim Smith is being introduced to some of the people who work for Business Travel Limited, a company in London. Listen to the conversations and fill in the missing names and job titles on the organization chart below.

Try to complete this task and the listening questions in **2.4** without reading the text of the conversation. Cover up the text while you are listening.

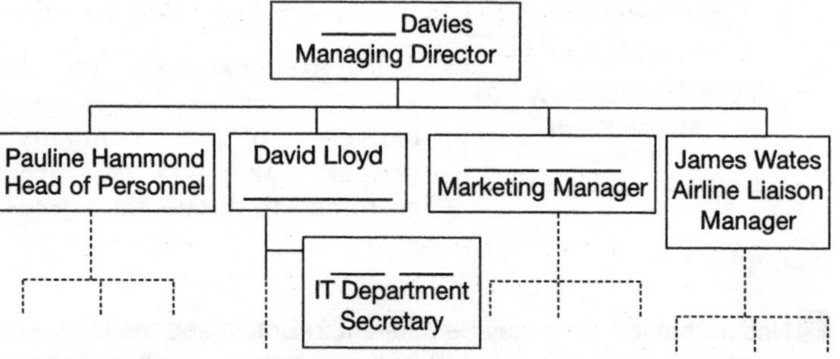

Conversation 1: in the MD's office

GD Come in. Ah, morning Pauline.
PH Hello Graham. Hope I'm not disturbing you.
GD No, I'm expecting a visitor at ten though.
PH I just wanted to introduce you to Jim Smith from the Los Angeles office. He's come over to work on the new internet project.
GD Ah, yes. Pleased to meet you, Jim. Welcome to London.
JS Thanks very much.
GD You're going to be here for three months, aren't you?
JS That's the plan. I'm really looking forward to spending so much time in England. The longest I've stayed before is a week.
GD I believe we are meeting next week to discuss our plans for the internet. On Monday, isn't it, Pauline?
PH Yes, that's right.
GD Well, I hope you settle in all right. If there's anything you need, just let Pauline or myself know.
JS Thanks very much.

Conversation 2: in the IT department of BTL

PH David, I'd like you to meet Jim Smith. Jim is co-ordinating the new website project. Jim, this is David Lloyd, he's the IT manager.
JS I think we met last year in New York. At the IT strategy meeting.
DL Yes, I remember. I was very interested in your presentation about new technologies in the travel industry. I'm very glad you agreed to come and work with us.
JS Thanks.

Conversation 3: in the IT department of BTL

PH Jim, this is Janet Andrews. She is David's secretary, and she'll also be looking after you during your stay.
JS Hello Janet.
JA Nice to meet you, Mr Smith.
JS Please, call me Jim.

Conversation 4: in Jim's new office

MH (Knocks on Jim's office door)
JS Come in.
MH Hello. Jim Smith?
JS Yes, that's right.
MH I'm Michael Hopkins. Marketing Manager. I just wanted to say hello and introduce myself.
JS Oh, right, pleased to meet you Michael. I guess we are going to be working together quite a lot.
MH Yes, that's the idea. Anyway, welcome to London. I'll leave you to settle in. Perhaps we can have lunch today or tomorrow.
JS Today would be great. Will you come and get me when you are ready?
MH Of course. At about one o'clock?
JS That's fine. See you then.
MH Okay.

2.4 Listen for the details

Listen to the conversations in 2.3 again.

True or False? Write T or F next to the statements below to show if they are True or False.

1 Graham Davies has met Jim Smith before. *F*
2 Janet Andrews is the Head of Personnel.
3 David Lloyd already knows Jim Smith.
4 Jim Smith works for an internet company.
5 Janet Andrews is going to be Jim's secretary.
6 Michael Hopkins is the Marketing Manager of BTL.
7 Michael Hopkins is going to have dinner with Jim Smith.
8 Jim Smith wants Janet to call him by his first name.
9 Pauline introduced the Marketing Manager to Jim.
10 Jim Smith is going to be working in London for about three weeks.

Correct the statements that were false. Rewrite them in your notebook.

Example:

Graham Davies has never met Jim Smith before. OR
Graham Davies is meeting Jim Smith for the first time.

Language focus

2.5 Forms of address

Look back at the conversations in **2.3** and answer these questions:

1 How do colleagues address each other at work?
   a Using *Mr/Mrs/Miss/Ms* + first name + second name?
   b Using *Mr/Mrs/Miss/Ms* + second name only?
   c Using first name + second name without *Mr/Mrs/Miss/Ms*?
   d Using first name only?
   e Using second name only?
   f Using their job title?

2 How does Pauline refer to Jim when she introduces him to different people?

3 Is this the same or different in your language?

Generally in Britain and North America people do not use titles (*Mr*, *Miss*, *Mrs*, *Ms*) when talking to colleagues. This reflects an informal working atmosphere between colleagues. However, more junior employees may use titles when addressing a senior colleague, as Janet Andrews did:

Nice to meet you, Mr Smith.
Good morning, Mrs Blackstone.

Even in this case it is normal for people who work together to use first names, so Jim says:

Please, call me Jim.

You would probably only address your boss or a senior colleague as *Sir* in very formal situations. It would be very unusual to address a senior woman colleague as *Madam* or *Ma'am*.

In some languages it is possible to address people by their title (*Herr Direktor*, *Monsieur le Directeur*). This is not usually possible in English in business situations.

Reflection and observation

- How is this different from the way you address colleagues in your first language?
- If you work in a company where English is used a lot, make a note of how different people are addressed. How formal or informal is your company?

2.6 Introducing people

Here is some useful language for introducing people:

Jim, I'd like you to meet …
I'd like to introduce you to … (more formal)
Peter, this is Jim Smith. (less formal)
Jim Smith, David Lloyd. (less formal)

In business situations, it's normal to say something about the person you are introducing.

Jim, I'd like you to meet Pauline Hammond. Pauline is the head of our Personnel Department.
This is Jim Smith. He's going to be working on the new website.
Jim, this is David Lloyd, the manager of the IT department.

I'd like you to meet Patrick Riordan from British Airways.
This is Sally Ryder, the head of customer relations at ...

This is how Michael Hopkins introduced himself:

I'm Michael Hopkins. The Marketing Manager.

Practice

Look at the business cards below. How would you introduce these people to (**a**) the MD of your company? (**b**) a colleague in your office? (**c**) each other?

David Black
IT Manager
Wentworth Travel Ltd

Andrew Jackson
Senior Marketing Manager
English Petroleum Products

Jane Saunders
Finance Director
First Class Computers

Jeremy Bowen
Personnel Assistant
Pearson-Riley Incorporated

Louise Watkins
Payroll Manager
Conway Transport

James Peterson
Sales Executive
Croydon Car Leasing

Maria Lopez
Customer Care Agent
Thomas Travel & Tours

Listening 2

2.7 Talking about jobs

Listen to these people talking about their jobs. Then choose the best job title from the list overleaf.

	Job		Job
Speaker 1:		Speaker 2:	
Speaker 3:		Speaker 4:	
Speaker 5:		Speaker 6:	
Speaker 7:		Speaker 8:	

a E-commerce Co-ordinator
b Sales Manager
c Secretary
d Personnel Manager
e PA to the MD
f Receptionist
g Accountant
h Finance Manager
i Technician
j Sales Executive
k External Relations Director
l Ticketing Agent
m Customer Care Agent

1 My job is to look after the employees in the company. I am responsible for recruitment, so if any department needs new staff my department prepares job advertisements and information about the post, draws up a shortlist of the best candidates, arranges interviews and then helps with the interview itself. I also co-ordinate staff training in the company, and deal with problems related to pay, pensions, promotion and so on. My department holds records on every employee in the company and so I have to make sure that we comply with the Data Protection Act.

2 My job is to work with the sales and marketing departments to help them develop a strategy for internet based commerce. We don't design the company site ourselves, we use an outside contractor, but obviously I have to work with them to make sure our website works the way we want it to, and gets maintained and updated regularly.

3 I'm responsible for sales and so obviously I'm in charge of a number of salesmen, salespeople I should say. I also help to devise the company's advertising policy, together with the marketing department.

4 Well, Charles Hawkson is the Managing Director of the company and I am his personal assistant. I organize his appointments diary, make the arrangements for meetings and business trips, answer the telephone and greet his visitors if they come to see him here. I do some typing – letters, reports and things like that, but Mr Hawkson also prepares a lot of documents directly on the computer himself. I think it's an interesting job because of the variety of things I do.

5 I'm on the front desk, greeting visitors, receiving deliveries, and also I answer the telephone. It does get pretty busy but there are usually two of us here.

6 I work under the Finance Manager and basically I keep the company's books. This means records of sales income, expenditure, taxes and so on. I'm also in charge of payroll. There is a payroll clerk who works in the personnel section but I also have to keep an eye on this area.

7 Well, basically, I sell my company's products. We are a travel company and what we do is sell airline tickets and hotel bookings. We only deal with business travel and the company advertises widely, so basically I am selling our products to people who write in or telephone. Quite a lot of our sales are done with e-mail now, and I think in the future that will become even more important.

8 I do PR for my company, which involves dealing with the press as well as members of the public. We are a large manufacturer of computer peripherals so we do prepare quite a lot of press releases about things that we are doing, new products, special deals and so on. When there are problems we tend to get a lot of enquiries from journalists so I deal with these. Also, major complaints from customers who have some sort of problem, for example if there is a very widespread problem with a particular product line, I get involved in that.

2.8 Talking about your own job

Think about your present job, or a job you had in the past, or a job you would like to have in the future.

You are going to practise explaining your job to a visitor or a new colleague.

First, make notes about these things:

- The job title
- The department or section you work in
- Your key responsibilities
- The tasks you do every day
- Who is your manager, and what is your relationship to other people in your department?

Now imagine you are explaining your job to the visitor or a new colleague. What would you say? Write down exactly what you would say and/or practise saying it out loud. If you need help, you can use the framework below or look at the **Lesson summary** at the end of this unit.

I'm the/a ______________________________
I work in the ________________________ section/department
I'm responsible for ______________________________________.
I ______________________ and ________________________.
I work under ________________________.
(I supervise the work of ____________________________.)
(I work with ___________________________________.)

Language focus

2.9 Job titles

Look at these words which are often found in job titles:

Senior	Sales	Director
Assistant	Managing	Manager
Vice	Personnel	Assistant
Deputy	Marketing	Accountant
Executive	Human Resources Development	Officer
Personal	Financial	Controller
Chief	Customer Services	Executive
Head of	Accounts	Secretary
Director of	IT	Technician
Assistant to	Public relations	Advisor

These words can be combined in different ways to describe different jobs:

Personal Assistant to the Managing Director
Senior Sales Executive
Sales Assistant
Customer Services Manager
Director of Financial Services
Customer Accounts Advisor
Personnel Officer
Chief Financial Officer
Head of Human Resources Development

Note the use of prepositions:

PA to the Accounts Manager
Head of Financial Services
Assistant to the Director of Marketing and Sales

Practice

Put these jumbled-up words back in the right order to make sentences about people's jobs. Check your answers with the recording.

Example: PA the to director I'm managing the — *I'm the PA to the managing director.*

1 head of he's the department the finance ______
2 an PricewaterhouseCoopers she's with accountant ______
3 Airways from British he's ______
4 sales department she works of the for ICL ______
5 for they American work in Express traveller's division the cheque ______

Try to find more ways of combining these in job titles. Look at the jobs pages in newspapers or on the internet and see which combinations you can find.

2.10 Duties and responsibilities

Here is some of the language that people use to talk about what they do in their jobs. Notice that the **present simple tense** is used to talk about job responsibilities and duties.

Chief Financial Officer: *I am in charge of the accounts and finances of the company.*
Personnel Officer: *I am responsible for recruitment and training of staff.*
IT Manager: *I run the IT section.*
Head of Sales Department: *I manage a sales team of 25.*
Customer Relations Officer: *I deal with customer complaints.*
Secretary: *I type letters and reports, answer the telephone and organize meetings.*
Purchasing Officer: *I liaise with our suppliers in different countries.*

Accountant: *I check that invoices are correct, I authorize payments and I prepare account statements for customers.*

See **Language reference** section at the end of the book for notes on present simple tense.

Pronunciation note

Notice that when you use the third person ending, (*-s* or *-es*) the verb sometimes has an extra syllable:

manage (two syllables), ***manages*** (three syllables), *liaise* (two syllables), ***liaises*** (three syllables).

1 Find two other verbs in the statements above that add an extra syllable like this.

____________ ____________

2 Practise talking about other people's jobs, like this.
The IT Manager runs the IT section.
The Head of the Sales Department manages a sales team of 25.

Lesson summary

Here are some of the things you practised in this lesson:

- Job titles and responsibilities:
  Managing Director
  Personal Assistant
  Personnel Manager
  Chief Financial Officer
  Sales Executive
  Senior Customer Relations Officer

  I liaise with airlines and travel companies, and I organize travel and accommodation for business travellers.
  Paul is in charge of the IT section and he manages the technicians and IT support staff.
  She deals with customer complaints.
  They prepare accounts for customers, check invoices and authorize payments.

- Introducing yourself and other people:
  Hello, I'm David Haynes, the Director of Marketing.
  This is Pauline Hammond, our Head of Personnel.
  David, I'd like you to meet Jane Bruton from KCLE.

- Ways to address colleagues:
  Hello, Mike. Morning Jan.
  Good morning Mr Matthews. Excuse me, Mrs Baxter.

Suggestions for further practice

1 Research job titles in your company. Find your company's organization chart (or make your own). Find out what the different job titles are and what they mean. Write about some of the jobs in more detail.

2 Imagine you are showing someone around your department. What will they see? Who will they meet? Think of some questions the visitor might ask you about people's jobs. Then practise the dialogue – say it out loud (if you are in a quiet place) or write it.

3 Look for job advertisements in a newspaper (for example the *International Herald Tribune* or the *Financial Times*) or a website that advertises jobs. Make a note of different job titles you find, especially jobs in your own field, or ones that interest you. Note down any information that is provided about the duties and responsibilities of the post. Look up any words that are not clear to you.

4 Look at some business dictionaries and some general English dictionaries and see which one is the most helpful and easiest for you to use. It is a good idea to consider both bilingual dictionaries (e.g. French–English) and monolingual dictionaries (where all the definitions are in English and there are no translations into your first language). Buy a good dictionary and spend a little time learning to use it well.

5 Have you started keeping a notebook of useful vocabulary? You can write down words you find in this book as well as business English words you find for yourself. Organize your vocabulary notebook so that you will remember the meaning of the words and how they are used. Review the words frequently until you have learned them.

6 Do some research on introductions in your company, or any English-speaking company you visit. Notice the way people introduce themselves and others. Make notes about what you have noticed.

7 Think of different situations where you might have to introduce yourself and/or other people. Write some dialogues and practise them.

multinational companies

In this unit you will practise

- **comparing two different accounts of a multinational company**
- **extracting information from tables of company figures**

Language

- **vocabulary building: international business**
- **word partnerships**

Introduction

3.1 Multinationals and countries

- Sony, which is based in Japan, and Coca Cola, based in the USA, are companies that operate in many countries. Can you name any other multinationals?
- What do you know about the following companies? Complete the table using the words in the box below:

	Country	Business Activity
Microsoft	*USA*	*computer software*
Volkswagen		
Unilever		
Hitachi		
Barclays		

Countries: UK Japan Germany UK & Netherlands
Business activities: automobiles electronic equipment banking household products

Reading 1

3.2 Skimming and scanning the text

Unilever is one of the biggest companies in the world. You are going to read an article about its history and development.

1 Which paragraph discusses brands?
2 When did the company begin to sell ice cream?

Unilever has a rich and colourful history spanning more than 70 years

A Unilever was formed in 1930 when the Dutch margarine company Margarine Unie merged with the British manufacturer of soap Lever Brothers. Both companies were competing for the same raw materials, both were involved in large-scale marketing of household products and both used similar distribution channels. Between them, they had operations in over 40 countries. Margarine Unie grew through mergers with other margarine companies in the 1920s. Lever Brothers was founded in 1885 by William Hesketh Lever. Lever established soap factories around the world. In 1917, he began to diversify into foods, acquiring fish, ice cream and canned foods businesses.

B In the 1930s, Unilever introduced improved technology to the business. The business grew and new ventures were launched in Latin America. The entrepreneurial spirit of the founders and their caring approach to their employees and their communities remain at the heart of Unilever's business today.

C Unilever NV* and Unilever plc are the parent companies of what is today one of the largest consumer goods businesses in the world. Since 1930, the two companies have operated as one, linked by a series of agreements and shareholders that participate in the prosperity of the whole business. Unilever's corporate centres are in London and Rotterdam.

D Today, Unilever is a supplier of consumer goods in foods, household care and personal product categories. The company also has other operations, mainly plantations in Africa and Malaysia. Famous brands include Dove, Lipton, Magnum ice cream, Omo and Cif.

[Source: http://www.unilever.com]

*NV (Naamloze venootschap) is Dutch for 'Public Limited Company'.

3.3 Understanding text organization

Choose a heading for each of the four paragraphs in the text from the suggestions below.

Early growth ___
Organization ___
Product range ___
A new company ___

3.4 Vocabulary

Choose the best meaning from **a**, **b** and **c** for each word or expression in **3.2**.

1 merged (*line* 2) means
- **a** worked closely together
- **b** became one company
- **c** bought

2 distribution channels (*line* 6) means
- **a** ways of getting the product to the consumer
- **b** ways of finding customers
- **c** ways of contacting suppliers

3 founded (*line 9*) means
- a discovered
- b established
- c acquired

4 entrepreneurial spirit (*line 15*) means
- a qualities needed for business success
- b a free spirit
- c a sense of responsibility

5 parent companies (*line 18*) means
- a a similar company
- b family of companies
- c principal company within a group of companies

3.5 Writing a summary

The following is a summary of the text in 3.2. Fill in the missing words. Listen and check your answers on the recording or in the **Answer key.**

When Margarine Unie and Lever Brothers __________ in 1930 they became a multinational __________ with interests in over 40 countries. The organization has continued to grow ever since and today is one of the largest __________ __________ businesses in the world. Famous __________ are Lipton, Magnum ice cream and Dove. The headquarters are in __________ and Britain.

Reading 2

3.6 'Unilever: A Company History'

Now read a different article about the history of Unilever.

From ice cream to washing powder, Anglo-Dutch group Unilever is one of the world's biggest makers of household goods. The consumer goods giant grew out of a merger in 1930 between Dutch margarine company Margarine Unie and British soapmaker Lever Brothers. Seventy years later, it has lost out to US rivals Proctor & Gamble and Colgate–Palmolive. Its response to the increased competition is to axe jobs and cull some of its brands.

The Sunlight company

Lever Brothers was founded in 1885 by William Hesketh Lever with his brother James. The company produced Sunlight, the world's first packaged, branded laundry soap. Mr Lever established a reputation as a social reformer, championing a shorter work day, savings plans, libraries and health benefits. He built Port Sunlight, a tree-lined employee village outside Liverpool. His empire originally consisted of soap factories. But in 1917, he decided to diversify into foods. He bought fish, ice cream and canned foods businesses. In 1930, he chose Margarine Unie as a merger partner. The Dutch company had grown through mergers with other margarine companies in the 1920s. The logic for the Anglo–Dutch merger was clear: animal fats were the raw materials for both margarines and soaps. The new company dabbled in many different areas. During the Second World War it helped make tank periscopes and soldiers' rations. In the 1950s, it moved into chemicals, packaging, market research and advertising. By 1980, soap and edible fats contributed to just 40% of profits, compared with an original 90%.

Persil power

In recent years, the company has faced increasing pressure from US rivals Proctor & Gamble and Colgate–Palmolive. The launch of Persil Power was scuppered by the finding that far from cleaning clothes, it destroyed them. Niall Fitzgerald, who introduced Persil Power, now heads the company. He got the job as UK chairman in September 1996, when Unilever streamlined its management. Since the mid-1980s, the company has got rid of its packaging companies, most of its agribusiness and its speciality chemicals business. This left it with home and personal care, and foods. The company then embarked on a spending spree in these three areas. It bought Brooke Bond tea in 1984 and later the Fabergé/Elizabeth Arden brands. Back in the UK, its ice cream brands – which include Magnum – have been hit by competition investigations. In 2000, the government called on the three ice cream companies to end the trading agreements with retailers which abuse their monopoly power.

[Source: BBC News Online 'Unilever: A Company History' (22 February 2000)]

3.7 Vocabulary

Find the words in the text which have the same meaning as the words listed below:

1 reduce staff (lines 5–10)
2 basic ingredients (lines 15–20)
3 reason (lines 15–20)
4 became involved (lines 20–25)
5 ruined (lines 25–30)
6 agricultural business (lines 35–40)
7 a period when there was much buying (lines 35–40)

Building your vocabulary

Language learners often try to learn lists of new vocabulary. While this is useful it can also mean that you have difficulty knowing how to use the words. Learning 'word partnerships' can be helpful. These are two (or more) word expressions which appear frequently, e.g. *raw materials*, *household products*, *parent company*. You will also find it helpful to build diagrams of word partnerships, for example the word company has many partners:

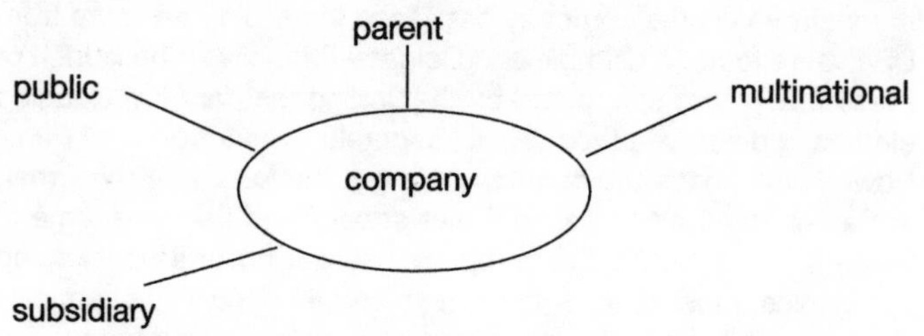

Can you add any more words?

3.8 Time line

Complete the time line of Unilever's history:

Year
1885 ____________________
1917 ____________________
1930 ____________________
1950s ____________________
1980s ____________________
1984 ____________________
1996 ____________________
2000 ____________________

3.9 Different types of text

Below is a list of different types of business publications. Do you read any of them in your work?

- Company annual reports
- Professional journals
- Company newsletters
- Business books
- Business travel guides
- Business newspapers

In which type of publication would you expect to see the following?

1 I am delighted to announce that Mr Chris Long has been appointed as the new Head of the Finance Department. Previously, Chris had worked as Assistant Director at Newbolds in the City.

2 City analysts were not surprised at today's dramatic announcement of Sir Christopher Blair's resignation. With falling profits and mounting debts, something had to be done to rescue the failing company.

Different approaches

An academic journal and a tabloid newspaper will vary in the way they treat a topic. The audience for the academic text will be scholars and students. The purpose will be to provide an objective and accurate account of a topic. The language will probably be formal. The tabloid newspaper on the other hand will have a mass audience and will want to entertain or persuade its readers. When reading a text ask yourself these two questions:

- Who is the intended audience for this text?
- What is the purpose (to entertain? persuade? inform? etc.)?

Answering these questions will help you to get a better understanding of the text.

Making a comparison

Compare the two histories of Unilever. How do they differ? Think about the following:

- Content: is the text critical/uncritical/trying to persuade/ trying to entertain?
- Style: Are there differences in the language, e.g. in the vocabulary?
- Interest: which was more interesting?

Where do you think the texts come from: textbook? official company history? financial magazine? newspaper?

3.10 Your company history

Produce a time line for your company. Then write a short history of your company or a company which is well known in your country.

Year ....

....

....

....

....

....

....

....

....

3.11 The world's biggest companies

This is a list of the some of the world's biggest companies:

Company	Industry	Country	Revenue ($m)	Net income ($m)	Assets ($m)	Market value ($m)	Employees (000's)
Citigroup	financial services	USA	82,005	9,994	716,937	209,613	173.5
General Electric	electronics	USA	111,630	10,717	405,200	520,686	316.5
Exxon Mobil	energy	USA	160,883	7,910	144,521	290,023	115.0
Bank of America	banking	USA	51,632	7,882	632,574	91,903	163.4

Royal Dutch Shell	energy	Holland	105,366	8,584	113,883	224,265	99.0
Ford	automobiles	USA	162,558	7,237	276,229	59,344	364.6
HSBC	banking	UK	39,348	5,408	569,139	94,105	146.9
General Motors	automobiles	USA	176,558	6,002	274,730	57,498	392.0
IBM	computer systems	USA	87,548	7,712	87,495	190,359	299.2
American Int'l Group	insurance	USA	40,656	5,055	268,238	173,503	52.3
Toyota Motor	automobiles	Japan	120,697	3,812	149,309	170,080	214.6
Wal-Mart	retailing	USA	165,013	5,575	70,245	258,963	1,025.0
Unilever	household goods	Holland	41,418	2,801	26,773	48,462	255.0

3.12 Comprehension – check your understanding

1 Match the terms and the definitions:

a revenue	i anything of value belonging to a company
b net income	ii the amount left after payment of all expenses and taxes
c assets	iii how much it would be worth if sold
d market value	iv all the money received by a company/ person during a specific period (also known as earnings)

2 Which company has the largest
- a revenue?
- b net income?
- c assets?
- d market value?
- e number of employees?

3 How many countries are represented in this table?

4 Does the list include any IT companies?

5 What kind of companies appear most often in the list?

6 Fill in the gaps in the report below. Listen to the recording to check your answers.

a There are ______ banking companies in the list. HSBC is from the ______ and the Bank of America is obviously from the United States. The figure for revenues from Bank of America, __________, is greater than the figure for HSBC, $39,348m. However, the __________ of HSBC, $94,105m, is greater than that of the Bank of America, $91,903m.

b Write a similar paragraph comparing the two energy companies in the list.

Suggestions for further practice

1 You can read more about Unilever at the company's website: http://www.unilever.com

2 You can read more about the world's biggest companies at http://www.forbes.com

04 job hunting

In this unit you will practise
- **understanding job advertisements**
- **talking about qualifications and experience**
- **keeping a conversation going**
- **the layout of a business letter**
- **talking about simple problems and suggestions**

Language
- **qualifications and skills**
- **work and study experience**
- **beginning and ending a business letter**
- **present perfect or simple past tense**

Introduction

4.1 Looking for a job

- Do you have a job at the moment? How did you find out about your job? Did you see it advertised? Where? In a newspaper or magazine? On a noticeboard? Did you hear about it from a friend? Or was it advertised on the TV or the radio?
- Are you looking for a job at the moment? Are you planning to start looking for a new job in the near future? What is the best place to find out about the kind of jobs you are interested in?
- Think about your present job, or, if you have not yet started working, ask a friend who has a job in business. Which of these things did you have to do to get your present job?

1 Telephone or send a letter/e-mail asking for further information.
2 Write a letter of application.
3 Fill in an application form.
4 Prepare a CV or résumé.
5 Telephone to arrange an interview appointment.
6 Attend an interview.
7 Do a test.

Which of these could you do in English?

Reading 1

4.2 Job advertisements

A Look at the job advertisements on pages 41–2 and make a list of the different job titles. There are six jobs.

1 ______________________ 4 ______________________
2 ______________________ 5 ______________________
3 ______________________ 6 ______________________

B Think about the jobs that are advertised. Which one looks most interesting to you? Why?

C Which job would you **least** like? Why?

4.3 Comprehension

Scan the advertisements below and on page 42. Which one(s)

a require a driving licence? ___
b state the exact salary? ___
c want you to send your CV? ___
d expect you to fill in an application form? ___
e do not give a postal address? ___
f ask for references or names of referees? ___
g require English plus another language? ___
h specifically mention a university degree? ___
i require some other professional qualification? ___
j offer more information on the internet? ___
k involve using computers? ___

1

Bilingual executive assistant needed. Must be efficient and well organized with fluent Spanish and English, good computing skills. US $2,500 a month.

Send a letter of application and CV to:

Personnel Department
International Insurance SA
C/Villanueva 29
28001 Madrid

2

Accountancy clerk required for expanding business and language training institute in city centre.

We are looking for a qualified accounts clerk/book-keeper who is able to handle student fees and staff salaries. Good English and Spanish. Familiarity with computerized accounts.

Certificate in book-keeping level 3 or equivalent.

Please send CV and the names and addresses of 2 referees to:

USA College of English & Business
Paseo de Gracia 116 bis
28078 Barcelona

3

Business Graduates

We are a large financial consultancy agency looking to recruit between 50 and 100 executive trainees for posts throughout our European network. After initial training, successful applicants will be based in one of our regional offices, providing financial consultancy and planning advice on products including pensions, life assurance, savings, investments and taxes.

Good package plus incentives. Interested?

Phone 01723 590 8080 or e-mail personnel@fse.com

FINANCIAL SERVICES EUROPE

4

ELNET ESPAÑA

Head of Marketing

We are looking for a dynamic, experienced marketing manager to develop the customer base for our Internet and Telecoms services.

For further details and an application form contact:

Srta Martha Caballero
Directora de Selección
ELNET ESPAÑA
Pº de la Castellana,
7–2a
28046 MADRID

5

Sales Executives

An established mail order and e-commerce retailer with branches in the UK and France is looking for sales executives to help us expand our presence in Spain. No experience necessary, training will be given. Reasonable salary + excellent commission. Interested? Write to:

Telemall International SA
119 Paseo de la Castellana
28046 MADRID

Or visit our website to apply online:
www.telemall.com.es/recruit/salesexec.htm

6

SOFTWARE SUPPORT MANAGER

ICS Ltd provides technical support and training to leading organizations throughout Europe.

We are seeking an experienced IT manager to run a team of 25+ software support specialists working in a major Spanish bank. The post is based in Madrid but will involve some travel within the country.

The successful applicant will have excellent knowledge of a wide range of systems and applications, good Spanish and English, excellent team management skills and the ability to deal with senior managers in our client's organization.

In return we offer an excellent salary + car and other benefits. Apply to:

David James, ICS Ltd, Waterloo Building, Stamford Street, London SE9 1NN
E-mail djames@ics.com, fax +44-20-8747 1357

Listening 1

4.4 Well qualified for the job?

Find jobs for these people. Listen to what they say about their qualifications and experience and choose the best job from the advertisements on the previous page for each person.

a My name is Patrick Kiely and I come from Dublin in Ireland. I'm 24 years old. I studied IT and business administration at Dorset College of Further Education. I speak fluent Spanish and reasonably good French. I worked in a bank in Dublin for two years but I gave that up six months ago when my girlfriend moved back to Spain. I have excellent IT skills, but I don't want to spend the whole day in front of a computer screen. I prefer people to computers. I've been living in Madrid for the last six months but I don't have a job at the moment.

b Hello, my name is Teresa Soliz. I'm a secretary. I'm 28. I've had several short-term jobs in Madrid, and London where I lived for two years. I have been working as the Personal Assistant to the director of a real estate company for the last three years, but I would like to change my job and if possible get out of secretarial work completely.

c Hi, my name is Miriam Jax, I'm 35 and I have a degree in international marketing from the University of Mainz, my home town in Germany. I have worked in marketing for 13 years, in Germany, the USA and Argentina. My present job, which I have had for three years, is marketing manager of a software company based in Madrid.

d My name is Michel Delain and I'm 26 years old. I studied accounts and book-keeping at a private college in France and for the last 18 months I have been working in the accountancy department of a travel company in Bilbao, northern Spain. I don't like my job and I would prefer to live in a big city. I'm from France but I am fluent in Spanish and I speak reasonably good English.

e Hello there, my name's David Delgado. I'm from Australia but my parents are originally from Spain. I've got a degree in computing and I've worked in a number of companies providing IT support and training. My present job is as an IT support manager in a further education college in London. I'm 31 years old. I am bilingual in English and Spanish and I would like to work in a Spanish-speaking country.

Language focus

4.5 Qualifications and skills

Here are some different ways to talk about your qualifications and skills.

I've got a diploma in Business Studies with IT.
I have a degree in marketing.
I have 'A' levels in economics, maths and German.
I've got a diploma in IT for business.
I have fluent French and I can speak German quite well too.
I have a driving licence.
I know how to use a number of software accounts packages.
I am pretty good with computers.
I'm good at working in teams and getting on with colleagues.
I know how to operate switchboards and fax machines.
I studied marketing at university.

Note that in British English it is common to use *have got* instead of *have*. *Have got* sounds less formal. In the USA it is less common to use *have got*. Be careful, we only use *have got* in the present simple tense. For all other tenses, use *have*.

i 'A' levels are the examinations that students in England, Wales and Northern Ireland take when they leave school at the age of 18, usually in three or four subjects. In Scotland many students finish school a year earlier and take 'Highers' in five or six subjects. At the age of 16, most children in the UK take exams called GCSEs (General Certificate in Secondary Education) in a larger number of subjects (six-ten usually).

Practice

Write about your qualifications and skills.

I've got ....

I also have ....

I know how to ....

I can ....

I'm good at ....

I'm pretty good with ....

I ....

I also ....

Practise talking about your qualifications and skills. Record yourself. You can read the things you wrote at first, but after a little practice you can record yourself talking without any notes.

4.6 Talking about your experience

Who might say these things? Try to remember, then look back at **4.4** to check.

1 I have been working for a software company for three years. ____
2 I worked in a bank for two years. ____
3 I've got two years' experience of managing an IT support team. ____
4 I worked in the USA for a number of years. ____
5 I've worked in a number of different companies in Spain and in London. ____
6 For the past 18 months I have been working for a travel company. ____

Simple past or present perfect?

When do you use simple past tense (*I worked …*) and when do you use present perfect tense (*I have worked …* or *I have been working …*)?

a Is Patrick still working for a bank in Dublin now? Yes/No? Tense? ____

b Is Teresa Soliz still working for a real estate company now? Yes/No? Tense? ____

To learn more about these tenses, see **Language reference** section at the end of the book.

Write about your own work and study experience. Concentrate on getting the tenses right.

I have been working in........... for ....months/years.
Before that I worked in .... for ....
From 199_ to 199_ I studied ....
I have been studying .... since ....
I studied .... in .... for .... years.

Practise talking about your work and study experience. Record yourself. You can read the things you wrote at first, but after a little practice you can record yourself talking without any notes.

4.7 Pronunciation of past tense endings

Regular verbs form their past tense by adding *-ed* (or just *-d* if the base form of the verb already ends in *-e*).

work → worked	live → lived
visit → visited	telephone → telephoned
call → called	decide → decided

Verbs ending in a consonant followed by *-y* usually form the past tense with *-ied* replacing the *-y* of the base form. But verbs ending in a vowel (*a, e, i, o, u*) followed by *-y* just add *-ed*

study → studied	enjoy → enjoyed
dry → dried	play → played

Pronunciation note

As far as the **sound** or **pronunciation** of the past tense is concerned there are three different endings.

/t/ as in *worked*
/d/ as in *lived, telephoned, called*
/id/ as in *decided, visited, started, ended* (where *-ed* follows *t* or *d*)

The difference between /t/ and /d/ is not important but where the ending is /id/ you should be careful to pronounce the extra syllable.

Which of these end in /id/? Practise saying these sentences. Record yourself and listen to the speaker on the recording.

I decided to come to Spain six months ago.
I worked in the USA before I came here.
I started looking for another job last month.
I finished a temporary job yesterday.
My contract with the company ended in February.

Listening 2

4.8 Conversation in a bar

It's six o'clock. Roberto has just finished work. He feels like a drink before he takes the bus home. He meets a friend, Patrick, in the bar.

Listen to their conversation and try to answer these questions. If you haven't got a recording to work with, read the conversation instead.

1 How is Patrick feeling? How do you know?
2 What happened to Patrick?
   a He lost his job?
   b His team lost an important game?
   c His job application was unsuccessful?
3 Which job is he going to apply for now?

Roberto What's the matter, Patrick? You look down in the dumps.

Patrick Oh, hi, Roberto. I'm okay. I didn't get that job I told you about. If I don't find something soon, I'll have to head back to Dublin.

Roberto Let me buy you a drink. What'll it be?

Patrick Oh thanks. A beer, please.

Roberto Two beers please.

Roberto Here you are.

Patrick Thanks.

Roberto Did you look in *El Mundo* today. I saw a couple of interesting jobs. Here, look.

Patrick Accounts clerk. Certificate in book-keeping level 3. No, you know what it's like here, you have to have the right qualifications for this type of thing. I haven't got a certificate in book-keeping.

Roberto Well, you could give it a go.

Patrick No, I hate working with figures all day anyway.

Roberto Wait a minute – what about this one? Bilingual executive assistant needed. Must have fluent Spanish and English, good computing skills, efficient and well organized. US $2,500 a month.

Patrick Hmm, that sounds okay. A bit vague, though. Probably looking for an attractive blonde secretary.

Roberto Well, you never know. It's worth a try.

Patrick I suppose so. Let me copy down the details. Got a pen I can borrow?

Roberto Oh, don't bother, just keep the paper. I've read it all anyway.

Patrick Thanks, Roberto. By the way, did you watch the match last night?

Roberto Yeah, what a disaster! It makes you wonder how they got this far. I can't see much chance of...

4.9 Listen for the details

Listen to the conversation in **4.8** again.

True or false? Write **T** or **F** next to the statements below to show if they are True or False.

1 Patrick has found a new job in Dublin. *F*
2 He doesn't have a book-keeping qualification.

3 He likes working with numbers and calculations.
4 He is optimistic about one of the jobs.
5 Roberto is trying to encourage Patrick.
6 He lent Patrick a pen.
7 The job of executive assistant is only for a woman.

4.10 Keeping a conversation going

What would you say? Choose an appropriate response to these questions and suggestions. Listen to the recording to check your answers.

Example: 1 c

1	Do you fancy going for a drink after work?	a	I know I should. But there's never a good time.
2	Have you got a pen I can borrow?	b	No, I didn't. Was it any good?
3	What'll it be?	c	No, not tonight. I have a lot of work to finish off.
4	Why don't you apply for it?	d	A glass of dry white wine for me, please.
5	You really should take a holiday.	e	I suppose I could give it a try.
6	By the way, did you watch the football last night?	f	Sure. Here you are.

Reading 2

4.11 Layout of a business letter

C/ Prim 19
4th floor
28004 Madrid

Telephone 91 523 97 80
E-mail pat.kiely@yahoo.es

The Personnel Manager
International Insurance SA
C/ Villanueva 29
28001 Madrid

20th April

Dear Sir or Madam

I would like to apply for the position of bilingual executive assistant, which I saw in today's edition of *El Mundo*.

As you will see from my CV, I have a diploma in Business and IT and experience of administration in the Bank of Ireland. English is my first language but I have very good spoken and written Spanish and I can also speak French. I have good IT skills and am familiar with a number of IT applications.

I am available for interview at any time and, if my application is successful, I will be able to start work almost immediately.

Yours faithfully

P. Kiely

Patrick D. Kiely

Look at Patrick's letter below and answer these questions.

1 Where does Patrick write his address?
2 Where does he put his name?
3 Where do you put the name and address of the person you are writing to?
4 What do you write at the beginning and end of the letter if you don't know the person's name?

The address of the person sending the letter goes here. Don't put your own name or job title. Your company name may already be at the top.

The full name, job title, company and address of the person you are sending the letter to goes here.

Today's date

Greeting. Title and surname or *Dear Sir or Madam.*

Introduction or opening. State the reason for writing the letter.

Main body. This is to tell the reader something about yourself in relation to the job advertised.

Polite ending. Use *Yours sincerely* if the letter is sent to a named person. Otherwise, *Yours faithfully.*

Signature

Name of person sending the letter.

> 49 Stamford Street
> West Dulwich
> London SE21 8LP
> ☎ 020-8674 2966
>
> Ms Janice Campbell
> Personnel Department
> London School of IT
> 79 Waterloo Road
> London SE2 4RR
>
> 19/02/04
>
> Dear Ms Campbell
>
> I am extremely interested in the position of Head of Administration which I saw advertised in *The Times* newspaper on 17th February.
>
> As requested, I am attaching my résumé. I think you will agree that I have the experience and qualifications you are looking for. In my present post with South London College, I am Head of Administration in the Student Admissions and Records Office, where I lead a team of six. This job, which I have held for almost three years, involves setting up and running new administration systems, training staff and managing the collection of students' fees.
>
> I look forward to having the opportunity to discuss my suitability for this post at interview.
>
> Yours sincerely
>
> *Helen R. Kennedy*
>
> Helen Kennedy (Mrs)

Ending the letter

In **British English** you end the letter with *Yours faithfully* if you don't know the name of the person you are writing to. If you know the name, it is important to put it at the top of the letter, and then end the letter with *Yours sincerely*.

It is much better to find out the name of the person who will receive your letter and then put that at the top of the letter.

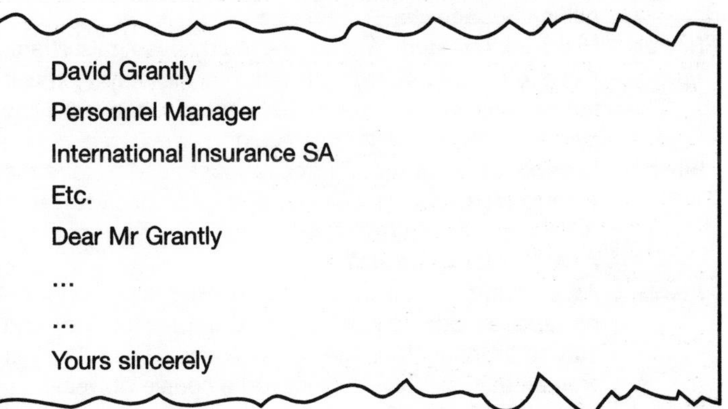

David Grantly
Personnel Manager
International Insurance SA
Etc.
Dear Mr Grantly
...
...
Yours sincerely

In **American English** the convention is slightly different. You can use the following options:

Personal, less formal	*Sincerely yours/Yours sincerely/ Sincerely/Cordially yours*
Fairly formal	*Yours truly/Very truly yours/Yours very truly*
Very formal	*Respectfully yours/Yours (very) respectfully*

Unit 5 gives more practice in writing application letters, CVs and résumés.

Listening 3

4.12 In the office

Pierre and Silvia work for International Insurance SA in Madrid, Spain. It is the end of the day but Pierre is still working. Listen to the conversation and identify some problems facing Pierre.

Silvia Hello, Pierre. I'm just on my way out. How about a quick drink?

Pierre Oh hi, Silvia. No thanks. I've still got a lot to do. I'm leaving for London on Tuesday and I haven't even sorted out all the arrangements, let alone prepared all the papers for the meeting.

Silvia Anything I can do?

Pierre No, thanks, it's all right. I'll manage. I'm leaving in about half an hour anyway.

Silvia You work too hard. You really should have an assistant.

Pierre I know, I know. There's no point in me staying much longer, anyway, I can't send these e-mails out. The system is giving me trouble again.

Silvia It works okay for me, Pierre. You just need to take the time to learn how to use it properly. Or get yourself a new assistant. Why don't you ask personnel to advertise for someone?

Pierre As a matter of fact I did. The advert came out in the newspaper today. I just hope that the person they find stays a bit longer than the last two people I had. The last woman they sent me only stayed a couple of weeks.

Silvia They will, Pierre, if you are a bit nicer to them. Just because you work 12 hours a day, it doesn't mean everyone else wants to.

Pierre All right, I know.

4.13 Listen for the details

Listen to the conversation in **4.12** again.

True or false? Write **T** or **F** next to the statements below to show if they are True or False.

1 Pierre is going to have a drink with Silvia. *F*
2 Pierre is not ready for his trip to London next week. ___
3 Pierre's secretary is still working too. ___
4 Pierre doesn't know how to use the e-mail system very well. ___
5 The personnel department is trying to find Pierre a new assistant. ___
6 Pierre's last assistant was a woman. ___
7 Pierre's last assistant worked for him for a long time. ___
8 Silvia thinks Pierre is not nice to his assistants. ___

Rewrite the false sentences in your notebook to make them true:

Example: *Pierre isn't going to have a drink with Silvia. He's too busy.*

4.14 Problems and suggestions

A Match the problems with a suggestion from the list below. Listen to the recording to check your answers.

Example: 1 e

Problems

1 I can't get this printer to work.
2 I'm having problems with these figures.
3 There's something wrong with the photocopier.
4 The lift isn't working, I'm afraid.
5 My car has broken down. Something to do with the steering lock.

Suggestions

a Why don't we take the lift at the other entrance?
b Have you tried switching it off and on again?
c You should take out breakdown cover.
d Why don't you let me have a look at them?
e Have you called the helpdesk?

B What suggestions would you give these people?

Mike: I don't have time to make all my own travel arrangements.
Alicia: I'm fed up with this job.
Alexandra: My boss expects me to work 12 hours a day!
Paul: I can't open my e-mails.
Julie: I never have any money left at the end of the month.

C Write some more problems and suggestions.

Practise with a friend. One of you describes a problem. The other one makes an appropriate suggestion.

Lesson summary

Here are some of the things you practised in this lesson:

- Understanding job advertisements.

- Talking about your qualifications:
  I've got a diploma in Accountancy.
  I have a degree in Business Studies from London University.
- Talking about work experience:
  I worked for the Bank of Ireland for three years.
  I've been working here since 1999.
- Problems and suggestions:
  I'm having trouble with this computer.
  Why don't you call the technician?

Suggestions for further practice

1 Write some more profiles of qualifications and experience, like the ones in **4.4**. You can think of people you know and write profiles for them.

2 Look for job advertisements in a newspaper (for example the *International Herald Tribune*, the *Financial Times*) or a website that advertises jobs. See how well you can understand them. If you find any words or abbreviations you do not know, first try to guess the meanings, then look in your business English dictionary to check if you were right. Use your vocabulary notebook to record any useful words or expressions.

3 Write a dialogue about a company problem and suggestions for solving it.

4 Find some business letters in different languages and compare the conventions for organizing information.

letters and CVs

In this unit you will practise

- **understanding job requirements**
- **analysing a job advertisement**
- **writing an effective job application letter**
- **writing a CV or résumé**

Language

- **professional qualities and characteristics**
- **positive action verbs to describe achievements**
- **useful phrases for opening and closing a job application letter**
- **key skills and abilities**

Introduction

5.1 Applying for a job

There are two kinds of job application. You may be applying for a job that is advertised, in which case you should have quite a lot of information about what the employer is looking for. Or you may be writing to companies to ask for a job, even though no job has been advertised.

In both cases, you need to make yourself seem attractive to the company as a potential employee, so that they will invite you to an interview. The main purpose of your application is to get an interview. So, you need to 'sell yourself'. The activity below will help you to do this.

A What kind of person are you? How would you describe yourself? Tick the adjectives and phrases you think apply to yourself? Add any others you think describe you well.

kind	ambitious	easy-going
hard-working	a good communicator	articulate
generous	a team player	helpful
smart (appearance)	determined	intelligent
well organized	careful	laid back
punctual	ruthless	sympathetic
enthusiastic	motivated	independent
good at managing people		

NB Notice that *smart* in British English refers to your appearance and your clothes. In the USA it is often used to mean intelligent or clever.

B Which of your qualities do you think an employer might like? Which qualities are relevant to all jobs? Which ones only apply to certain kinds of jobs, e.g. a salesman, a manager, a secretary?

more than one job available

computing knowledge

design

able to work with business clients

initiate change

solve problems

complete projects

E-Commerce Consultants

At Multimedia Solutions Incorporated we have been designing and managing state-of-the-art commercial websites since 1993. We provide e-commerce solutions for large and small companies in a number of sectors, including business consultancy, travel and tourism and insurance services, from a simple web presence to complete e-commerce solutions. We are looking for highly motivated graduates in business, computing or multimedia design, preferably with some industry experience. If you have a flair for design, skill in using a range of design packages, and experience in dealing with business customers, we have the perfect position for you. Successful candidates will be based in London but expected to travel regularly to different parts of the UK and other EU countries, working with our clients and participating in all aspects from concept to website launch and beyond.

An attractive salary package will be offered and career development opportunities will be available and actively encouraged.

Please apply by post or online to:

Barry Hopton
<bhopton@msi.co.uk>
Multimedia Solutions Incorporated
Wellington House
195 Waterloo Bridge Road
London SE2 3LH

knowledge about this established company

knowledge of world of business

qualification

experience

mobile, driving licence

good communicator

teamwork

ambitious

Reading 1

5.2 A job advertisement

If you are writing a letter in response to an advertisement, it is very important to match yourself to the selection criteria in the advertisement or job description. Look at the advertisement on the previous page for clues about what this company is looking for.

Which ones would you include in a letter applying for this job? Tick (✔) the ones that you think are appropriate and put a cross (✘) next to those that are not appropriate.

a I have a full driving licence and I would be happy to travel.
b I am married with two young children.
c I have experience of providing IT support for a range of businesses including travel and retail.
d I am in good health and I enjoy sports activities.
e When I was a student I also did voluntary work caring for children in a hospital.
f Although my main degree is in distributed computing systems, I also completed courses in graphic design and usability design.
g I prefer to work on my own but I would be prepared to cooperate with others and work in a team.
h While I am able to work independently, successful teamwork has been a key part of my present job.
i This post interests me as an opportunity to build on my skills and develop a career in my chosen field.
j I am interested in improving my salary and conditions and this job seems to offer me this opportunity.
k My communication and teamwork skills, together with strong commitment and enthusiasm, have helped me to complete a number of challenging projects.
l My father ran his own business, and many of my friends and relatives are in the business field.

See **Answer key** on p. 203 for suggested answers. It is essential to match your skills and qualifications to the job that is advertised. Sometimes an employer will send a detailed job description and or a person specification. You should try to address all the points asked for.

9 Greenfields Avenue
South Ealing
London W5 5RN

Mr Barry Hopton
Personnel Manager
Multimedia Solutions Incorporated
Wellington House
195 Waterloo Bridge Road
London SE2 3LH

17th May

Dear Mr Hopton

I would like to apply for one of the posts of e-commerce consultant with your company which I saw advertised in today's *Daily News*. This post is exactly what I am looking for, and at the same time I am confident that I have the skills and experience your company needs.

My first degree, in IT with Business Studies, has given me a good understanding of how these two fields are related, as well as the practical IT skills to advise business clients on their needs and implement solutions. In the two years since I graduated I have put these skills to practical use as Web Designer with West London College of Higher Education. In addition I have completed freelance projects for small businesses and taken courses in graphic design and usability design. The post you advertised interests me greatly as an opportunity to build on my skills and develop a career in my chosen field. I'm also attracted by the variety of work that your company would offer and I would enjoy the opportunity to work in other parts of the UK and Europe.

My CV is attached and further information about myself, and links to internet projects I have worked on can be found at my website: http://www.aol.com/homepages/andrewscj/index.htm. I am available for interview at any time and I would like the opportunity to demonstrate that I have the necessary qualities.

Yours sincerely

C. Andrews

Chris Andrews

Reading 2

5.3 An application letter

Read the letter on p. 59 and answer the following questions.

1 Where does Chris Andrews live?
2 What is his present job?
3 What qualifications does he hold?
4 What is the title of the job he is applying for?
5 What date was the job advertised in the *Daily News*?
6 What is Barry Hopton's position?
7 Who does he work for?
8 Do you think Chris looks like a suitable applicant for this job? Why?/Why not?
9 Do you think he has written an effective job application letter? How could it be improved?

5.4 Tips for writing an application letter

Look at this list of 'Do's and Don'ts' for writing application letters. Choose some of the tips and decide if they are do's or don'ts. Tick (✔) the do's and put a cross (✘) next to the don'ts.

Do's and Don'ts

1 Apply for a job that the company doesn't have.
2 Be clear and concise.
3 Be positive – use positive words like *'achieved'* and *'success'*.
4 Focus on what you have to offer an employer.
5 Have your cover letter checked by at least one other person before you post it.
6 Know what job you are applying for.
7 Make your enthusiasm for the job and the company very clear.
8 Be dishonest. Make sure you are able to discuss or explain any sentence in your application. Any information you give may be used in the interview.
9 Match yourself to the selection criteria listed in the advertisement/ position description.
10 Sound desperate.
11 Use a word processor and laser printer to produce your letter.
12 Use negative language, e.g. talking about the bad things in your present job.

13 Use simple and uncomplicated sentences.
14 Clutter up the page with too much information.
15 Use your cover letter as an example of the fact that you can write a professional looking business letter.
16 Give examples of things you have done, to show that you have the skills you say you have.

Check your answers in the **Key** at the back of the book.

Can you think of any more tips? Write them in your notebook. For example:

- Don't send a handwritten letter, unless you are specifically asked to.
- Do try to find out the name of the person your application should be addressed to.

5.5 Analysing an advertisement

Look at this job advertisement and analyse it in the same way as the advertisement in **5.1**. Or, if you prefer, find an advertisement for a job you are interested in, and use that instead.

The questions below might help you. Underline or draw an arrow to the relevant information in the advertisement.

1 Does the job require IT skills?
2 What qualifications are required?
3 How much experience is required?
4 What kind of products or services are involved?
5 Are there opportunities for promotion?
6 Will the job require travel?
7 Do you think communication skills are important?
8 Do you think foreign language skills are required?
9 Is the job only for British people?
10 What information is provided about the company's activities?
11 How many jobs are available?
12 Will training be provided?

Business Graduates

We are a large financial consultancy agency looking to recruit between 50 and 100 executive trainees for posts throughout our European network. After initial training, successful applicants will be based in one of our regional offices, providing financial consultancy and planning advice on products including pensions, life assurance, savings, investments and taxes.

Good package plus incentives and long term prospects. Interested?

Phone 01723 590 8080 or e-mail personnel@fse.com

FINANCIAL SERVICES EUROPE

Make some notes on some things about yourself that you would highlight in your application letter or CV.

Language focus

5.6 More tips and useful language

Here are some ideas about how to describe yourself effectively in job application letters and CVs.

1 Think carefully about the purpose of writing an application letter. This can include the following things:

- To inform the employer that you are interested in the job;
- To persuade the employer that you are a suitable candidate;
- To make sure that they look at your CV and invite you for an interview;
- To suggest areas that will be discussed in the interview;
- To show that you can communicate clearly and effectively in writing;
- To show that you know how to write a business letter and present it in a professional, attractive way;
- To make you look professional;
- To give the reader some idea about your personality.

2 **The opening** should state which job you are applying for, possibly say where you found out about it, and show that you are positive and enthusiastic about the job. Here are some possible phrases that you could include:

Your advertisement for the post of executive assistant in today's Times interests me greatly because ...
I am confident that I have the skills and experience you are looking for.
I have the commitment and expertise that I believe are necessary to succeed in this job.
From your advertisement it seems that you need a person who can ...
I believe I am exactly the kind of person you are looking for.
I can offer the professional skills and motivation needed to ...
Given the opportunity I am sure that I could successfully fulfil your requirements.

3 In **the main body of your letter** you should match the job requirements to the skills and refer the reader to relevant parts of your CV or résumé. It is enough to write about two or three key skills you have. Write a short paragraph about each of these. It is important to provide examples of specific skills and achievements relevant to the job.

As you will see from my CV, I graduated from ...
In my previous job, I successfully trained the customer care team to ....
I was responsible for introducing a new system for recording contacts which contributed to a 25 per cent increase in sales.

Use **positive action verbs** that highlight your achievements:

I started	*I introduced*	*I developed*	*I completed*
I trained	*I achieved*	*I increased*	*I organized*
I led	*I managed*	*I improved*	*I accomplished*
I trained	*I planned*	*I prepared*	*I was responsible for*

4 **Closing the letter**

I would be happy to discuss my suitability for this position further.
I look forward to meeting you in person to discuss what I can offer your company.
An interview would give me the opportunity to show you the commitment I could offer in this job.
I look forward to meeting you and finding out more about the challenges this job could offer me.
I am confident that an interview will confirm my suitability for this post.
I will be happy to supply references and any further information you require.
Thank you, in anticipation, for considering my application.
I am sure that the attached CV will convince you that I have the necessary skills for this position.

5.7 Your own letter of application

1 Write your own job application letter for one of the job advertisements in **Unit** 4 or 5. Or find a suitable advertisement in a newspaper or on the internet to apply for.

2 Books on business letters, books on applying for jobs, and several internet sites include sample job application letters.

Find one or more of these and compare them with your letter. Some suggestions for further reading and links are provided at the end of this Unit.

Patrick David Kiely

Contact Details

Calle Prim 19
4th floor
28004 Madrid

Telephone 91 523 97 80
E-mail <pat.kiely@yahoo.es>

Education

1995–1998	Dorset College of Further Education, Dublin. Advanced Diploma in IT and Business Administration.
1989–1995	St Joseph's College, Dublin. (Leaving Certificates including grade A in Spanish, Maths and Economics, grade B in Physics, English and Art.)

Employment History

1999–2001	Bank of Ireland, Dublin. Banking officer. All aspects of local branch banking. Counter cashier, responsible for receiving and issuing money, foreign exchange, accurately debiting and crediting accounts; advising customers on loans and financial products; sorting out problems and customer care.
1996–1998	(Part time) Salesperson in National Gallery of Ireland, Publications Department. Sales and packaging of art books, prints and cards. Stocktaking and record keeping.
1998–1999	(Summer vacation job) Comlink computers. Advising private customers and small businesses on their IT requirements. Sales, delivery and installation of PCs. Answering technical queries and dealing with IT problems.

Other Professional Courses

June 2000	Bank of Ireland. One-week course in foreign exchange.
1996–1997	Dublin Community College (part time evening course). Business French.
May 2001	USA College of English & Business, Madrid. HTML & web design. Introductory course on web page design and maintenance.

Other skills

Good IT skills. Proficient user of Word, Excel, Access. Internet and E-mail packages. Basic knowledge of HTML and Microsoft FrontPage (web page design).
Fluent Spanish (written and spoken).
French (fairly fluent spoken, good written).
English (mother tongue).

5.8 CVs and résumés

A Here are some questions about Patrick. Find the answers in the CV on p. 64. N.B. if the information is not available in the CV, just write *No information*.

1 Where does Patrick live?
2 How many years did he study at Dorset College?
3 What was the name of his secondary school?
4 What is his date of birth?
5 Is he married?
6 Does he have any children?
7 Does he have an e-mail address?
8 What is his postal address?
9 Where did he work part time while he was a student?
10 What subjects was he good at in his secondary school?
11 Which language does he speak better, French or Spanish?
12 What were his duties at Comlink Computers?
13 Which job does Patrick put first on his CV, the earliest or the latest?

B How could this CV be improved? Do you think Patrick should include more information? Is there anything he should leave out? Would you advise him to add extra sections to his CV (for example, about his hobbies and interests)?

C From the information in his CV, does Patrick seem to have the right experience and qualifications for the job of bilingual executive assistant?

5.9 Your own CV or résumé

1 Have you already prepared a CV or résumé? Is it up to date? Are you happy with it? Write/rewrite it keeping in mind one of the jobs advertised in **Unit** 4 or 5, or a real job advertisement.

2 Find some sample CVs and compare them with your own. Some suggestions for further reading and links are provided at the end of this unit.

Lesson summary

Here are some of the things you practised in this lesson:

- Adjectives to describe your qualities: *well organized, articulate, punctual, ambitious, motivated* (see **5.1**).

- Looking carefully at job advertisements to see what kind of person they are aimed at (see **5.2** and **5.5**).
- Writing effective application letters (see **5.1–5.7**).
  Useful opening phrases:
  Your advertisement for the post of executive assistant in today's Times *interests me greatly because …*
  I believe I am exactly the kind of person you are looking for.

  Highlighting your key skills:
  As you will see from my CV, I graduated from …
  In my previous job, I was responsible for introducing …

  Using positive language and describing your achievements:
  I achieved …; I introduced…; started, trained, improved, was responsible for, planned

  Useful closing phrases:
  I look forward to meeting you in person to discuss what I can offer your company.
  I will be happy to supply references and any further information you require.
  Thank you, in anticipation, for considering my application.
- CVs and résumés (see **5.8–5.10**).

Suggestions for further practice

1 Look at two different job advertisements for similar jobs that you might apply for. Make lists of the key skills and qualities that are asked for in both advertisements. What things are the same for both advertisements? What things are different?

2 Write your CV and give it to a colleague to look at. Ask your colleague to suggest improvements.

3 Find some sample application letters, either in your company, or on the internet or in books. Draw a circle around sentences and sections you think are very good, and underline the parts you don't like so much. Make a note in your notebook of useful sentences and expressions used in the opening, the main body and the closing of the letters. Make a note of the positive verbs used to describe achievements.

4 The following websites have useful information on writing job application letters and CVs.

http://www.ruthvilmi.net/hut/help/writing_instructions/
http://owl.english.purdue.edu/handouts/index2.html/
http://www1.umn.edu/ohr/ecep/resume/

09 a job interview

In this unit you will practise

- **taking part in a job interview**
- **discussing candidates for a job**

Language

- **qualities and characteristics**
- **similarities and differences**
- **present perfect continuous and past simple tense**
- **expressing opinions, agreeing and disagreeing**
- **making decisions and giving reasons**

Introduction

6.1 Interview questions

- How many job interviews have you had? Were any of the questions unexpected or were you well prepared for everything? How did you feel? Nervous? Confident? Relaxed?
- What questions do you expect to get asked in a job interview?
- Have you ever interviewed someone for a job yourself? How did you prepare for the interview? How did you plan the questions?

Interviewers are likely to include some questions based on the candidate's CV and application letter, as well as some general questions that all the candidates will be asked. There may be some areas that the interviewers cannot ask about because of company policy or employment laws. For example, in the UK it is not usual to ask about a candidate's family, number of children, their childcare arrangements, etc.

A Look back at Patrick Kiely's application letter in Unit 4.11 and his CV in Unit 5.7. Imagine you are going to interview him for the job at International Insurance. Write down some questions you would like to ask him.

B Write down answers to the questions you thought of.

Do you think it is important to be completely truthful in a job interview? Or is it okay to lie about things like your interest in the company and the job you are applying for, or your reasons for leaving your previous job?

Listening 1

6.2 An interview

Patrick Kiely is having an interview at International Insurance, for the job of bilingual executive assistant. There are three interviewers, David Grantly, the Head of Personnel, and Silvia Becatto and Pierre Croyden, who are senior executives in the company. If Patrick gets the job, he will be working with Pierre.

The interview has already been going on for about 15 minutes and Patrick has already talked about his business studies and his previous job.

Look at David Grantly's interview notes. He has made a note of three questions he wants to ask Patrick. As you listen to the interview, note down Patrick's answers.

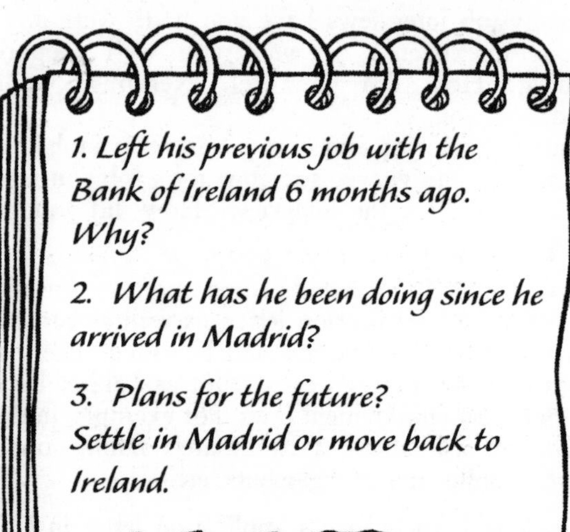

1. Left his previous job with the Bank of Ireland 6 months ago. Why?
2. What has he been doing since he arrived in Madrid?
3. Plans for the future? Settle in Madrid or move back to Ireland.

Silvia From what you have told us, Mr Kiely, it seems that you were doing well with the Bank of Ireland. Would you mind telling us why you decided to leave?

Patrick Yes, of course. Really there were a number of reasons. Firstly, I really wanted to travel and work abroad, particularly in Spain. That has always been my ambition. Secondly, my partner, who is from Madrid, was offered a very good job with an American bank here in Madrid. So we decided that this would be a good time to move here. I felt I had been at the Bank of Ireland long enough to gain a lot of useful experience, and there was not much opportunity for me to get an overseas posting with the bank, not in the near future anyway.

David You left that job about six months ago, is that right? What have you been doing in that time?

Patrick Well, as I said in my letter I have been working really hard on my Spanish and doing some other courses as well. Obviously I have been applying for jobs, too. There

	are not that many opportunities in the banking sector at the moment, although that is not the only area I'm interested in. I've had a number of interviews and I have turned down a couple of offers. This job is one that would match my skills well, though, and I really feel that it is the kind of thing I am looking for.
Pierre	How about your long-term plans, do you think you will stay in Spain or do you hope to move back to Ireland, or somewhere else, perhaps?
Patrick	Well I wouldn't like to promise that I'll definitely be here for the rest of my life, but I really like Madrid, my partner's family live here, and so at the moment we feel pretty settled in Madrid.
David	Right. Well, I don't think we have any more questions for you. Pierre? No, okay, perhaps there are some things you would like to ask us about the job or the company?
Patrick	Yes, you mentioned opportunities to travel, and that was one thing that attracted me to this job. Could you tell me some more about that?

6.3 Listen for the details

Listen to the conversation in **6.2** again.

True or false? Write T or F next to the statements below to show if they are True or False.

1 Patrick is interested in travelling.
2 His girlfriend is Irish too.
3 This is his first interview since he arrived in Spain.
4 He has been offered some jobs already.
5 He has been doing some language classes in Madrid.
6 He left the Bank of Ireland because he didn't like his job.

Language focus

6.4 The right tense

Choose the right tense. Try to complete the exercise first, without reading the dialogue or listening to it. Then listen to the recording to check your answers.

1 From what you have told us, Mr Kiely, it seems that you were doing well with the Bank of Ireland. Would you mind telling us why you *decided / have decided* to leave?

2 I *felt / have felt* I had been at the Bank of Ireland long enough to gain a lot of useful experience.

3 You left that job about six months ago, is that right? What *did you do / have you been doing* in that time?

4 Well, as I *said / have said* in my letter I *worked / have worked / have been working* really hard on my Spanish and doing some other courses as well.

5 Obviously I *applied / have been applying* for jobs, too.

6 *I had / I've had* a number of interviews and I *turned down / have turned down* a couple of offers.

In general we use **present perfect continuous** (*have been doing / has been doing*) for recent activities, for the things happening in the period up to the present. These activities might still be continuing, or they might have stopped. We use **past simple** tense for activities in a time period that is finished. So, for example, Patrick left Ireland six months ago. If he talks about the time he was in Ireland, or his previous job, he will probably use the past simple tense.

Practice

A Think about your recent activities. Have you been playing a lot of sport recently? Have you been taking a course or learning something? Have you been working hard? What have you been working on over the last few days and weeks? Write some sentences.

Examples:

I've been working extremely hard the last three weeks. I have been preparing a report on a new product my company would like to offer.
I've been playing tennis regularly for the last two years.

B Think about your last job, your last school, or, if you have finished studying, think back to the time when you were a student. Write about some of your activities then. What was your life/work/studies like then? What kinds of activities were you involved in?

Examples:

I played a lot of tennis and football when I was a student.
I shared an apartment in New York with two of my colleagues.
I worked on product development for a year, then I worked in the marketing department.

For further information, see the **Language reference** section at the end of the book. Look out for more examples of these tenses in the dialogues and in your reading.

Listening 2

6.5 Another interview

Now David, Pierre and Silvia are interviewing another candidate, Teresa Soliz.

Listen to the conversation and make notes about Teresa.

Pierre According to your CV you work for a real estate company. You've been there for quite a long time, haven't you?
Teresa Yes, that's right, three years.
Pierre So I was wondering, why do you want to leave now?
Teresa Well, I do like my job, and the money is good. But anyway three years is the longest I've been in any job and I feel it's time for a change. Besides, I really want to do something a bit different from just secretarial work. I feel this job will offer me that.
Pierre Oh yes, definitely. The work is very varied and we are looking for someone to take on quite a lot of responsibility working in my department. But there would also be administrative duties, some correspondence, typing reports and handling e-mails. Is that what you expected?
Teresa That sounds okay.
Silvia Well, thank you very much, Miss Soliz. Perhaps there are some questions you would like to ask us?
Teresa Yes, of course, I think you have explained everything about this job, and I am really interested in it. I wanted to find out about longer-term prospects in the company.

Silvia Of course, well we are looking for someone to work with Pierre and support him in all aspects of his work. It would be a good opportunity to learn about all aspects of insurance, not just loss adjustment which is Pierre's responsibility.

David This is a large company, and we advertise posts internally wherever possible, so once you have some experience in this post there would certainly be opportunities for promotion.

Teresa How about training?

David Yes, of course, we offer quite a few programmes in-company and we also send people on courses outside. We would look at your needs and put together an initial package of courses. But it is also our policy to allow employees to . . .

6.6 Listen for the details

Listen again to the conversation in **6.5**.

True or false? Write **T** or **F** next to the statements below to show if they are True or False.

1 Teresa is working for a real estate company at the moment.
2 Teresa left her job with the real estate company after three years.
3 Pierre's department at International Insurance deals with loss adjustment.
4 The job Teresa has applied for only involves secretarial work.
5 There are opportunities to transfer to another job in International Insurance.

6.7 Vocabulary

Try to complete these phrases without listening again or reading the scripts of the interviews (**6.2** and **6.5**). Then look at the scripts to check your answers. If no words are missing, just leave the space blank.

1 Patrick's interview

a There was not much opportunity ______ me to get an overseas posting ______ the bank.
b What have you been doing ______ that time?

c I have been working really hard ______ my Spanish.
d I have turned ______ a couple of offers.
e I really feel that it is the kind of thing I am looking ______ .
f Do you think you will stay in Spain or do you hope to move ______ to Ireland?
g Perhaps there are some things you would like to ask us ______ the job.
h Could you tell me some more ______ that?

2 Teresa's interview

a I feel it's time ______ a change.
b You have explained everything ______ this job, and I am really interested ______ it.
c I really want to do something a bit different ______ just secretarial work.
d We are looking for someone to take ______ quite a lot of responsibility.
e We would look ______ your needs and put ______ an initial package.

3 Find the phrases above that mean the same as these words:

a to refuse, not to accept
b not the same as
c to be responsible for
d examine, discuss, think about

Language focus

6.8 Qualities for the job

What do you think are the most important things that business employers look for when they are recruiting new staff? Knowledge of business? Knowledge about a particular sector of industry? IT skills? Punctuality and smart appearance?

Obviously it depends on the job. But a recent survey of employers showed that there was a lot of agreement about the most important things they look for when they recruit graduates.

The list below shows the top 17 out of 62 different attributes (or characteristics) employers would like graduate employees to have. Look at the list. Which ones do you think are surprising? Are there any other things you expected to see on the list?

The most important attributes employers expect from graduates

1 Willingness to learn	2 Commitment	3 Dependability
4 Self-motivation	5 Teamwork	6 Communication skills
7 Co-operation	8 Drive & energy	9 Self management
10 Motivation to achieve	11 Problem-solving ability	12 Analytical ability
13 Flexibility	14 Initiative	15 Logical argument
16 Adaptability	17 Numeracy	

[Source: Managing Higher Education, Issue 2, 1996]

Practice

A Rate yourself in relation to these characteristics. Give yourself a score out of 10.

B Write sentences about yourself using the adjectives that correspond to the attribute. You can use the following modifiers:

High amount of the characteristic: *very, highly, extremely, really*
Medium amount of the characteristic: *fairly, reasonably, quite, pretty*
Low amount of the characteristic: *not very*

Examples:

*I'm **very** willing to learn.*
*I'm **extremely** committed.*
*I have got **quite a lot of** drive.*
*I'm **fairly** good at working in teams.*
*I'm **not very** good at oral communication skills. / I'm **not a very** good communicator.*
*I'm **pretty** good with figures (numerate).*
*I think I'm a **fairly** flexible person.*
*I'm **highly** motivated.*

Listening 3

6.9 Making a choice

After the interviews, David, Silvia and Pierre discussed the candidates. Listen to their discussion and answer these questions:

1 How many candidates did they interview for this job?
2 Which one did they choose?
3 Who was their second choice?
4 Which candidate did they feel was more relaxed? More ambitious? Had better Spanish? Better English? Was better qualified?

David Well, what do you think?

Silvia My feeling is that it is a choice between the last girl and the Irish chap. They both seemed very competent and enthusiastic.

David I agree, they were clearly the best of the five we interviewed. What about you, Pierre? After all, whoever gets the job will be working closely with you.

Pierre It's a difficult choice. Miss, er, Soliz, has a lot of experience, and she is clearly ambitious. She seems to have all the qualifications we are looking for. But so does Mr Kiely.

David He hasn't worked for six months, since he came to Madrid.

Pierre I know. But it can't be easy for someone coming here from abroad.

Silvia And he hasn't wasted his time. He has taken some IT courses and he has been studying Spanish.

Pierre I think we should take him. I have a feeling he would be more likely to stay with the company. He made it very clear how keen he was to get the job.

David Do you think his Spanish is up to it?

Pierre His Spanish seemed pretty good. I suppose he would need someone to check any important letters he wrote. And his English is obviously not a problem.

Silvia Yes, I felt that his Spanish was as good as her English. And he seemed to be very confident and relaxed. That should make it easier for him to get on with you, Pierre.

Pierre Are you suggesting I'm difficult to work with?

Silvia	Only joking, Pierre. Seriously, what do you think?
Pierre	I agree with you. Also, he did say he could start immediately. We are desperate for the help in my department. David?
David	That's fine with me. I'll offer him the job, to start as soon as possible. Miss Soliz is our second choice. If you agree, I'll let her know that if a similar job comes up, we would be happy to offer it to her.
Pierre	Fine. Thanks a lot David, Silvia.
David	You are welcome. I'll talk to you after I have spoken to Mr Kiely.

6.10 Useful expressions

Find these expressions in the conversation in **6.9**. Then try to match them with their synonyms.

1 to get on with someone ____
2 to let someone know ____
3 to be up to it ____
4 to come up ____

a to inform someone
b to be able to do something, to be good enough
c to happen unexpectedly
d to have a good relationship with someone, able to work together

Look for any other words or expressions in the conversations.

Language focus

6.11 Comparisons

Look at these different ways of comparing people.

Same:

*Both candidates were **equally** enthusiastic/well qualified/ good at expressing themselves.*
*Teresa and Patrick **both** have very good IT skills.*
*I felt Teresa was **just as** ambitious **as** Patrick.*

Different:

*Patrick seemed **more** confident **than** Teresa.*
*Teresa seemed **less** confident **than** Patrick.*

*I felt Teresa was **not as confident as** Patrick.*
*Patrick **had more confidence than** Teresa.*
*Patrick could start **sooner**.*
*Teresa was **better qualified** for the position.*

Small differences:

*Patrick could start **a little/a bit/slightly** sooner than Teresa.*
*Teresa was **not quite** as enthusiastic as Patrick.*
*Patrick's Spanish is **almost** as good as Teresa's English.*

Big differences:

*I thought Teresa was **much** more experienced.*
*She didn't seem **nearly** as enthusiastic as Patrick.*
*In my opinion she was **nowhere near as enthusiastic about** the job.*

Practice

A Look at the interview notes about two candidates for a secretarial job with International Insurance services. Write sentences comparing the two candidates.

B Write a dialogue of the discussion about these candidates, based on these notes. You can use the conversation in **6.9** as a model.

Marisol Delgado	*Virginia Ferrufino*
Very fast typing speed! Made a mistakes though	*Fast typing. Very accurate few typist – only made one mistake*
7 years' experience	*4½ years' experience*
Very good English, also a little Italian	*Speaks excellent English, good French, some German*
Could start in 2 weeks	*Could start immediately*
Present job – she earns around $1,700 a month	*Earns $2,000 in present job. Can we match that?*
Very ambitious. Would she stay in this job long??	
No problem with 8.30 a.m. start time	*Cannot start work before 9.30 a.m.*

Seemed a little nervous. Perhaps not a very confident person	*Seems very relaxed and confident*
Excellent knowledge of computers. Good with PowerPoint, Excel, knows about databases	*Seems very knowledgeable about Word but not much experience with PowerPoint and other applications*

Lesson summary

Here are some of the things you practised in this lesson:

- Talking about recent activities:
  I've been working on a number of projects for my company.
  I've been playing football quite a lot recently.
  I've been working in the marketing department since last May.
- Talking about activities in the past:
  In my previous job I worked on a number of similar projects.
  I took courses on e-commerce and web page design as part of my degree.
  I worked in teams a lot when I was with the Bank of Ireland.
- Talking about your attributes, using modifiers:
  *I think I'm **pretty good** at working in teams.*
  *She is **extremely** good at solving problems.*
  *He's **not very** confident but he seems highly motivated.*
  *According to her previous employer, she is **not very** dependable.*
- Comparisons, similarities and differences:
  *Teresa has **more** experience than Patrick.*
  *He is not **as well** qualified for the job **as** she is.*
  *She is **much more** enthusiastic about the job.*
  *He is **not quite** as confident **as** her.*

Suggestions for further practice

1 Find a book or a website which has advice for successful interviews. Make a list of 'do's' and 'don'ts' for job interviews. Choose some questions and write answers (for yourself).

2 Practise job interviews with one or two friends. Take it in turns to be the interviewer(s) and the candidate(s).

3 Write a dialogue of part of a job interview, in your company, perhaps for your own job.

4 Think about two people, perhaps two colleagues that you know well. Write some sentences comparing them. Focus on their similarities and differences.

5 Imagine you have interviewed two people for a job or a promotion within your company. Write a dialogue of the discussion between yourself and another interviewer in which you discuss which candidate is most suitable.

6 Make a list of some of the useful expressions in this unit, especially the expressions which combine verbs and prepositions (e.g. *get on with someone, take on, give up*). Practise using them in sentences.

07 check your progress

7.1 Vocabulary

Fill in the missing letters. Can you add any more words?

1

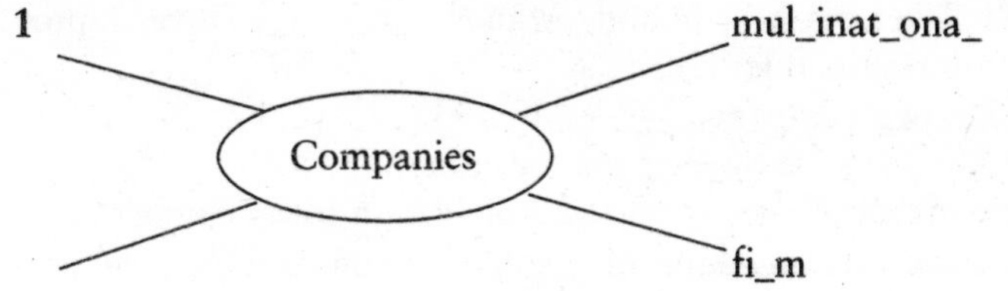

2

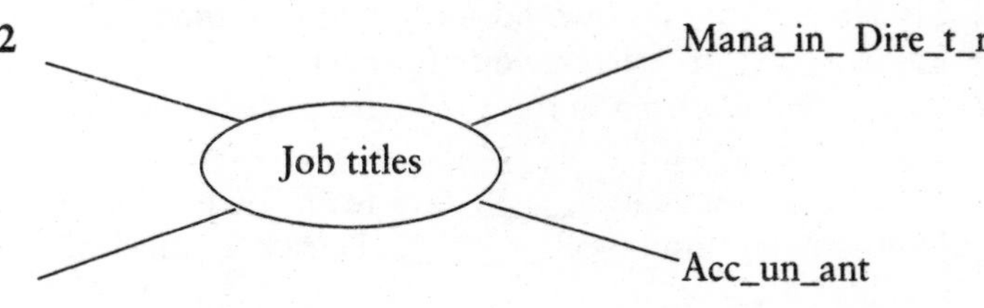

3

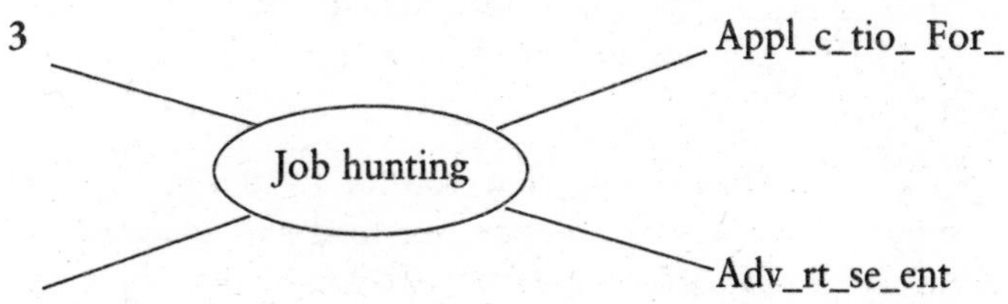

4

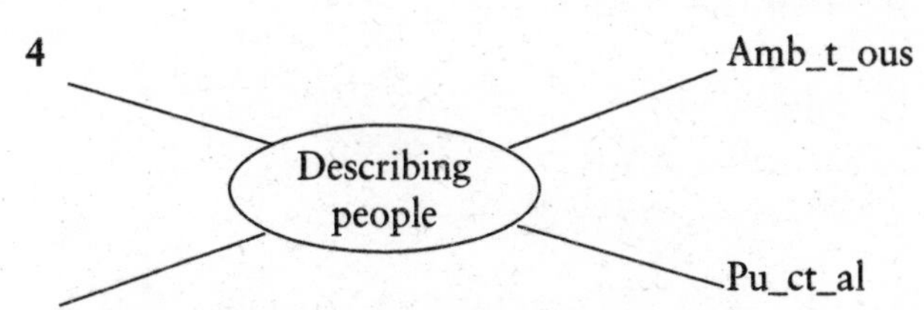

7.2

Complete these sentences with appropriate words which appeared in **Units 1–6**.

1 Comet is a _______ of Kingfisher plc.
2 Ryanair was __________in 1985.
3 Paul is in charge of the IT section and he ______ the IT support staff.
4 The Customer Relations Manager ____ ___ complaints from customers.

5 I'd ____ you to meet my colleague David Brown.
6 Both Unilever and Margarine Unie were ________ in marketing household goods.
7 Unilever markets famous brands _________ Dove, Lipton and Magnum ice cream.
8 The two companies ______ in 1930.
9 I know ___ to operate fax machines.
10 For further _______ and an application form, contact ...
11 I have been working in a software company ___ the past three years.
12 My father _____ his own business until he retired last year.
13 I look _______to meeting you in person.
14 As you will see from my _____ I have a degree in Business Studies.
15 How many candidates ______ they interview for this job?
16 International Insurance ________ Patrick a job and he accepted it.
17 Patrick ________ more confident than Teresa.

7.3

A reporter would like to interview you for a radio programme about work. Listen to the recording or read and answer these reporter's questions. (If you are not working at the moment, imagine you already have a job.)

1 Who do you work for?
2 What kind of company is that?
3 How long have you been working there?
4 What is your job title?
5 What did you do before you started your current job?
6 How many hours a week do you work?
7 What do you like/dislike about your job?
8 What's the most important quality you need to do this job?

When you have finished, listen to the second part of the recording which contains the complete interview with the questions and suggested answers.

7.4 Jumbled sentences

Fit the two parts of each sentence together, e.g. 1 and f.

1 Microsoft designs and ...
2 I'd like you to meet ...
3 Unilever NV and Unilever plc are the parent companies of what is ...
4 I don't have time to make ...
5 Why don't you ask ...
6 I have a lot of experience ...
7 Paulo was not as ...

a your colleagues to help?
b of working in teams.
c well qualified as Maria-Teresa.
d Patrick Corbet from British Airways.
e all my own travel arrangements.
f manufactures computer software.
g today one of the largest consumer goods businesses in the world.

In this unit you will practise

- **talking about figures**
- **listening to a radio broadcast for specific information**
- **making comparisons**

Language

- **currencies and money**
- **numbers and prices**
- **comparative adjectives**
- **approximate times and figures**

Introduction

8.1 Money and finance questions

- The *Financial Times* and the *Wall Street Journal* are famous business newspapers in Britain and the United States. What is the most famous business newspaper in your country?
- Bill Gates, the founder of Microsoft, is one of the richest people in the world. How much money do you think he has? $100 million? $500 million? $1,000,000 million? $5,000,000 million?
- Which of the following are connected with stock markets?

  The Nikkei, American Express, the FTSE100, Wall Street?
- In Britain the largest note is worth fifty pounds. What's the largest note in your country?
- How much is one US dollar worth in your currency?

Here are three news items. What are they about?
Stock markets? Currency rates? Inflation? Unemployment? Interest rates?

1 The most spectacular decline at the start of the year was British Airways, whose share price fell from 420p to 260p in the first quarter of 2000.

2 The government's aim to bring the number of jobless to below 3.5 million before the next election is not impossible, though it is an ambitious target.

3 The Bank of Japan has reduced its rate to zero to revive its economy, which has suffered a long-term recession since the early 1990s.

Language focus

8.2 Discussing figures

Currencies

In written English, currency symbols are placed before the number but when speaking we usually say the symbol after the number, for example:

$8,000	eight thousand dollars	SR25	twenty-five riyals
€120	one hundred and twenty euros	Y969,000	nine hundred and sixty-nine thousand yen

Note:

£5.94	five pounds ninety-four
$10.87	ten dollars eighty-seven

Decimals

In Britain and the USA we use a point (.) for decimals not a comma (,):

12.56	twelve point five six
2.1 m	two point one million

(However, be careful, as in most other countries it is common to use a comma for decimals e.g. 12,56.)

Long numbers

We use commas (,) for writing long numbers: thousands and millions:

15,000	fifteen thousand
29,568	twenty-nine thousand, five hundred and sixty-eight (*British English*)
29,568	twenty-nine thousand, five hundred, sixty-eight (*American English*)
250,789	two hundred and fifty thousand, seven hundred and eighty-nine (*British English*)
250,789	two hundred and fifty thousand, seven hundred eighty-nine (*American English*)
5,000,000	five million
£5m	five million pounds
5,000,000,000	five billion
$5.8bn	five point eight billion dollars

8.3 Currencies

According to *The Economist* magazine the average price for a McDonald's 'Big Mac' hamburger in the USA is $2.51. Can you match the countries, currencies and hamburger prices in other countries?

Country	Currency	Price of a 'Big Mac' Local currency	Hamburger Dollars
Japan	Dollar	Real 2.95	1.65
European Union	Rouble	£1.90	3.00
Brazil	Yen	Y294	2.78
Russia	Sterling	€2.56	2.37
United Kingdom	Yuan	$2.51	2.51
China	Real	NT $70.00	2.29
USA	New Dollar	Y 9.90	1.20
Taiwan	Euro	R39.50	1.39
Indonesia	Rupiah	Rp 14,500	1.83

[Source: 'Big MacCurrencies' © The Economist Newspaper Limited, London (April 27 2000)]

Listening

8.4 A news broadcast

Listen to this radio broadcast of the business news and complete the text below.

In the currency markets today the Euro fell against the dollar and sterling. This followed the announcement that Germany would hold a general election in the Autumn. Earlier in the day there were rumours about industrial unrest in France and the threat of more strikes. The euro was adversely affected, losing **(a)** ____ against the US dollar.

British exporters continued to express concern about the growing strength of sterling. British exports were increasingly expensive and uncompetitive overseas, they said. The value of sterling is now up significantly against most major currencies compared with **(b)**___ and **(c)**____months ago: **(d)**____ against the dollar, **(e)** ____ against the euro, and **(f)**____ against the Japanese yen.

Fast food giant Kentucky Fried Chicken will create **(g)** ____ new jobs over the next five years as part of a large expansion programme in Britain. Over **(h)** ____ new restaurants will open following the chain's **(i)** ____ growth in sales over a five-year period. The announcement followed the opening of KFC's 500th UK outlet in Cardiff, Wales, raising its employment levels to more than 12,000 workers. The company predicts it will have about **(j)** ____ workers in Britain by 2005.

The number of jobless in Germany unexpectedly rose by 12,000 to **(k)** ____ million in March. The German Chancellor has pledged to bring unemployment down to below **(l)** ____ million by 2004.

Language focus

8.5 Numbers

People often have difficulty using numbers. Write out the following numbers in words:

Example: €368

You write: *three hundred and sixty-eight euros*

1 3.5% ____________________
2 22,000 ____________________
3 10.5 ____________________
4 $2.78 ____________________
5 Y294 ____________________
6 £1.90 ____________________
7 9,784,596____________________
8 5,483,495____________________

Reading 1

8.6 McDonald's

Read the following article, which refers to the figures in 8.3 about the price of a 'Big Mac' hamburger, and answer the questions below:

McDonald's is the largest food service company in the world. In 1997 world-wide sales exceeded $33 billion and net income was over $1.6 billion. The company has over 23,000 restaurants in 109 countries. Its flagship product is the 'Big Mac' hamburger. The Big Mac index was launched about 15 years ago by *The Economist* magazine as a light-hearted guide to the exchange rate between currencies and the cost of living around the world. The first column of the table shows the local currency prices of a Big Mac. The second converts them into dollars: the average price of a Big Mac (including tax) in a typical American city is $2.51. The cheapest hamburger among the countries in the table is in China ($1.20). At the other extreme the most expensive is $3.00 in the United Kingdom. However, there are obvious faults in using this data to compare the cost of living in different countries, e.g. local prices may be affected by trade barriers on meat, sales taxes or significant differences in other items, such as rent.

Match a word or phrase in the text with the following words below:

1 were more than __________
2 the most important __________
3 started __________
4 not serious __________
5 changes __________
6 costly __________
7 information __________

True or false?

a McDonald's has approximately 230 restaurants in each country where it operates.
b *The Economist* created the Big Mac index.
c The cost of living is highest in the UK.

Language focus

8.7 Making comparisons

Adjectives

cheap	*cheaper*	*cheapest*
expensive	***more** expensive*	***most** expensive*

The ***cheapest*** hamburger among the countries in the table is in China ($1.20).

One or two syllables	Add *-er* or *-est*	*cheap**er***
One syllable ending with a single consonant	Double the last consonant and add *-er* or *-est*	*bigg**er***
Two syllables ending with *-y*	Change y to *i* and add *-er* or *-est*	*loveli**er***
Two or more syllables	*more* or *most* before the adjective	***more** expensive*

Other ways to make comparisons:

than — *Computers are cheaper in Hong Kong **than** in France.*
as ... as — *France imports **as** many cars **as** Italy.*

When we say that things are different we use

not as ... as — *France imports cars but **not as** many **as** Britain.*

Practice

A How do these adjectives change when making comparisons?

1 hard ________
2 dear ________
3 efficient ________
4 good ________
5 lucky ________
6 ambitious ________
7 interesting ________
8 expensive ________
9 cheap ________
10 costly ________

B Use the appropriate form of the adjectives to complete (1) the extract from the radio programme and (2) the dialogue below:

(1) Cisco Systems, the global internet specialist, is not only one of the ______ *(big)* companies in the world (based on its market value) but also the ______ *(good)* employer in the United Kingdom. According to a survey carried out by the *Sunday Times* newspaper, its staff are ______ *(happy)* and ______ *(satisfied)* with their work than any other group of employees in the country.

(2) **Mark:** Hello. How are you? Haven't seen you for a while. How are things in your new job?

Eloise: Fine, thank you. I like the work. The hours are ______ *(long)* and I have more responsibility now, so it can be very stressful at times. But it's a good career move. The company's one of the ______ *(large)* in the country so there are plenty of opportunities for promotion.

Mark: What are the people like? Is there a good work atmosphere?

Eloise: Most of the employees are ______ *(young)* than me. In fact the boss is only in his mid-thirties.

Reading 2

8.8 Skimming and scanning

Read the following article and answer these questions:

1 Who was responsible for the £32 billion loss?
2 What was the reaction when the trader sold £300 million in shares instead of £3 million?

Two zeros add up to £32 billion loss

A city trader's typing error cost his bosses more than £2 million and led to a £32 billion plunge on the London stock market. By accidentally keying in a couple of extra noughts on his computer screen, the trader sold £300 million of shares instead of the £3 million he meant to.

The error, made during share deal in the closing minutes of trading on Monday, caused the FTSE-100 Index to fall 140 points and sparked an inquiry into the safety of the computer system involved.

City trading floors were buzzing with speculation about the identity of the investment bank and the trader. US firm Lehman Brothers has been linked to the incident but has declined to comment. The trader's bank will almost certainly have to buy back the shares at higher prices. Analysts put the losses at about £2 million.

Despite attempts yesterday morning to rectify the situation, the stock market refused to cancel the trade. A Stock Exchange spokesman said: 'We are continuing to speak to the firm in order to investigate how tight their internal controls are. We expect a certain standard of integrity from member firms and if we find that adequate controls aren't in place we have the power to fine them.'

The sell order involved a clutch of stocks and sent prices of some of the market's biggest names, including Vodafone and BP, significantly lower. Henk Potts, of Barclays Stockbrokers, said: 'There would have been a few traders staring in disbelief at their screens for a few minutes.' But, he said, most traders would soon have grasped there had been a mistake.

The Footsie recovered most of the losses, gaining more than 130 points in the first 15 minutes of trading yesterday.

[*Source*: 'Two zeros add up to £32 billion loss' by Rebecca Mowling, *Metro*, 6 May 2001]

8.9 Vocabulary

Choose the best meaning from **a**, **b** or **c** for each word or expression in 8.8.

1 led to (*line 3*)
- **a** brought to
- **b** resulted in
- **c** followed through

2 keying (*line 4*)
- **a** typing
- **b** opening
- **c** turning

3 sparked (*line 9*)
- **a** stopped
- **b** started
- **c** delayed

4 rectify (*line 17*)
- **a** correct
- **b** prevent
- **c** control

5 tight (*line 20*)
- **a** good
- **b** helpful
- **c** united

6 integrity (*line 21*)
- **a** honesty
- **b** ability
- **c** competence

7 clutch (*line 23*)
- **a** a number
- **b** a bag
- **c** a small group

8 in disbelief (*line 26*)
- **a** feeling incredible
- **b** not believing
- **c** in good faith

9 grasped (*line 28*)
- **a** wondered
- **b** understood
- **c** said

10 Footsie (*line 29*)
- **a** FT 100 SE
- **b** the Ft company
- **c** Foot group of companies

8.10 Comprehension

Are the following statements true or false?

Read the article in 8.8 again.

- **a** The trader sold too many shares.
- **b** The problem was the result of a computer error.
- **c** Lehman Brothers have admitted it was their mistake.
- **d** The Stock Exchange will fine Vodafone.
- **e** Traders immediately knew that there had been a mistake.
- **f** The Footsie gradually recovered the losses over the next few days.

8.11 Approximating

Analysts put the losses ***at about £2million.***

Match these questions and answers.

1 How long did it take to get there?
2 What time is your meeting?
3 What's the rate at the moment?
4 How much are they?

a *They cost about $450 each.*
b *I think £1 sterling is worth about US $1.20.*
c *It's round about three o'clock*
d *About an hour or so.*

Lesson summary

In this lesson you have practised:

- Using figures to discuss currencies and money.
- Extracting information from a radio broadcast.
- Making comparisons between companies.
- Approximating.

Suggestions for further practice

1 Is it possible to buy shares in your company? Look in the financial press and find out the cost of a share.

2 Make a list of statistics about your company. For example, its value, the number of employees, sales. This kind of information may be publicly available in printed form or on the web.

3 Practise listening to numbers in English. For example, listen to the BBC financial news and keep a record of how much your country's currency changes against the dollar in one week.

09 using the telephone

In this unit you will practise

- understanding and using telephone language
- making offers and requests on the phone
- making plans and arrangements
- understanding and leaving voicemail messages

Language

- phone numbers
- the English alphabet and spelling aloud
- the future tenses

Introduction

9.1 Telephone questions

- Do you use the telephone a lot?
- How often do you use English on the telephone?
- What do you find difficult? Understanding the other person? Giving information clearly? Knowing appropriate expressions? Anything else?

Listening 1

9.2 On the phone

Christos Georgiou is telephoning the office of Jim Smith. However, Christos is unable to speak to Jim. If possible, listen to the recording first, before you read the conversation below and try to understand why Jim Smith can't talk to Christos Georgiou. Don't worry about trying to understand everything you hear/read.

Secretary Good morning. Business Travel Limited.
Christos May I speak to Jim Smith, please?
Secretary Sorry. His line's busy. Do you want to hold?
Christos Yes, please.
(*phone ringing*)
Secretary Sorry to keep you waiting, caller.
(*phone ringing*)
Secretary Sorry. His line's still engaged. Do you want to hold or would you rather leave a message?
Christos Could you ask him to ring Christos Georgiou from Multimedia Solutions Incorporated on 020 85983? I'll be at this number all morning but I'll be out of the office this afternoon.
Secretary Sorry. Could you spell the name?
Christos The first name is C-H-R-I-S-T-O-S. The surname is G-E-O-R-G-I-O-U.
Secretary Okay. Thank you. I'll make sure he gets your message, Mr Georgiou.
Christos Thank you. Goodbye.
Secretary Goodbye.

9.3 A telephone message

Jim Smith's secretary puts the note below on his desk. Compare the note with the phone conversation. There are five errors in the note. Can you find them? Listen to the conversation again if necessary and write your answers below. Then check your answers in the Answer key.

1 The caller's name is Mr Georgiou, not Mr Christos.
2 ....
3 ....
4 ....
5 ....

Business Travel Ltd
<u>MESSAGE</u>

Day: *Monday* Date: *14-05* Time: *11:05* am/pm
To: *Jim Smith* Extension: *3175*

While you were out...
Mr/Mrs/Ms : *Christos*
Phone number: *020 85993* Company: *Multimedia Solutions Corporation*

called
came to see you
will call you back
call him/her back
is waiting to see you in...
has left the following message

He will be in his office this afternoon.

Received by: *Andrea*

9.4 What would you say?

1 You are telephoning a client. He picks up the phone and says 'Hello'. What is your reply?
  a Hello. Here is Juan.
  b Hello. I am Juan Garcia.
  c Hello. Juan Garcia speaking.

2 The phone rings. Somebody wants to speak to a colleague who is not in the office today. What do you say?
  a I'm sorry. She's not here. Can I take a message?
  b I'm sorry. She's not here. I'm taking a message.
  c I'm sorry. She's not here. Do you like me to write a message?

3 A client you are talking to on the telephone also needs to talk to your colleague Peter Gray in another department. You are going to transfer the call. What do you say?
  a Just hold on and I'll put you across to Peter Gray.
  b Just hold on and I'll put you through to Peter Gray.
  c Just hold on and I'll turn you on to Peter Gray.

4 You're talking to a client but you didn't catch the name of the client's company. What do you say?
  a I didn't catch the name of your company. Can you repeat it, please?
  b Repeat, if you please, the name of your company. I didn't catch it.
  c I didn't catch the name of your company. Repeat it again please.

Language focus

9.5 Telephone numbers

Telephone numbers in English are spoken as separate digits.

You read/write	You hear/say
5980 3761	*five nine eight zero, ... three seven six one*
8499 3872	*eight four double nine, ... three eight seven two* OR *eight four nine nine, ... three eight seven two*

Practice

Listen to these telephone numbers and say them:

a 5599 0921	d 8574 0021
b 7846 2254	e 8593 0900
c 0466 8777	f 3364 0986

9.6 The alphabet and spelling

How do you spell your family name? You often need to spell names on the telephone. Do you know how to pronounce the letters of the English alphabet?

It is easy to get confused about the vowel sounds of letters. For example, some people get confused between J and G, or I and E and A. The chart below shows the letters sorted into six groups. All the letters in the same group have the same vowel sound. Listen and try to say them.

AHJK: These all have the /eɪ/ sound.
BCDEGPV: These all contain the /i:/ sound, as in *bee* or *tree*. In American English the last letter of the alphabet is also pronounced like this. Z (zee)
FLMNX: These contain the sound /e/ as in *help* or *red*. In British English, the last letter of the alphabet is pronounced like this. Z (zed)
IY: These contain the /aɪ/ sound as in *try* or *high*.
O: This is the only letter with the /əʊ/ sound as in *boat*.
QUW: These all contain the /u:/ sound as in *blue* or *zoo*.

Here are some more characters in English that sometimes form parts of names and serial numbers that you have to spell out to people.

/ slash or stroke	\ backslash	- dash or hyphen
( ) brackets or parentheses	(open bracket	) close bracket
' apostrophe	@ at	

Don't forget that we say the number 0 in different ways in English:

Zero, O, and *nought* are the most common ones.

When spelling out names and other words which have two letters the same, or reading out numbers, we sometimes say 'double' instead of repeating the letter or number, for example:

Little is spelt L-I-double T-L-E (LITTLE).
The telephone number for reservations and tickets is double nine five, three two double seven (9953277).

There are different ways to ask someone how to spell something:

How do you spell your name?
How do you write that?
Can you tell me how to spell that?

Practice

Practise spelling these names. Say them out loud:

Christos Georgiou   Millennium Systems   Wickham Displays

Your name______________________________
The name of your company/college______________________

Listening 2

9.7 Voicemail messages

It's particularly important when listening to telephone messages to be able to recognize the letters of the alphabet and numbers.

Jim Smith is checking the messages on his voicemail. Listen and complete the table below.

	Message 1	Message 2	Message 3	Message 4
Name		*Liam Dwyer*		*Yasuko Kitamura*
Date				
Dept./ Company	*Anglo-Spanish Travel Services*			
Tel no.				

9.8 Telephone requests and offers

Match a line from column **A** with a line in column **B** to create mini-dialogues.

Example: 1f.

A	B
1 I'd like to speak to Judy Davies, please.	a Go ahead. Dial 9 for an outside line.
2 Can I take a message?	b Certainly. Has he got your number?
3 Could you give him a message?	c It's M-O-L-E-W-S-K-I.
4 Would you mind spelling your last name?	d No, that's okay, I'll call again later.
5 Can you tell me when she will be back in the office?	e Of course, sir, no problem.
6 Do you think I could use your phone? I need to contact my office.	f Hold on, I'll put you through.
7 Could you ask him to give me a call back this afternoon?	g She should be here this afternoon.

9.9 In your own language

Look at these expressions. How would you say them in your language?

1. I'll call/phone/ring you tomorrow. OR I'll give you a call tomorrow.
2. Hello, this is Jim Smith from BTL. OR Jim Smith from BTL speaking.
3. His line is engaged. OR His extension is busy.
4. I'll transfer you to my colleague Michael White. Hold on a minute, please. OR I'll put you through to my colleague Michael White. Hold on a minute, please.
5. Sorry, could you repeat that? I didn't catch it. OR Sorry, I didn't catch your name. Would you mind saying it again?
6. How do you spell that? How do you spell your last name?
7. Can you speak more slowly please? My English isn't all that good.
8. Can you speak a bit louder? OR Can you speak up a little?
9. Would you like to hold, or leave a message?
10. I'll call back later.

Listening 3

9.10 Second phone call

Jim Smith from Business Travel Ltd has received the telephone message from Christos Georgiou. He is telephoning Multimedia Solutions Incorporated to return Christos Georgiou's call.

If possible, listen to the recording before you read the conversation in **9.12**. Don't try to understand everything. Just listen for the answer to this question:

Question: What was the main problem discussed in the telephone call?

a a problem with MSI's website?
b a delay?
c a mistake with delivery of new software?

9.11 Listen for the details

Answer these **True/False** questions. Circle **T** or **F**. Then listen to the conversation in **9.10** again to check if you were correct.

1 Christos Georgiou is returning John Smith's call. T / F
2 Christos called Jim Smith earlier. T / F
3 Jim wanted to tell Christos about a problem. T / F
4 Multimedia Solutions is designing a new website for Business Travel Limited. T / F
5 The delay will not cause serious problems. T / F
6 Jim is angry about the delay. T / F
7 The product will be delivered at the end of next week. T / F

9.12 Second phone call – the script

Here is the script of the conversation you heard in **9.10**. Fill in the missing words. Then listen to the recording again to check (PA = personal assistant).

PA	Multimedia Solutions Incorporated, Development Section, good morning.
Jim	Oh hello, I'd ________ to speak to Christos Georgiou.
PA	He's on the other line at the moment. I'm his PA. Can I ask who's ________?
Jim	Yes, ________ is Jim Smith from Business Travel Limited. I'm ________ his call from this morning.

PA	Oh yes, Mr Smith. _________ on just a second, I think he's just finished.
Christos	Hello Jim, sorry to _________ you waiting.
Jim	No problem. What's up?
Christos	_________ about the new version of your website. We had some problems with the changes you asked for last week, but it's all _________ out now. However, we are behind schedule and we are not _________ to be able to deliver next week.
Jim	Well, when do you think you will _________ able to deliver?
Christos	We only need two extra days. It'll be _________ for installation by Tuesday of the week after next.
Jim	As long as we get it on the Tuesday there should be no problem. Are you sure there _________ be any more delays?
Christos	Yes, I'm sure.
Jim	Okay, that's fine. But if anything else does come up, please let me _________ as early as possible.
Christos	Of course. If we have any more problems, _________ let you know immediately.
Jim	Thanks a lot. I'll give you a _________ at the end of next week anyway.
Christos	Fine. _________ speak to you then. Have a good weekend.
Jim	Bye.

Practice

Now practise saying the dialogue on your own or with a friend. Look at **Suggestions for further practice** for some other ideas.

Language focus

9.13 *Will* and *going to*

Look at these four mini-dialogues. Then answer the questions below.

1

A The new designs are ready.
B Okay, I'll come and have a look at them this afternoon.

2

A I'm going to have a look at the new designs.

3

A I'm flying over to New York next week.
B Oh, really? When are you leaving?
A Monday afternoon.
B How long for?
A I'm coming back on Thursday.

4

A I've got all these reports to check by Friday. It's impossible.
B I'll give you a hand, if you like.
A That would be great. Will you check the ones from the finance department?

a Which conversations are about plans already made?
b Which conversations are about plans just being made at the moment of speaking?
c Which sentence is an offer to help?
d Which sentence is a request?
e Which conversation is about definite travel arrangements for the near future?

Now complete these grammar rules by matching the phrases on the left with those on the right.

1 We use *will* future
2 We use *going to* + infinitive
3 We use present progressive future
4 We also use *will*

a in offers and requests.
b to talk about definite travel plans in the near future.
c to talk about future plans just as they are being decided.
d to talk about plans already made.

See **Language reference** for further details.

9.14 Further practice of the future

Choose the best reply to complete each conversation. Then listen to the recording to check your answers.

1 Any plans for the holidays?
  a Yes, I'm going to go to the USA for a week.
  b Yes, I'm flying to the USA for a week.
  c Yes, I will visit the USA for a week.

2 Your secretary called.
  a Okay, I'm going to call her back.
  b Okay, I'm calling her back.
  c Okay, I'll call her back.

3 How is the new website design coming along?
  a Fine, I think, but I will meet the designers this afternoon.
  b Fine, I think, but I'm going to meet the designers this afternoon.
  c Fine, I think, but I meet the designers this afternoon.

4 Has the company made a decision on the new products yet?
  a Not yet, but we will discuss it in the development meeting on Friday.
  b Not yet, but we are going to discuss it in the development meeting on Friday.

5 **Secretary** I'm afraid Mr Jones isn't in the office this morning. Can I take a message?
  Caller Yes please. It's Jim Smith from Business Travel Limited. Could you tell him I'll call him tomorrow?

Secretary a Certainly, Mr Smith. I'm going to give him your message as soon as he arrives.
b Certainly, Mr Smith. I'm giving him your message as soon as he arrives.
c Certainly, Mr Smith. I'll give him your message as soon as he arrives.

9.15 What would you say?

1 The receptionist tells you there is an English-speaking client on the telephone, then she puts the call through to you. What would you say?
For example, you could say:
Hello, John Clinton here, how can I help you?

2 You telephone a supplier, and they answer the phone like this: 'Comlink Limited, good morning.'
You say: ....

3 The person you are visiting tells you that your Managing Director called earlier and wants to talk to you urgently.
You say: ....

4 Someone asks you about your plans for the weekend.
You say: ....

5 You are on a business trip abroad. Someone asks you when you are returning home.
You say:..

6 You want to know about delivery dates for a product on order.
You say: ....

Some suggested answers have been recorded for you. Listen to check your answers.

Lesson summary

Here are some of the things you practised in this lesson:

- Telephone language:
  Hello, this is ...
  I'd like to speak to ...

I'll put you through.
The line's engaged/busy. Do you want to hold?
Sorry to keep you waiting.
Can I take a message?

- Offers and requests:
  Would you like me to take a message?
  Shall I get him to call you back?
  I'll tell him you called, if you like.
  Do you think I could use your phone?
  Would you mind spelling your name again?
  Could you ask him to call me back?

- Talking about future plans:
  We're going to discuss this at tomorrow's meeting.
  I'm flying back on Thursday evening.
  I'll let you know tomorrow.

- Telephone numbers:
  764 1966 'seven six four, one nine six six'
  020 895 4322 'oh two oh, eight nine five, four three double two'

Suggestions for further practice

1 Play the recording without looking at the script. Pause the recording at the end of each line and try to remember what comes next.

2 Write a similar dialogue using your own company's name and products, or changing the situation to something that happened to you recently.

3 Think of other situations where you need to make requests or offers. What would you say?

4 Find a telephone conversation on a British or American video. Write out the conversation and practise it.

5 Practise the dialogues with a friend, first looking at the script, then without looking at the script.

6 Work with a partner. Each writes down 10 telephone numbers. Dictate your numbers to your partner in English.

7 Ask a good English-speaking friend to record telephone messages for you. Listen and write down the messages.

10 e-commerce

In this unit you will practise

- **discussing the role of computers in business**
- **talking about advertising on the web**
- **giving a presentation**

Language

- **information technology**
- **presentations: useful expressions**
- **pronunciation: stress**

Introduction

10.1 Are you computer literate?

- Do you use the internet in your work?
- What is the difference between the internet and the web?
- Do you have an e-mail address?
- Do you know the names of any IT companies? Can you use any software packages?
- Which of the following are famous international IT companies? Cisco systems; Sun; Sony; McDonald's; Ford; Mercedes?

The following terms are used when discussing IT. Can you match the words on the left with their definitions?

software	electronic business, e.g. via the web
hardware	program which searches through a database
PC	system of interconnected PCs
telemarketing	computing program, e.g. Word, Excel
e-commerce	physical components of computing, e.g. disks
network	selling only via the telephone
search engine	personal computer

Listening 1

10.2 Computer talk

Listen to the recording or read these conversations and decide which of the terms described in **10.1** the speakers are talking about.

1 ....

2 ....

3 ....

4 ....

1 **A** Which would you recommend then?
B Well, there are a lot of them now on the web and they can vary in quality a great deal. With the bad ones you can spend ages searching to find what you're looking for. Yahoo is my favourite but I sometimes use Lycos and Altavista too.

2 A Where do you get yours from?
B A company called Computer Inc. They import the components from the Far East and assemble the PCs and printers here.

3 A Hello. Helpdesk here. Can I help you?
B Hi. This is Steve Robbins from Marketing. I don't seem able to get access to the customer database. Another person in my department is having the same problem.
A I'm afraid the whole system is down at the moment. Try again in, say, 15 minutes and hopefully the engineers will have fixed the problem by then.

4 A Thank you for applying for the job and coming to this interview. For the position of administration officer, we are looking for someone who is comfortable using Microsoft Word and Excel.
B I'm familiar with both. I used them regularly in my last position.

Reading

10.3 IT and banking

How has e-commerce changed business activity? What effect have computerization and the internet had on the world of commerce?

A Read the article below. What does it say about the impact of new technology on business?

THE IMPACT OF E-COMMERCE ON BANKING

The cost of an ordinary banking transaction in a branch is 100 times that on the web

Information technology has radically changed the way many industries work. The ability of computers to store and handle information has allowed businesses to get rid of paper records. Computers can store vast amounts of information in a small space, so companies are able to keep much more detailed information about their clients and suppliers. IT has also speeded up the handling of information, so that data can be found easily, sorted instantly and accessed from many different places.

The internet and e-mail have revolutionized business communication. Intranets allow employees to 'talk' to each other, to distribute memos and to access company documents and databases without moving from their desks. The internet allows business people to access all kinds of essential information and to communicate almost instantly with clients, suppliers and other contacts.

Within the traditional banking sector, electronic commerce has brought about radical change. The high-speed transfer of information has allowed customers to access their accounts through ATMs (Automatic Teller Machines) – also known as 'hole-in-the-wall' banking machines. Customers not only withdraw money from wherever they are, they can also check their account balances, order a statement and even print out a mini-statement of their banking records. One of the major reasons banks have encouraged the greater use of technology is cost efficiency. The cost of an ordinary banking transaction in a branch is 100 times greater than that on the web (Digital Britain 1999 Microsoft limited). With online banking, customers can access their account from their home or office PCs and carry out banking business without ever going near a 'real' bank. As a result banks need fewer branches and fewer employees to deal with customers' needs.

B Now read the article again and answer these questions:

1 How much cheaper is it to carry out a transaction on the internet than in a branch?
2 Complete the following table:

The impact of e-commerce on banking	
Advantages	**Disadvantages**
__________	__________
__________	__________
__________	__________
__________	__________
__________	__________

10.4 Vocabulary – Word partnerships

A Join together words from each column to make word partnerships.

Example: 1e

1 service	**a** records
2 information	**b** changes
3 paper	**c** technology

4 radical — d information
5 essential — e industries

B Now complete these sentences using one of the word partnerships in A.

1 The computer system is not working again. Fortunately we have ________ ________ of the data you require.
2 The impact of ____________ ____________ has caused the banking industry to experience enormous changes in recent years.
3 One result of the ____________ ____________ in banking has been the redundancy of large numbers of staff.
4 In certain parts of the country as much as 70 per cent of the workforce are now employed in the ____________ ____________.
5 ____________ ____________, such as clients' details, are kept on a database in the marketing office.

Language focus

10.5 Pronunciation – Stress

When we speak the emphasis we give to a particular syllable in a word is called stress. For example the stress in *num*ber is on the first syllable. In the word ad*vise* it is on the second syllable.

Dictionaries usually indicate the pronunciation of a word using phonetic symbols, e.g. /ˈsimbəl/. However, if you do not know phonetics, you can still work out the stress. Normally, there is a ˈ symbol (e.g. /ˈnʌmbə/, /ədˈvaɪz/) before the stressed syllable.

A Listen and repeat the following words, in particular noting the stress.

B Listen again and mark the stress. The first one has been done as an example:

mobile	*ˈmobile*	borrow
important		easy
clever		exchange
advertisement		increase
total		special
afford		advise

Listening 2

10.6 Advertising online

A Pre-listening questions: It is now possible to buy everything from books and CDs to airline tickets and house insurance on the web. Most business people believe that buying and selling online will become increasingly important.

- Have you ever bought something online?
- Does your company advertise online?
- Have you seen adverts on the web? Do you think they are effective?

B Listen to Wang Yi, an IT consultant. Make notes as you listen. How many different types of advertising methods does she discuss?

Wang Yi Well, the most popular form of web advertising is the banner ad. These appear as a rectangular block which flashes or moves on the screen trying to attract your attention. In my opinion they don't achieve very much. Most people just ignore them. The bottom line is that people simply do not click on ads.

Peter Blake So they are a waste of money?

Wang Yi In my opinion, yes, I think so. However, I know others take a different view and feel that if the ad is compelling enough it can reinforce the company's brand in the consumer's mind. But, personally I'm not convinced it's worth the money.

Peter Blake What other forms of advertising are there?

Wang Yi Classified advertising has better results than banners.

Peter Blake With classifieds you pay to have your product or service listed in specific categories, don't you?

Wang Yi Yes, that's it. The same as the classified ads in the newspaper.

Peter Blake I guess it's probably more successful because users are searching for a specific item, such as accommodation, a builder or whatever.

Wang Yi Yes. What is more, it can suit all budgets. Also, it's sometimes possible to get a free basic listing and then to upgrade to include hyperlinks and email enquiry forms.

Peter Blake	Anything else worth considering?
Wang Yi	I would recommend e-zines.
Peter Blake	These are electronic magazines?
Wang Yi	That's right. An advert in an appropriate e-zine can be a highly effective form of promotion. If the marketing message is sufficiently targeted to its audience, then it is estimated that as many as one in five users will click through your website. This compares with the average click rate of between 0.3 and 0.1 per cent for the banner advertising.

Comprehension

1 Which is the most successful kind of advertising on the web? Why?
2 Which method of advertising would you use if you didn't have much money to spend?
3 Which is the least successful way of advertising?
4 You are also at this meeting on advertising on the web. What questions would you ask?

Listening 3

10.7 Preparing a presentation

A Can you think of a person, famous or perhaps someone you know at work, who is a good public speaker? Nelson Mandela? The American President? The president of your country? What are the qualities of a good speaker? Which of the following are important? not very important? unhelpful?

	important	not very important	unhelpful
appear confident	✔		
to speak loudly and slowly			
lots of good jokes			
give detailed information			
use visual aids			
read your presentation from your notes			
knowledge of the audience			

B Roberto Diaz is going to give a presentation on web advertising. Although he knows a lot about the topic he doesn't feel confident about his presentation skills and has asked a colleague, Paulo Gonzalez, to advise. Listen to the two versions of the start of Roberto's presentation, one before and one after receiving advice. Which one is better and why?

Introduction 1

Good morning everybody. My name is Roberto Diaz from Webmaster Incorporated and I'm very pleased to be here today to talk to you about starting up online advertising. The presentation will be divided into two parts. I'd like to start by offering some general guidelines concerning online advertising, then I will discuss the costs involved and finally my recommendations for your company. Of course, I will be happy to answer any questions either during or at the end of the presentation.

Introduction 2

Hi everybody. My company, Webmaster Incorporated, sent me here to talk about online advertising. I believe you're thinking about doing some advertising on the web. Basically, I'm going to talk about the kind of work I do at Webmaster and you can ask questions. I don't know if I'll be able to answer them but I'll try.

C Listen to the recording or read the dialogue between Paulo and Roberto. What advice does Paulo give for the following:

1 the introduction

2 the main body of the presentation

3 the conclusion

Paulo Well, most people are nervous when giving a presentation. And some find it more difficult to speak in public than others. However, there are certain things you can do to make sure that your presentation is effective. Find out about the audience. How much do they know about the subject? I think your audience for this talk know very little about on-line advertising so you will have to include some basic information about doing business on the web. Also, check out the location. You will feel more comfortable if you know what the room will be like. Will it be here at Webmaster or is the presentation elsewhere?

Roberto It's in the conference room upstairs.

Paulo Fine. You should separate the presentation into three parts: introduction, main body and conclusion. In the introduction you introduce yourself, the purpose of the presentation and say how you will organize things... you know... something like... first, I'm going to discuss this, then I'll talk about that... and so on. Oh, and say whether you want the audience to ask questions during or at the end of the presentation. I put a lot of time and effort into getting the introduction right. Usually I memorize the words of the introduction just like an actor does with a script. First impressions are very important. Then, in the main part of the presentation clearly signal each of the points. I use Microsoft Powerpoint and have each main point displayed on an overhead screen. Finally, in the conclusion a brief summary, thank them for their attention and ask again about questions.

Roberto You make it sound easy.

Paulo Well, it isn't. But if you spend some time preparing yourself I'm sure you will be fine.

Language focus

10.8 Useful phrases for presentations

Here are some useful expressions for making an effective presentation:

Introducing yourself:

Good afternoon. My name is Paulo Diaz and I'm the Marketing Director at Webmaster Inc.

Hello. I'm Paulo Diaz and on behalf of Webmaster Inc I'd like to welcome you to today's presentation.

Telling the audience about the structure of your presentation:

My talk will be divided into five parts. Part one will deal with ... and part two ...

First of all, I'm going to look at ... Then ...

Introducing the first point:

I'd like to begin by discussing ...

To start with, I'd like to consider ...

Starting a new point:

Moving on ...

Next ...

Referring to a previous point:

As I said before ...

In part one of my talk I mentioned ...

Concluding:

That brings me to the end of my presentation. Thank you for your attention.

That concludes my talk. Thank you very much.

Inviting questions:

Are there any questions?

If you have any questions, I will be glad to answer them.

Under which of the above headings would you put the following expressions?

1 That covers everything I wanted to say.
2 Next we come to ...
3 Let me introduce myself.
4 So, to summarize ...
5 As I said previously ...
6 I'd like to conclude here.

Listening 4

10.9 The presentation

Listen to Roberto's practice presentation.

1 How many of the expressions in **10.8** does he use?

2 Does he follow Paulo's advice?

Hello. I'm Roberto Diaz, Marketing Director of Webmaster Inc and on behalf of the company I'd like to welcome you to this presentation about online advertising. This is a new, exciting and powerful way of increasing your company's presence in the marketplace and today I want to offer some general guidelines.

To start with, you should do some research and make a list of those websites that sell advertising space and therefore are likely to attract your target customer. For example, a travel agent might advertise on the National Tourist Organization website.

Secondly, some sites are much more popular than others, so find out how many people visit the site. For e-zine advertising you should find out the number of subscribers your message will be going to. The owners of the site should be able to provide these statistics, called 'site demographics'.

Thirdly, think carefully about which page on your website you'd like to send visitors to. For large organizations the home page is hardly ever the best place. However, if it's a product information page or an enquiry from deep within your site you need to ensure that this page has sufficient links for the user to be able to continue navigating. If there is a danger that your visitors will get lost, then consider designing a 'bridging' page to welcome visitors from your adverts.

Fourthly, having an e-mail enquiry form on another website is an efficient way to capture new enquirers if the e-mail is set up to go to the right person. This may seem obvious but it can be a problem in large organizations with centralized marketing departments. Whose responsibility is it to respond? Is it policy to acknowledge enquiries within a specified time limit?

After a set period – say, three months – results can be measured in terms of an increase in the number of visitors to your site (which is good); an increase in the number of e-mail enquiries received (which is better); an increase in the number of products/services bought (which is best of all).

A regular analysis of these figures against your expenditure on marketing will help you calculate the return on your investment. Online advertising is simply a way to get surfers to the right part of your website more quickly, ensuring that their expectations are fulfilled...

...Well, that brings me to the end of my presentation. If you have any questions I will be happy to answer them.

[Source: 'A look at the most effective options available to online advertisers' by Fiona Joseph, EL Gazette, June 2001]

10.10 Prepare a short presentation

Try to prepare your own presentation using the following information:

Subject: Your job and your ambitions.

Audience: Your old school has invited past students to talk about their work to those currently in the final year of their school education.

Main body: Qualifications and skills needed/responsibilities of the job/ advantages and disadvantages/career future.

Record your presentation on cassette or, even better, on a video tape. When you have practised your presentation think about these questions.

1 What do you think someone listening to your presentation would say about it and why? What were the strengths of the presentation?
2 Did you keep to your time limit? If not, why?
3 Do you feel the presentation was well-organized? For example, did you indicate clearly when you were moving to another point?
4 Did you have any visual materials, such as drawings or plans, to help illustrate your talk?

5 What questions do you think the audience might ask? Do you have answers for these questions?
6 If possible, ask a friend who speaks English to watch your presentation and comment on the delivery, e.g. was your voice loud enough? Did you speak too quickly or too slowly? Could you remember what to say or did you keep looking at your notes?
7 When you do the presentation again how will you do it differently?

(See also **Useful web addresses** on page 237.)

socializing

In this unit you will practise

- making and responding to invitations
- social conversations with business contacts
- entertaining business clients (in a restaurant and in a bar)

Language

- accepting and declining invitations
- small talk
- business idioms
- formality
- polite requests

Listening 1

11.1 Invitations

Establishing good personal relations can be very important for success in business. Consequently, entertaining clients and socializing with prospective business partners is a regular part of commercial life. A lot of business deals take place outside the company office, in conversations in a bar or during a meal at a restaurant.

Michael Blythe works for an international accounting firm and his job frequently includes entertaining foreign clients. You are going to hear extracts from two telephone conversations involving Michael Blythe.

1 In which dialogue is Michael Blythe's invitation to go for a meal not accepted?
2 In which dialogue is Michael Blythe talking to someone he already knows?
3 Listen to the dialogues again and fill in the missing words.

Dialogue 1

Michael Blythe	Hi Faisal. Good to talk to you again. How are you?
Faisal Ali	Fine, thanks Michael. How are you?
Michael Blythe	Very good, thanks.
Faisal Ali	Can you remind me about the timetable on Friday when I'm coming to your office?
Michael Blythe	We're meeting Peter Bowles, the marketing manager, at 2 pm and then Fred Johnson, the general manager, will join us at 4 pm. I think you met Fred when you were here last time but you won't have met Peter before as he only started here a couple of months ago.
Faisal Ali	That's fine. I look forward to meeting them. So, do you think we will be able to get everything sorted out by the end of the day?
Michael Blythe	Yes, sure. We should be finished by 5 pm.
Faisal Ali	Great.
Michael Blythe	Faisal, would you be free before 2 pm? ________________ first for lunch, say at 12.00? We could go to a local restaurant just near our offices.

Faisal Ali	Yes. _______________. Shall I meet you at, say 11.50, in the foyer of your office block?

Dialogue 2

Andrea Hall	Hello. Andrea Hall here.
Michael Blythe	Good morning Ms Hall. Michael Blythe here from Wisbech International.
Andrea Hall	Oh hello, Mr Blythe.
Michael Blythe	I'm ringing in connection with the arrangements for your visit to our offices later this week. We had arranged to have the meeting on Friday afternoon, probably finishing around 5 pm. And _______________ you and your colleagues would let us take you to dinner afterwards.
Andrea Hall	_______________. I'm afraid I will have to say no. Unfortunately our flight back to Glasgow leaves at 6.30 so I doubt if there will be enough time for a meal. However, we could perhaps go for a drink if there's a suitable bar near your offices?
Michael Blythe	Yes. We're in the centre of town so there are lots ...

Language focus

11.2 Accepting and declining

Inviting
(a new business client)

We were wondering if you and your colleagues would let us take you to dinner?
Would you care to join us for dinner?
We would like to invite you to dinner.

(someone you know well)
How about dinner later on?
Why not join us for dinner later?
Do you fancy a drink later?

Accepting invitations

(a new business contact)
Thank you very much. That would be nice.
Thank you. I'd be delighted to join you.

(less formal, someone you know)
Thanks. A good idea.
Thanks. Great.

Refusing an invitation

(a new business contact)
Thank you for inviting me. Unfortunately I have a prior engagement. Maybe we could arrange something for another time?
That's very kind of you. However, I'm afraid I have another commitment on Friday evening.

(less formal, someone you know)
Thanks. But, I'm sorry. I can't that particular evening. Another time, perhaps?

Listening 2

11.3 More invitations

Listen to the recording. Respond to the invitations using the expressions given in **11.2**.

a Accept the invitation.
b Decline the invitation.
c Accept the invitation.

a If you're free later this evening, we were wondering if you would like to meet us for a drink?
b As it's your first time in Minsk, I would be happy to show you round the city's main sites. Would you be interested?
c Do you play golf? There is a fabulous course on the outskirts of the city. If you like, we could arrange to play a few rounds at the weekend.

Listening 3

11.4 New contacts and old friends (formality)

You will hear two conversations. Read the information given below about the speakers. What differences would you expect to hear in a conversation between business people who know each other well and people who meet for the first time?

Conversation A

Anna Smith is part of a British Government trade delegation to South Korea. After the official speeches are over she attends a cocktail reception where the delegates have a chance to socialize and to network. She is introduced to Mr Sang Hoon.

Conference Organizer	May I introduce Mr Sang Hoon?
Sang Hoon	How do you do Ms Smith?
Anna Smith	How do you do?
Sang Hoon	I enjoyed your presentation very much.
Anna Smith	Thank you.
Sang Hoon	May I give you my card? My name is Mr Sang Hoon from *Dysanne* Engineering plant.
Anna Smith	Thank you. And here's mine. My apologies again for arriving a little late this morning at the presentation and keeping you all waiting. The plane into Seoul was delayed by bad weather.
Sang Hoon	Oh, not at all. That's quite all right. Would you care for a cigarette?
Anna Smith	No thank you. I gave up a couple of years ago.
Sang Hoon	Is this your first visit to Korea, Ms Smith?

Conversation B

Mark Greenspan from New York and Julio da Silva from Mexico City have done business together many times. Julio is visiting New York and has arranged to meet Mark in a bar in the evening.

Mark Greenspan	Hi Julio. Good to see you again.
Julio da Silva	Mark! Hello. How are you?
Mark Greenspan	Sorry I'm late.
Julio da Silva	Oh, that's okay.
Mark Greenspan	I'm fine, thanks. How are things in Mexico City? How's business?
Julio da Silva	Good. Very good in fact. There's talk of expansion and opening new offices in Acapulco.
Mark Greenspan	Really! Let me get you a drink and then you can tell me all about it. What would you like? A beer?
Julio da Silva	Yeah. That'd be great. Is it okay to smoke in here?
Mark Greenspan	Go ahead. We're in the smoking area.
Julio da Silva	Thanks. Well, cheers!
Mark Greenspan	Cheers, Julio. How's the family?
Julio da Silva	They're great. Maria sends her regards. How are your kids getting on?
Mark Greenspan	Oh, pretty much the same as usual. So tell me about these expansion plans.
Julio da Silva	Well, they're already pretty far advanced. We're hoping to get the green light this month to rent the place in Acapulco.
Mark Greenspan	Who's going to be working down there?
Julio da Silva	I think Juan has got it all sewn up. It was his baby in the first place.

Comprehension

1 Who smokes?
2 Who has just given a presentation?
3 Where does Julio work?
4 What did Sang Hoon give to Anna Smith?
5 What did Mark offer Julio?

Note:

1 'How do you do?' is only used when you meet someone for the first time. Also, it is not really a question but a formal way to say Hello.
2 'How are you?' is a question and requires an answer. 'Fine, thanks'.

Language focus

11.5 Small talk

'Small talk' describes the remarks we make to friends and people we meet to start a conversation or just to be friendly. In English-speaking countries we often use topics such as the weather or sports for small talk.

A What would you say?

a It's the start of the week and you meet a colleague on the way into the office.
b You are meeting a regular client who is also a keen golfer.
c A supplier has just given you a small gift.
d You are in the lift in your office building. A colleague, who you haven't seen for a while, gets in the lift too.
e You are meeting a client at the airport and then taking him to your offices for a meeting. As you haven't met before, you don't know what he looks like but you see someone who could be him.

B Match the situations (a–e) above with one or more of the following remarks:

1 How was your weekend?
2 Was the journey all right?
3 Have you played much lately?
4 That's very kind of you.
5 Hello, Peter. How are things in the IT section?
6 Excuse me. Are you Mr Andrews? I'm ... from MS Development.
7 Did you watch the football yesterday?
8 Great weather we are having at the moment.
9 I'm afraid the weather hasn't been very good recently.

11.6 Business idioms

In less formal settings people tend to use more idiomatic language. Idioms can be difficult to use appropriately and successfully in conversation. So, be warned! However, it is useful to be familiar with some expressions so that you can understand what people are talking about.

A The following are idioms that you might hear in a business context. Match the idioms on the left with their explanation on the right.

1 to get the green light	a to be very busy
2 red tape	b a plan which will probably not succeed
3 to put on hold	c to start something happening
4 in the pipeline	d official rules that seem unnecessary and cause delay
5 on the blink	e in debt
6 to start the ball rolling	f to receive permission or approval to proceed
7 to be tied up	g not working properly
8 in the red	h planned for the near future
9 a long shot	i decide not to continue for a while

B Fill the gaps using one of the above idioms. You may have to adapt them to fit the context.

1 We've ______ ______ ______ ________ to go ahead with the project.
2 It's taking such a long time to finalize the deal. It's because of all the government ______ ______ .
3 The decision has been ______ ______ ______ until the end of the year.
4 We've got a new website ____ ______ ________ for next May.
5 I'm afraid I can't give you the exact figures right now. The computer network has been ____ ______ ______ all morning.
6 Webmaster Inc. __________ ______ ______ ________ when they reduced their prices by 10 per cent. All the other computer hardware companies were forced to do the same.
7 Let me look at my diary. I'm afraid I don't have any free time on Thursday. I'm ______ ____ all day.
8 This is a statement from the bank. As you know we've been overdrawn for the past two months. This situation hasn't changed. We're still ____ ______ ______.
9 It's ____ ______ ______ but we're so desperate I'm willing to try anything.

11.7 Entertaining in a restaurant

A Business meetings often continue in social situations such as in a restaurant or a bar.

Can you match the food with the country?

Food	**Country**
curry	Mexico
pâté	Italy
spaghetti bolognaise	India

borscht	Tunisia
tacos	Russia
couscous	Japan
sushi	France

B Here are descriptions of two of the dishes above. Which ones?

1 In Britain it's now more popular than fish and chips. There are many varieties, some are very hot and spicy and others quite mild.
2 It looks rather like a plateful of string covered in meat and tomatoes.
3 What is a typical dish from your country? How would you describe this to a visitor?

Vocabulary: *It's rather spicy...*
It's a bit like... / It's rather like...
It's the speciality of this region/restaurant

4 An important client is visiting your company and you have the responsibility of choosing a restaurant and deciding on the meal. Write down the menu.

11.8 Entertaining in a bar

Match the requests on the left with the answers on the right.

What would you like to drink?	I'd better not. I'm driving. Thanks all the same.
What kind of wine would you like?	Cheers.
This is on me./It's my round.	A pint of Guinness, please.
Cheers.	A dry white wine, please.
Another one before you go?	Thank you very much.

Listening 4

11.9 Polite requests

What would you say?

A What would you say if you are in a bar with some new business contacts who are being very generous and they insist on buying you more drinks than you want. You do not want to get drunk but you are keen not to offend your hosts.

B You have been invited to the home of an important client. It's getting late. You are keen to leave and return to your hotel room to do some work to prepare for the meeting tomorrow. Your host then brings out his holiday photographs to show you.

C Listen to the dialogues and note down the language used for asking questions politely.

Asking questions politely	Answer: Yes	Answer: No
1 *Excuse me, Could you...?*	*Certainly*	
2 *Is it alright to...?*		*Sorry. I'm afraid ...*
3 *Do you mind if...*	*Please do*	
4		
5		
6		
7		
8		

1 Excuse me, could you tell Ms Chin that Linda Scott is here to see her?
Certainly. Please take a seat while I contact her office.

2 Is it all right to smoke in here?
Sorry, I'm afraid it isn't. This is a no-smoking area.

3 Do you mind if I open the window for a minute? It's a bit stuffy in here.
Please do.

4 Sorry to disturb you. Can I get my coat?
Yes, of course. Sorry, I didn't realize I was in the way.

5 Could I have a glass of water, please?
Here you are.

6 May I use your phone to make a quick call to the office?
Yes. Please help yourself.

7 Would you like some coffee while you're waiting?
That would be lovely. Thank you.

8 Could you tell me where the toilet is, please?
Sorry. I'm a visitor here.

Practice

What would you say to make the following more polite? Listen to the recording for some suggestions.

a Put your coat there.
b Coffee?
c How do you spell your name?
d What company are you from?
e What do you want?
f Where can I smoke?

Listening 5

11.10 Intonation and politeness

It is not only the words you use that make a request polite. Intonation is very important too.

A Listen to these two versions of the same sentence. In the first version the speaker is angry and in the second version the speaker is polite. Can you hear the difference? Listen again and try to copy the speaker:

> Could you sort out this problem by tomorrow?

B You will hear two versions of each request. Decide which is the more polite, version **a** or **b**?

> 1 I have been waiting over half an hour now. How much longer do you think it will be before I can see Mr Jameson?
> 2 Could I have the bill, please?
> 3 Excuse me. What did you say?

Lesson summary

Here are some of the things you practised in this lesson:

- Invitations:
  Would you care to join us for dinner?
  Thank you. I'd be delighted to join you.
  Thank you for inviting me. Unfortunately I have a prior engagement. Maybe we could arrange something for another time?

- Formality:
  Would you care for a cigarette?
  That would be great.
- Small talk:
  Did you have a pleasant flight?
- Business idioms:
  The computer's on the blink.
- Entertaining:
  It's the speciality of this region.
  This is on me.
  Just a soft drink for me.
- Polite requests:
  May I use your phone to make a quick call to the office?

Suggestions for further practice

Two of your company's important business clients (one male and one female, both aged about 35) will be visiting your city for the first time. Plan a weekend's entertainment for them.

12 making contact

In this unit you will practise

- **making an enquiry about the services a company offers**
- **describing your company and saying what it does**
- **talking about requirements and abilities**
- **exchanging contact details and suggesting further meetings**

Language

- **business sectors and activities**
- **capability**
- **polite requests and offers**

Introduction

12.1 Attracting the customers

Think of the company you work for or another company you know about.

- What products and/or services does the company provide?
- Who buys these products/services? Is it private individuals, other companies, government organizations?
- How do potential customers find out about the company? Tick all the ones that apply, and write any more ideas you can think of.

  1 Advertisements in the media (television, radio, newspapers and magazines).
  2 Advertisements and features in trade journals.
  3 Trade fairs.
  4 Listing in directories (such as Yellow Pages).
  5 Web pages on the internet.
  6 Direct mailing to potential customers.

- What publicity material is given to customers who contact your company to make an enquiry?

Listening 1

12.2 Making an enquiry about a company

Jim Smith is at an e-commerce business exhibition. He is talking to the representative from an internet design company. Read the questions then listen to (or read) the conversation to find the answers.

1 Who does Jim Smith work for?
2 Why is he at the exhibition?
3 What does Mike Saunders give Jim?
4 What do you think Jim is going to do after the conference?
   a Have dinner with Mike Saunders.
   b Look at some of the websites designed by Mike Saunders's company.
   c Write a letter to Mike Saunders offering him a job.
   d Arrange a meeting with Mike Saunders.

Mike Good morning

Jim Hello there. Do you have any more information about the services you provide? A brochure or something?

Mike Yes sure. Here you go. This tells you quite a lot about us. There are some contact details inside as well. What exactly is it you are looking for?

Jim Oh, well we are looking to expand the capabilities of our website, and I am trying to find out what sort of support we can get from specialized companies.

Mike We have some brochures here about the kinds of services we offer. What area are you in?

Jim Travel. I don't know if you have heard of us, Business Travel Limited. My name's Jim Smith.

Mike Mike Saunders. Here's my card.

Jim Thanks very much.

Mike Basically we can provide help at different levels – from providing consultancy and advice to setting up, running and maintaining a fully interactive e-commerce site. What sort of services are you looking for?

Jim Well, actually we already have a website that basically just gives information for our clients. We also use the internet to book flights directly from the airlines, and the same sort of thing with the hotels. But now we would like to allow our clients to access our services directly for themselves. Online booking and so on.

Mike Right, well, I'm sure we can help. We have already set up interactive sites with full e-commerce capability for a number of clients. There is a list of our websites on the back of this brochure. You might like to take a look at some of these sites.

Jim Thanks. I'll take a look. I'll be in touch.

Mike Okay, that's fine. Goodbye.

12.3 Listen for the details

True or false? Write T or F next to the statements below to show if they are True or False.

1 Jim Smith has met Mike Saunders before. *F*
2 BTL already has a website.
3 Jim Smith is interested in getting a specialist company to develop BTL's website.
4 Jim gave Mike his business card and a brochure about BTL.

5 Mike Saunders's company has never designed e-commerce sites before.
6 Jim thinks Mike Saunders's company might be able to help BTL.
7 Jim suggested that Mike should look at BTL's website.

Language focus

12.4 Making enquiries

Here is some useful language for making an enquiry about a company:

Can you tell me a bit more about your company/about the services you offer?
I'd like some more information about your products.
Do you have a brochure or something with some more information?
What areas do you specialize in?
Where are you based?
How long have you been doing this kind of work?
Can you give me some idea about prices?

This language is useful for dealing with enquiries:

What area are you in?
What exactly are you looking for?
This brochure gives information about our services and costs.
Here's my card. You can call me on this number.
If you could give me your contact details, I'll get back to you/I'll send you some more information.
Would you like me to ask our sales manager to get in touch with you?

12.5 You make an enquiry

You are at a trade fair. You see that one of the exhibitors is offering a product (or service) you are interested in.

1 Decide what the product/service is and write a list of possible questions about it.

2 Write and/or record the conversation between yourself and the representative of the company. If you like, you can imagine that the person you are talking to is helpful, unfriendly, polite, enthusiastic about his products, etc.
3 Replay the recording or review the written conversation. See if you can improve it in some way.

Listening 2

12.6 Making contact by phone

Mike Saunders is calling a recruitment agency. He needs some temporary staff to work on an IT project. There are some words missing from the conversation. Try to fill in the missing words, then listen to the conversation to check your answers. If you need extra help, choose the words from the box below.

Receptionist	Project Personnel, good morning.
Mike	Oh good morning, I want to talk to someone about getting some IT consultants in, on a temporary basis.
Receptionist	I'll put you _______ to our IT department. Hold on a minute.
Celia	IT recruitment. Celia Robins _______.
Mike	Oh, good morning. My name is Mike Saunders, I work with a company called Multimedia Solutions. I don't think we have used your agency before.
Celia	How can I _______ you Mr Saunders?
Mike	We need to recruit extra web designers for a new contract. The project will probably _______ about one and a half to two months.
Celia	Right. How _______ people are we talking about exactly?
Mike	Five. We need people with _______ in e-commerce, using Dreamweaver and Oracle database. Do you have anyone like that?
Celia	Yes, that should be no problem. When do you _______ them for?
Mike	As soon as _______. Say next week? I know that is short notice but we need to get them in pretty urgently.
Celia	Okay. We do have some suitable people, I need to check if they are _______ for starting next week. I

	could fax or e-mail some CVs over to you this afternoon.
Mike	That would be great. Can you give me some _______ about cost?
Celia	If you need people for more than a month, around £50 an hour.
Mike	Right. Well if you have _______ people that would be fine.
Celia	Okay, well _______ it with me and as I say I should be able to send you the details this afternoon.
Mike	Okay, I'll _______ you my e-mail. It's M dot Saunders S-A-U-N-D-E-R-S at M-S-I dot co dot U-K. And the phone number is 020 7648 6868.
Celia	Fine. I'll be in _______ this afternoon.

available	experience	give	help	leave
idea	need	speaking	suitable	take/last
through	touch	many	possible	

Language focus

12.7 Polite requests and offers

There are a number of ways to be polite when you are asking for help, or when you need other people to do something for you. In English it is common to use this polite language even if you are asking for something routine.

- Make the request a question, using *would you…?*, *could you…?*, *will you…?* or *can you…?*:

  Can you give me a brochure about your products?
  Could you tell me a little more about the services you offer?

- Add *please* usually at the beginning or end of the sentence.

  Can you tell me your name, please? (on the phone, to a caller)
  Please could you despatch the order as soon as possible as it is required urgently? (in an order letter)

- Use some of these expressions:

Could you possibly ...;
I would be grateful if you could ... (very formal, usually in written English);
Would you mind ...ing ...?
I was wondering if you could ...

Could you possibly send us five copies of your catalogue?
I was wondering if you could come and talk to our MD about this new system.
Would you mind faxing over a price list this afternoon?
We would be grateful if you could give us a breakdown of costs as soon as possible.

- When you are offering to do something for someone else the following expressions are useful:

Can I help you?
Would you like us to quote for different quantities?
I'll send over the specifications this afternoon, if you like.
Let me give you a catalogue. It contains all our products and prices.

Practice

Complete these mini-conversations with one of the expressions in the box below, then listen to the recording to check your answers.

1 Could you tell me the times of flights to Frankfurt, please?
2 Mrs Williams will be down in five minutes. Would you like me to get you a coffee or something?
3 Would you mind sending us two extra copies of your price list, please?
4 I'm arriving in Munich tomorrow at 10 in the morning.
5 We are very interested in your new software, but I was wondering if you could come here and give a demonstration to our finance department.
6 Do you think you could send some more information about the new light bulbs? Specifications and prices, etc.?

a Certainly sir. When do you want to fly?
b No problem. I'll put them in the post today.
c Yes please. Black coffee with two sugars, please.
d Okay, that's fine, I'll send a car to the airport to meet you, if you like.
e Of course, that would be no problem. When would you like me to come?
f Of course. Would you like us to send you a sample as well?

Now choose one of the conversations and extend it to make a complete conversation.

Example:

Good morning. Business Travel Limited. How can I help you?

Can you tell me the times of flights to Munich?

Certainly sir. When do you want to fly?

Well, leaving London around 10 tomorrow morning. I have to arrive before lunchtime.

Okay, well there is a flight with Lufthansa at 9.45. That arrives in Munich at 12 exactly. And there is a British Airways flight at 10.05, which gets into Munich at 12.30.

I'll take the British Airways flight then. I need two tickets, business class, coming back the following day around the same time. *etc.*

12.8 Saying what your company can do

Listen to the mini-conversations and texts and fill in the missing words below.

1 Are you ________ ________ supply 200 units from stock?
Yes, I think we ________ ________ that. Let me just check on the computer.

2 The new machine is ________ ________ producing 75 copies a minute. And it ________ ________ programmed for double-sided, sorting, stapling and hole punching ________ ________ 100 sheets at a time.

3 Do you have any __________ __________ supplying personnel for overseas assignments?
Oh, yes, we __________ __________ dealt with a number of overseas placements.

4 Would it __________ __________ to deliver our order before the end of this month?
Yes of course. We __________ __________ delivery within two weeks.

can do	able to	can guarantee	capable of
experience of	can be	have already	
be possible	up to		

12.9 Talking about your company

How would you handle an enquiry about your company? Think about some of the questions you might get asked by someone who is interested in your company's products or services. (If you are not working for anyone at the moment, think of a company you know well.) Write a telephone conversation between yourself and a customer. Include offers and requests, and questions about your company's capabilities and experience.

If possible, record the conversation. Then review your work and think about ways to improve it.

Listening 3

12.10 Starting a conversation

Peter and Geoff are at a conference. They do not know each other, but they have been sitting together during a talk.

Listen to (or read) the conversation and answer these questions.

1 What kind of business does Peter work for?
2 What services does his company provide?
3 Who does Geoff work for?
4 What is his job?
5 What do they both think of the talk they have just heard?
6 Why does Peter want to contact Geoff?

Peter Well, that was very interesting, didn't you think?

Geoff Oh, definitely. Although I'm not sure that I agree with everything she said. The effect that e-commerce is going to have on jobs, for example. I really don't see that it will mean fewer personnel, at least not in the short term.

Peter Oh, yes, I guess you are probably right there. But some of the other issues are things we have already come across. I wish I had heard about them a year ago – we could have saved ourselves a lot of problems when we first set up our internet presence.

Geoff I'm sure that's true. What kinds of things do you use the internet for?

Peter Well, at the moment we are mainly using it to provide information to our customers. They can find out about the services we offer, contact details, customer reviews, that kind of thing. But we are planning to make it more interactive, to put our core business on the website.

Geoff What's your area?

Peter Travel. Business travel. We're one of the largest business travel providers in the UK. We basically organize travel for other companies – mainly flights and hotels. How about you?

Geoff I work for Western Credit Group – it's a small banking organization in the States. But my field is IT and my main concern at the moment is advising clients on the uses of the internet and e-commerce.

Peter Are you based here in London?

Geoff Yes I am. Here's my card.

Peter Thanks. Let me give you mine. Perhaps I can give you a call sometime. At the moment as I said, we are using our website to provide information, but our people also use it to book tickets and hotels for clients. So we are looking to develop our own capabilities in e-commerce.

Geoff By all means, give me a call and we'll set something up.

12.11 Roleplay – Networking

Networking means making contact with other people who might be able to help you, or who might be useful contacts for you or your company. For many business people this is an important activity when attending conferences, seminars, receptions and similar functions.

A What do you normally do when you meet someone in the business world, for example at a conference or a reception? Tick the ones you would do in your own country. Then put a star next to the ones you think would be normal in an English-speaking country. Add your own ideas to the list.

- Give them your business card
- Introduce yourself
- Ask their name
- Ask who they work for
- Ask how much they earn
- Find out what field they work in
- Talk about something neutral
- Tell them what you think of the conference/the reception/the seminar
- Discuss the possibility of meeting
- Arrange a meeting

B Which of these did Geoff and Peter do? In what order?

C Here is some useful language to use when you first make contact with someone.

May I introduce myself? I'm ... from ...
Well, that was an interesting presentation, wasn't it?
What did you think of the last presentation?
Here's my card.
Do you have a business card?
I work for ... . I don't know if you have heard of us, we are in ...
Whereabouts are you based?
What field are you in?
What line of work are you in?
Perhaps we could meet up sometime. We might be able to use your services.

D Write a conversation between yourself and one of these people who you have just met.

ABC Online Training Systems **John Smith** *Managing Director*	Asia Tours **Dewi Sutanto** *Head of Marketing*	MRS Industrial Machinery **Noriko Kensuke** *Technical Sales Executive*

If possible, record the conversation. Then review your work and think about ways to improve it.

Lesson summary

Here are some of the things you practised in this lesson:

- Useful language for making and dealing with enquiries. (see **12.4**)
- Polite requests:

  Could you tell me a little more about the services you offer?

  Please could you despatch the order as soon as possible as it is required urgently?

  I would be grateful if you could let us have your reply before the end of this week.

  Could you possibly send us some samples over this afternoon? (see **12.7**)
- Offers:

  Can I help you?

  I'll call him for you, if you like.

  Would you like us to send you over some catalogues and price lists? (see **12.7**)
- Useful language to use when you first make contact with someone:

  May I introduce myself? I'm ... from ...

  Well, that was an interesting presentation, wasn't it?

  What did you think of the last presentation?

  Here's my card.

  Do you have a business card?

  I work for ... . I don't know if you have heard of us, we are in ...

  Whereabouts are you based?

  What field are you in?

  What line of work are you in?

  Perhaps we could meet up sometime. We might be able to use your services.

Suggestions for further practice

1 Make use of opportunities to meet people, at international trade fairs, business seminars and similar gatherings. If you cannot take part in these conversations, listen to other people introducing themselves.

2 Choose some of the exercises in **12.5**, **12.10** and **12.11** and do them again, using different contexts. Try to improve on your previous attempt. Think carefully about ways to improve your performance.

3 Look in a grammar reference book for more explanation and practice about polite requests, offers, introductions and ability.

4 Go through the conversations and exercises in this unit and look for words you are not familiar with. Try to find groups of words, for example make a list of all the words relating to ability and capability (*can, able to, ability, capable of, capacity for*). Record these groups of words in a vocabulary notebook and learn how to use them.

13 the energy business

In this unit you will

- **read about changes in the energy industry**
- **practise your reading skills**
- **develop your understanding of vocabulary: synonym and metaphor**

The two texts in this section concern one of the world's most important and valuable commodities. The first text provides basic information about the oil industry while the second deals with the search for alternative sources of energy.

Text 1: The Oil Business

13.1 Warm-up questions

- Which energy sources do you use in your home? In your place of work? Oil? Gas? Electricity? Nuclear power? Wind? The sea? Solar power?
- Which is the most important in your country?
- Which is the most expensive? How much is a litre of petrol in your country?

Reading

13.2 Skimming and scanning

Read the text below to find answers to these questions.

1 What do the letters OPEC stand for?
2 Will we always need to use oil as a source of energy?

The Oil Business

What are the world's oil resources?

The world has about 1,000 billion barrels of proven crude oil reserves with the largest amounts to be found under Saudi Arabia, Iraq, United Arab Emirates, Kuwait and Iran in the Gulf. Venezuela has the next largest reserves, while in North America there are major deposits in all of Mexico, the US and Canada. Russia and China also have large proven reserves but, along with the US, they are pumping at rates which will cease to be sustainable far sooner than their Middle East counterparts. In Central Asia, Kazakhstan has large oil reserves which have not been fully exploited to date. Africa has significant deposits in Libya, Nigeria and Algeria, while large North Sea deposits are exploited mainly by Norway.

Are we running out of oil?

Oil is a finite resource which could eventually run out. World consumption today is about 70 million barrels a day and oil producers expect this to rise to 100 million barrels by 2020. The Organization of Petroleum Exporting Countries (OPEC) says its reserves are sufficient to last another 80 years at the current rate of production. What is more likely is that there will always be oil around, it will just become harder to extract, of poorer quality and more expensive. That is why many energy companies are currently investing large sums to find alternative sources of energy to reduce the world's reliance on oil.

What is the significance of Opec?

The 11 members of the OPEC produce about 40% of the world's crude oil. However, non-OPEC countries consume large amounts of the oil they produce, so about 60% of the oil traded internationally comes from OPEC countries. OPEC's share of world oil production has been much higher in the past and is set to rise considerably in the coming decades, as member countries hold more than 75% of the world's proven oil reserves. This is partly the result of a tendency for producers outside OPEC to pump oil at full capacity while members subscribe to a quota system to regulate market prices.

What causes fluctuations in oil price?

Events on the international stage can create a climate of uncertainty which can lead to rises in oil prices. More important – like any market – is the equation between how much oil is pumped by the producers and the demand for oil among consumers. Politics have also played a part in the past, as in 1973 when OPEC members – led by Saudi Arabia – cut the oil supply to punish the West for supporting Israel in the Arab–Israeli war. The move caused oil to jump from $3 a barrel to $12, causing economic crises in the developed world which had come to rely on cheap energy. Since then, OPEC's share of the oil market has dropped because more oilfields outside the organization have come on stream. For many years OPEC was also unsuccessful in getting members to stick to their own quotas. Higher prices since March 1999 came about as OPEC members agreed to cut their output – and stuck to quotas – to address an oil glut caused by a drop in demand after the Asian financial crisis. The oil cartel was joined by a number of other exporters, notably Mexico, Norway and Oman, increasing the OPEC-plus group's share of world output to 56%.

Who benefits from high oil prices?

The current buoyancy of oil prices offers most to cash-strapped non-OPEC countries like Russia. It is unrestricted by OPEC quotas yet reaps the rewards of high prices created by OPEC. Having seen the cycle of oil boom and bust over the years, OPEC itself now has 'market stability' as its watchword. An example of this ethos was seen in 1990 when Iraq invaded Kuwait, threatening to send oil prices rocketing. Prices did rise amid the uncertainty, but OPEC also agreed to raise quotas to replace the 3 million barrels per day removed from the market. On the other hand, the spikes of 1973 and in the

1980s may have brought prosperity, particularly in the Gulf oil sheikhdoms, but they also reduced demand and disrupted investment in oil projects in the medium term. Ironically, it tends to be non-OPEC countries which are hurt more by extremely low oil prices. Ease of access and quality mean that Middle Eastern oil, in particular, is the most profitable and cheapest to produce in the world.

Can the world wean itself off oil?

It will have to eventually, but oil is too important on too many levels for that to happen soon. Experts say the world's energy future could lie in renewable sources like wave, solar, hydro-electric and wind power, and fuel cells, which release energy from hydro-carbons chemically rather than through combustion. But while oil remains an available and relatively inexpensive resource, it will no doubt remain the backbone of economic power and political influence in the world.

[*Source*: *BBC Business News*, 24 March 2000]

13.3 Vocabulary

Choose the best meaning:

1 billion (*line 1*)
- **a** 1,000,000
- **b** 1,000,000,000
- **c** 1,000,000,000,000

2 sustainable (*line 6*)
- **a** able to increase
- **b** able to make a profit
- **c** able to continue

3 finite (*line 12*)
- **a** fine
- **b** limited
- **c** final

4 alternative (*line 19*)
- **a** opposite
- **b** reverse
- **c** other

5 is set to (*line 25–6*)
- **a** has
- **b** will
- **c** established

6 come on stream (*line 40*)
- **a** started production
- **b** failed
- **c** started slowly

7 glut (*line 43*)
- **a** disaster
- **b** over-supply
- **c** crash

8 cash-strapped (*line 48*)
- **a** having too much cash
- **b** short of cash
- **c** having no cash

9 cartel (*line* 44)
- **a** group of companies which work together, e.g. to fix prices
- **b** group of companies which regularly meet together
- **c** group of companies with same policies

10 wean (*line* 62)
- **a** gently break the habit
- **b** change
- **c** become aware of

13.4 Comprehension

Read the text in **13.2** again.

1 What do the following numbers refer to?
- **a** 70 million barrels a day
- **b** 80 years
- **c** 11 members
- **d** 1990

2 With reference to the text, are the following statements true or false?
- **a** Russia and China will probably exhaust their reserves of oil before the Gulf states do.
- **b** Finding oil in the future is likely to become harder.
- **c** OPEC is able to control the price of oil.
- **d** Politics is the main factor causing price fluctuations.
- **e** Non-OPEC countries are most affected by low oil prices.

3 The following paragraph is based on information found in the text. Fill in the missing words. Then check your answers by listening to the recording or looking in the **Answer key**.

> Oil can be found on all the continents of the world, the largest __________ being in the Gulf states. Although it is a __________ resource, OPEC believes it has enough for at least another 80 years. However, the oil companies are nonetheless investigating __________ sources of energy. OPEC is the key figure in the oil business and produces about __________ of the world's production – its share may well increase in the future. OPEC tends to favour a policy of __________ __________ and will increase supply if for any reason, e.g. __________, supplies to the world markets are reduced. While it continues to be a comparatively __________ source of energy it will continue to play a vital role in the political economy of the world.

4 Abbreviations: OPEC means the Organization of Petroleum Exporting Countries.

Do you recognize the following?

a NAFTA
b WTO
c EC
d FTSE
e ASEAN
f IMF
g PAC

Text 2: Alternatives to Oil

13.5 Pre-reading questions

- Why are people searching for alternatives to oil as a source of fuel?
- What alternatives do you know?
- How important is nuclear power in your country?
- How much pollution is there in your capital city?

Reading

13.6 Skimming and scanning

Read the text below to find answers to these questions.

1 How many serious nuclear accidents have there been?
2 What is the future for coal as a source of energy?

Alternatives to oil

by BBC News Online's Environment Correspondent Alex Kirby

The industrialized world stands aghast at the prospect of rising oil prices. Paying more for oil means increases in the price of almost everything that drives the rich economies. The possibility that oil prices could continue to rise appals the Northern countries, who see no other way to fuel their growth. But they have little room for manoeuvre, because they cannot determine the prices. In the grip of a crisis, it is hard to argue that there may be a silver lining. But the benefit of the present oil price hikes could be to focus attention on the possibility of a world far less dependent on oil. Environmental groups have for years been arguing that we shall all have to live radically different lives when the oil reserves are finally exhausted. The truth is that they probably never will be. Oil will simply become too expensive to compete with other fuels. Amory Lovins, of the Rocky Mountain Institute, is fond of reminding audiences: 'The Stone Age didn't end because the stone ran out, and the Oil Age will be just the same'.

The Age of Coal

Before oil's supremacy, coal was king. It was the bedrock of the industrial revolution in Europe and North America, and it still has a role to play. There are enormous reserves of coal available, but it does give off large quantities of the gases which are causing climate change, especially carbon dioxide (CO_2) and sulphur dioxide (SO_2). Technology can help, up to a point, with improvements like fluidized bed technology, which burns coal much more efficiently and results in much less pollution. But it seems highly unlikely that coal will ever recover its once-dominant position.

Nuclear puzzle

Some people still pin their hopes on nuclear power, which makes far less of a contribution to global warming (though it is not entirely neutral). But in half a century the world's nuclear industry has had at least three serious accidents. Windscale (UK, 1957), Three Mile Island (US, 1979) and Chernobyl (USSR, 1986) are names etched into the global memory, synonyms for horrific brushes with catastrophe. Many people therefore reject new nuclear plants in the belief that more accidents are inevitable. And apart from that, the industry still shows no sign of being able to get rid of its waste in safety.

Renewable fuels

A third category of fuel comes under the heading of renewables. Some are tried and tested, like hydro-electric power, and many countries, for instance Norway, are already exploiting them to the full. Wind and wave power have promise, as does biomass – crops like willow which grow quickly and are increasingly being used for fuel. Transport fuel based on renewable oilseed crops such as soybeans and rape seed also has potential. Solar power is coming on by leaps and bounds. There are already photo-voltaic cells which will provide power on a cloudy British winter's day, or even by moonlight. They are expensive, but a lot cheaper than similar cells were a few years ago. For vehicles, many motor manufacturers believe the future lies in fuel cells, which will power cars as effectively as now, but without relying on oil. They foresee a change from an oil-based economy to one based on hydrogen.

Conservation

And there is what its supporters are fond of calling 'the fifth fuel' – energy conservation. Most of us still waste fuel on a prodigious scale, and the savings we could make by greater efficiency, and by just switching off, are immense. The environment minister of an eastern European country told me in the early 1990s: 'In the Soviet days, we did have thermostats in our homes and factories. When we got too hot, we just opened the windows.'

Rising oil prices are the perfect excuse for second thoughts.

[*Source*: *BBC Business News*, 8 September 2000]

13.7 Comprehension

1 What do the following refer to?
   a (*line 17*) it
   b (*line 31*) apart from that
   c (*line 44*) They

2 Are these statements true or false?
   a In the future oil will become the most expensive fuel.
   b Coal is a major cause of pollution in the world.
   c People do not like nuclear power because it is too expensive.
   d Hydrogen will be the main source of energy in the future.
   e A lot of energy is wasted.

3 What do you think? Will oil be replaced by other forms of energy?

Language focus

13.8 Pronouns

Pronouns (e.g. *some*, *they*) are the important words used by writers to connect together ideas in a text. A good reader must be able to understand what the pronouns refer to.

What do the following refer to?

1 (*line 5*) they
2 (*line 10*) they
3 (*line 16*) It
4 (*line 23*) its
5 (*line 26*) it
6 (*line 34*) Some
7 (*line 52*) we

13.9 Vocabulary

A Synonyms

In line 29 the text refers to 'synonyms'. A good writer uses a wide range of vocabulary and tries to avoid repeating words by looking for *synonyms* (words with the same meaning). The words in the list **1–7** are from the text. Find a synonym from the list **a–g**.

1 aghast
2 radically
3 exhausted
4 neutral

a predict
b enormous
c completely
d worn out

5 exploiting
6 foresee
7 prodigious

e without effect
f horrified
g taking advantage of

B Metaphors

When we use a word which belongs to one area, e.g. politics, in a different area, e.g. business, we are using a *metaphor*. For example, line 16, '...coal was *king*'. The writer is using the word *king* metaphorically. Other examples are:

drives (*line 3*)	(as in motor vehicles)
bedrock (*line 16*)	(as in geology)
role to play (*line 17*)	(as in the theatre)
etched (*line 29*)	(as in drawing)

Practice

Look at these words again in the text. Choose the meaning closest to the text:

1 drives
- **a** moves forward
- **b** turns
- **c** rides through

2 bedrock
- **a** heart
- **b** beginning
- **c** foundation

3 has a role to play
- **a** is involved
- **b** has a responsibility
- **c** is playing

4 etched (into the global memory)
- **a** well remembered by everybody
- **b** drawn from memory
- **c** little known by most people

14 check your progress

14.1 Vocabulary

Find one word that doesn't fit in each of these groups. Cross the word out. Add two or three more words to each group.

Finance	Currencies	Companies	Energy
stock market	sterling	Microsoft	renewable
currency	baht	American Express	fluctuations
application form	rouble	British Airways	oil
interest rates	euro	FTSE 100	nuclear
shares	gold	Honda	reserves

14.2 Telephone language – jumbled sentences

Put these sentences in order to make a telephone conversation.

a Bye.
b Do you know when she'll be back?
c Good morning. Interactive Systems. How can I help you?
d I'd like to speak to Erika Stolle, please.
e I'm afraid she's not here today. Can I take a message?
f Okay, in that case I'll call again tomorrow.
g She should be here tomorrow.
h Thank you. Goodbye.

Correct order: ____ ____ ____ ____ ____ ____ ____ ____

14.3 E-commerce and banking

Fill in the missing words to complete this summary. Choose words from the box below.

Information technology has radically __________ many industries, especially banking. Banks can __________ more information, use __________ paper, and process transactions more __________ and more cheaply. As a result, customers can check their __________, pay bills and __________ money without ever __________ a bank.

accounts	changed	different	entering	immediately	less
money	much	pay	quickly	store	withdraw

14.4 Idioms

a After several years i______ t______ r______ , Amazon.com finally became profitable in 2001.

b Sorry I didn't get back to you earlier – I was t______ u______ in a meeting.

c Plans to expand the company have been p______ o______ h______ because of the recession.

d Can you call Xerox? The photocopier is o______ t______ b______ again.

making arrangements

In this unit you will practise

- **making appointments and organizing times to meet**
- **making travel arrangements**
- **talking about requirements**
- **talking about schedules, plans and arrangements in the future**

Language

- **future tenses and definite plans**
- **travel timetables**

Introduction

15.1 Travel arrangements

- Do you enjoy travelling? Do you like flying? Why/Why not?
- Do you travel a lot in your job? Where to? How often?
- Who makes your travel arrangements for you? You yourself? Your secretary? The travel coordinator in your company?

Look at the letter below and the following e-mail and answer these questions:

1 Where is Ray Smith planning to travel to?
2 When does he have to be there?
3 What is the purpose of the trip?
4 Who is he meeting?
5 Where is he going to stay?

SUNRISE PRODUCTS PTE
Head Office: Jalan Gajah Mada 279
Kota, Jakarta Utara 37106
Telephone: +62 21 860 3700 fax: +62 21 866 3715
e-mail: ho@sunrise-products. co.id

Ray Smith
Head of Overseas Marketing
International Plastics
35–75 Greenhurst Place
Croydon
Surrey CR8 4EZ

6th April

Dear Ray

I have made the arrangements at this end for your visit to us. Our chairman can meet you on May 9th and we have set aside May 11th for negotiations between yourself and the key people here. So can you arrive the weekend of 6th–7th May? This would give me a chance to show you round our plants on Monday 8th May and answer questions you may have. Please let me know ASAP if these dates suit you.

I suggest you stay at the Hotel Borobodur Intercontinental. It is the closest to our offices. Let me know your time of arrival and I will arrange for a car to pick you up at the airport.

Hope to hear from you soon
Regards

David Sitorus

David Sitorus
Operations Manager

From: Ray Smith <rsmith@mda.com>
To: Kate Jones <kjones@mda.com>
Date: Wednesday 28th April
Subject: trip to Indonesia

Kate

Can you make all the arrangements for this trip for me. I would like to leave on the Thursday and arrive on Friday so that I have the weekend to recover and prepare! Any airline will do (within reason!), business class of course. Send the arrival times to David Sitorus as he offered to send a car to meet me at the airport. I'd like to get the return flight on Friday (12th May) if possible – if not, the next day would be okay but I need to be back in time for my son's birthday on Sunday 14th.

Can you organize the room bookings too? If possible go with the one they have suggested.

Thanks

Ray

15.2 Vocabulary

Match these expressions from the letter and e-mail message with their meanings:

1 will do	a not late, before something starts
2 in time for	b to rest (after a journey)
3 to recover	c as soon as possible, urgently
4 go with	d will be okay, will be acceptable
5 to pick up	e to agree with, to use what someone has suggested
6 ASAP	f to meet someone (in a car)
7 be back	g return (home)
8 to show round	h to organize a visit or a tour (of a factory, a house, a tourist attraction)

Listening 1

15.3 A phone conversation

Kate Jones is on the telephone to Janet Brown of BTL. She is organizing Ray Smith's business trip to Indonesia. Before you listen, look back at 15.1 and write down some of the things that

Kate is going to ask for. When you listen, check whether your predictions were right.

Janet Good morning, Business Travel Limited. Janet Brown speaking. How can I help you?

Kate Oh, hello, this is Kate Jones from International Plastics. I want to arrange a trip to Indonesia for next week for my boss.

Janet Right, is it to Jakarta?

Kate Yes, leaving next Thursday if possible.

Janet 4th May?

Kate Yes that's right.

Janet Any preference as to airline?

Kate Not really, as long as it is a good one.

Janet Okay, well there is a Singapore Airlines flight via Singapore. That leaves at 9 pm and arrives at 11.30 pm the next day.

Kate Gosh that's a long flight. Isn't there anything direct?

Janet Don't forget there's a time difference of six hours between London and Indonesia. But anyway let me check what else is available. ... There is a KLM flight via Amsterdam. It leaves Gatwick at 7 am, arrives Amsterdam at 8 and the connecting flight leaves Amsterdam at 10. That would get you into Jakarta at 10.30 am on Friday.

Kate So that is ... 17 and a half hours. That's a bit better. I think 7 am is a bit early though, have you got anything else? Heathrow would be better than Gatwick.

Janet Let me check, hold on a minute. Oh yes, Emirates, there is a flight at 12.30 midday on Thursdays, with a good connection in Dubai, then arriving in Jakarta at 13.10.

Kate What is Emirates like, is it a good airline?

Janet Oh, yes definitely. It won the Business Travel Magazine airline prize for two years running. It's very good.

Kate Okay, that's fine. Can you check availability?

Janet Of course. Business class?

Kate Yes.

Janet When is the return?

Kate The following Friday.

Janet 12th May. Okay. Oh, Emirates don't have any flights from Jakarta on Friday. There's a flight on Saturday morning, 8 am arriving back at Heathrow on Saturday evening at 8 pm. Or there is a flight on Thursday morning, same times.

Kate I think Saturday would be better. Can you book that provisionally and I'll confirm it in an hour or two?
Janet Certainly. Just one passenger?
Kate Yes.
Janet Can I have the name?
Kate It's Ray Smith. How about the price?
Janet Three thousand two hundred and seventeen pounds, including airport taxes.
Kate One more thing, can you book the hotel in Jakarta. It's the Hotel Borobodur Intercontinental. Just a standard single room.
Janet Fine. I'll book that for you. Will you ring back to confirm the booking after you have spoken to Mr Smith?
Kate Yes, sure. Sorry, what is your name again?
Janet Janet Brown. My direct line is 020 7844 3775.
Kate Okay, I'll talk to you later. Thanks a lot.

15.4 Listen for the details

Listen to (or read) the telephone conversation again and fill in this booking form.

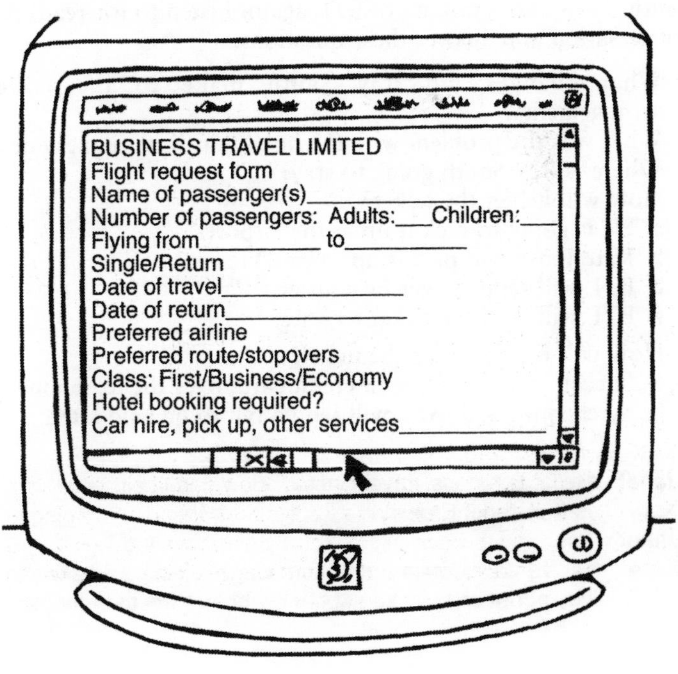

BUSINESS TRAVEL LIMITED
Flight request form
Name of passenger(s)__________
Number of passengers: Adults:___ Children:___
Flying from__________ to__________
Single/Return
Date of travel__________
Date of return__________
Preferred airline
Preferred route/stopovers
Class: First/Business/Economy
Hotel booking required?
Car hire, pick up, other services__________

Writing

15.5 Over to you

Choose A or B

A Look back at the letter in **15.1**. Write a letter inviting a visitor from overseas to your company. Include relevant details about when to come, where to stay, what you have planned for your visitor.

B Look back at the e-mail in **15.1**. Write a similar e-mail to your secretary, or to the travel section in your company, asking them to organize a trip for you. Make sure you include all the relevant details.

When you have finished, check your work and try to improve it.

Listening 2

15.6 Confirming travel arrangements

Kate Jones has confirmed the travel arrangements with Ray Smith. Now she is talking to BTL again. Listen to (or read) the conversation and answer these questions.

1 What changes did Ray Smith make to the travel arrangements?
2 What was the problem with the hotel that Kate requested?
3 Where is Ray Smith going to stay?
4 How will he get the ticket?
   a He is going to pick it up at the airport.
   b Kate Jones will pick it up from BTL.
   c BTL will send it over by courier.
   d BTL will mail the ticket to Kate.
5 How will Kate pay for the ticket?
   a In cash
   b By cheque
   c Using a credit card, over the telephone
   d BTL will send a bill to be paid later.

Janet Hello, Business Travel Limited. How can I help you?
Kate Is that Janet Brown?
Janet Yes.
Kate Hi, it's Kate Jones from International Plastics. I talked to you about an hour ago about my boss's trip to Indonesia.

Janet Yes, that's right. Hello Kate. Is everything okay?

Kate I've spoken to Mr Smith and those flights are fine. Can you confirm them for us?

Janet Sure, I'll do that right now. I'll fax you over a copy of the itinerary just to check all the details are correct. You have an account with us, don't you?

Kate Yes, that's right.

Janet So I can just invoice you for the tickets. I'll send the tickets out in the post tonight, unless you want them couriered over?

Kate No the post should be fine, as long as they arrive by Monday at the latest. Did you manage to get the hotel booking?

Janet Just let me check. ... Oh, there's an e-mail from our Jakarta office. *(reading)* 'The Hotel Borobodur is completely full next week'. There is an international conference of some sort. Our agent in Indonesia suggests the Hilton hotel. It's also very nice and it's quite convenient for the airport and the business district.

Kate Okay, I'm sure that will be fine. Can you just go ahead and book that?

Janet Sure. What we can do is book the room, and charge you a booking fee. Then Mr Smith can pay the hotel bill directly. Is that okay?

Kate That's fine.

Janet Okay, I'll get a fax from the hotel confirming the booking and send that to you with the airline tickets.

Kate Great. Thanks a lot. You've got our address for the tickets, haven't you?

Janet Yes, we have. Who shall I address it to?

Kate Can you mark it 'For the Attention of Kate Jones or Ray Smith, Marketing Department'?

Janet Sure. Anything else?

Kate No I think that is all. Thanks a lot, Janet.

Janet You are welcome. Bye.

Now complete this itinerary from BTL:

BUSINESS TRAVEL LIMITED
ITINERARY

Ticket for Mr Ray Smith

Thursday ____ May	Depart London ________ Airport	Flight EMI 7721	_____
	Arrive Dubai International		21.45
	Depart Dubai International	Flight EMI 2190	23.00
Friday 5th May	Arrive Jakarta Soekarno-Hatta		_____
________ 13th May	Depart Jakarta Soekarno-Hatta	Flight EMI 2191	_____
	Arrive Dubai International		14.05
	Depart Dubai International	Flight EMI 7720	15.20
	Arrive London ________ Airport		_____
Special meals:	normal meals / vegetarian / vegan / other (please specify)		

Hotel __________ International. 5th May – 13th May (___ nights).
Type of room: single / double / suite
Invoice to: _________ Account Number IP23Z
Tickets: courier / first class post / customer collects / pick up at airport

Language focus

15.7 Talking about future plans

There are several ways to talk about the future in English (see **Unit 9**). When you want to talk about definite plans and arrangements, especially travel plans, you normally use present tenses.

Use the **present progressive** to talk about travel arrangements.

*I'm **flying** to Paris this afternoon.*
*I'm **staying** at the Intercontinental Hotel.*
*I'm **meeting** the finance director tomorrow morning.*
*What time are you **meeting** him?*

Use the **present simple** tense to talk about scheduled flights and travel timetables.

*The plane **leaves** at 10 am and **arrives** in Amsterdam at 10.45 local time.*
*What time **does** the train **arrive** in London?*

Practice

A Answer these questions about Ray Smith's trip to Indonesia.

1 When is Ray Smith going to Indonesia?
2 Where does his plane leave from?
3 What time does it take off.
4 How many days is he staying there?
5 Which hotel is he staying in?
6 What is he doing on Monday 8th May?
7 When is he meeting the chairman of Sunrise Products?
8 What day is he flying back to the UK?
9 What time does his flight arrive back in the UK?
10 Who is meeting him at the airport in Jakarta?

B Make up your own itinerary. Then imagine you are explaining your plans to your secretary. Write a note telling her your travel plans.

I'm going to .... next week. My plane leaves at ... from ....

C Write a conversation between yourself and a colleague. One of you is going on a business trip. The other one is asking about the details of the trip.

Check what you have written and see if you can improve it. Check the tenses carefully.

Listening 3

15.8 Arranging a meeting

- Do you attend a lot of meetings in your job? Who with? Where?
- Who makes the arrangements for meetings? You yourself? Your secretary? Your manager or his/her personal assistant?

Sometimes it is difficult to arrange a meeting with several people involved. It's almost impossible to find a time when everyone is free.

Look at this e-mail, and Ray Smith's diary on page 169. Suggest a good time to meet. Then listen to the two conversations and find out when the meeting will be held.

From: Ray Smith <rsmith@mda.com>
To: Kate Jones <kjones@mda.com>
Date: Wednesday 28th April
Subject: Meeting re IT recruitment

Kate

Can you set up a meeting with Barry Donovan and Helen Thomas from Personnel for next week? We need to sort out the proposal to recruit more IT staff. Must be Tuesday or Wednesday as Monday is a bank holiday and I'm off to Indonesia on Thursday early morning.

You have my diary. Any time we can fit it in would be fine with me. Shouldn't take more than 45 minutes.

Thanks

Ray

15.9 Listening for details

A Now listen to Kate telephoning Helen Thomas and Barry Donovan and answer these questions:

1 What is the problem with Thursday?
2 What is Helen doing on Tuesday morning?
3 Why can't the meeting be held on Wednesday afternoon?
4 Where will Barry be on Tuesday?
5 What appointment will Barry have to rearrange?
6 Where will the meeting be held?

TUESDAY 2ND MAY		WEDNESDAY 3RD MAY	
9:00	*Visit BRF factory*	9.00	*Dentist*
10:00	*10.30 video conference Jakarta office*	10:00	
11:00		11:00	
12:00		12:00	
13:00	*Lunch with Mike*	13:00	
14:00	*Meeting with architects*	14:00	
15:00		15:00	
16:00		16:00	*Export seminar 4–6*
17:00	*Meeting with finance director re. Indonesian partners*	17:00	
18:00		18:00	
19:00	*Dinner with Paul Davies*	19:00	
20:00		20:00	*Pack for Indonesian trip*

Helen Hello.
Kate Is that Helen Thomas?
Helen Yes.
Kate Oh, hello, this is Kate Jones, Ray Smith's secretary.
Helen Oh yes, hello Kate.
Kate Ray wants me to fix up a meeting with you and Barry Donovan next week. It's about recruitment of IT staff.
Helen Okay, let me just check my diary. I'm free all day Thursday.
Kate That's no good, I'm afraid. He's leaving for Jakarta on Thursday. It will have to be Tuesday or Wednesday.

Helen Okay, can you suggest some times?

Kate Tuesday between 11 and 1, or Tuesday afternoon between 3 and 5.

Helen I can't make Tuesday morning, I'm afraid. We're interviewing for the post of technical director. I could do Tuesday afternoon from 4 to 5. Any idea how long the meeting will take?

Kate Ray thought no more than 45 minutes.

Helen Okay, so that's a possibility. Wednesday afternoon is no good. I have a meeting in Birmingham. Wednesday morning would be okay though, up until about 12. I'm catching the 12.40 train up to Birmingham.

Kate Okay, let me talk to Barry and see if he can make it on Tuesday afternoon. Can I call you back in a few minutes?

Helen Sure. I'll be here until 6 tonight.

Kate Okay.

Kate Hello, Barry?

Barry Yes.

Kate Kate here. I'm trying to fix a meeting with you, Helen Thomas and Ray. Are you free on Tuesday afternoon at 4?

Barry Sorry, Kate, I'm not coming in on Tuesday. I'm taking the kids to France for the bank holiday weekend and I've got the day off on Tuesday too. I'll be back on Wednesday morning.

Kate Could we meet around 10.30?

Barry Erm. I'm supposed to be meeting a supplier at 10.45. They are demonstrating some new software we are thinking of buying. I'm free all of Wednesday afternoon. Couldn't we meet then?

Kate I'm afraid not, Helen has to go to Birmingham.

Barry Okay, well, I'll tell you what, I'll see the software people in the afternoon. How's that?

Kate Thanks, Barry. 10.30 on Wednesday 3rd May. I think it will be in Ray's office.

Barry Okay, see you on Wednesday then.

Kate Sure. Have a great weekend if I don't see you before.

B Fill in the diary for **either** Barry **or** Helen.

TUESDAY 2ND MAY		WEDNESDAY 3RD MAY	
9:00		9.00	
10:00		10:00	
11:00		11:00	
12:00		12:00	
13:00		13:00	
14:00		14:00	
15:00		15:00	
16:00		16:00	
17:00		17:00	
18:00		18:00	
19:00		19:00	
20:00		20:00	

C Match these words from the conversations above with their meanings in **a–h** below.

1 a day off, the day off	a a job
2 bank holiday	b a one-day holiday
3 fix (a meeting, an appointment)	c computer programs
4 free	d not busy, available
5 post	e public holiday
6 software	f somebody who sells goods or services to another company
7 supplier	g the children, (my children)
8 the kids	h to arrange

Lesson summary

Here are some of the things you practised in this lesson:

- Useful language for negotiating arrangements:
  How about Thursday morning?
  Could you make it on Wednesday afternoon?
  I'm afraid I'm not coming in on Tuesday.
  I can't make it on Tuesday but I could manage Wednesday morning.
- Talking about plans and arrangements:
  We're interviewing on Wednesday morning.
  He's flying to India on Friday.
  What time are you leaving?
  Flight GA 332 leaves at 7.30 in the morning.

Suggestions for further practice

1 Go through the conversations and exercises in this unit and look for useful expressions for making arrangements. Write them in your vocabulary notebook and practise using them in conversations and e-mails.

2 Think of some questions to ask someone about the arrangements for a trip. It could be a business trip that you are going on. Write the questions you would ask the travel agent who has made the arrangements. Or it could be a trip your colleague or your boss is going to make. Write the questions you would ask them about their trip.

3 Look in the **Language reference** section at the back of this book and/or in a grammar reference book for more explanation and practice about the future tenses.

4 Look at the dialogues in this unit. Write similar dialogues making arrangements in your own company. Then write letters and e-mails confirming the arrangements.

meetings

In this unit you will

- **practise the language of meetings**
- **discuss cross-cultural differences in business**

Language

- **seeking and giving opinions**
- **expressing reservation and disagreement**
- **seeking clarification**
- **modal verbs**

Introduction

16.1 Going to meetings

- Do you attend meetings at work? How often? How long do they usually last? Who attends the meetings?
- Many people complain that much time is wasted in meetings and they often achieve very little? Do you agree?
- What are the main purposes of the meetings you attend?

16.2 Vocabulary

B Match the following words (**1–7**) with explanations (**a–g**).

Example: 1e.

1 agenda
2 chairperson
3 minutes
4 apologies for absence
5 item
6 to chair a meeting
7 to circulate (the agenda)

a the person in charge of the meeting
b to send copies of a document (e.g. an agenda) to a group of people
c the written record of what was said or decided at the meeting
d to be in charge of a meeting
e the list of items to be discussed
f something you say or write to say sorry for not attending
g one of the topics on the agenda

B Choose words from the list **1–7** above to complete the sentences.

1 The secretary will __________ the __________ for the next meeting to all participants at least one week in advance.

2 If anyone would like to add to the list of __________ on the agenda, please notify the chairperson beforehand.

3 Please read through the __________ of the previous meeting. If you feel they are inaccurate in any way, please let me know.

4 Only eight will be attending the meeting. The representatives from New York cancelled and sent their __________ .

Listening 1

16.3 The meeting

A Pre-listening exercise

Which of the following expressions would you expect to hear at a business meeting?

1 Could you put me through to Marcia Solanas?
2 I really can't agree.
3 Yes, that's right.
4 Thank you for your application.
5 Please find enclosed my CV.
6 Can I take a message?
7 How do you feel about this?
8 If I could just interrupt here?
9 Who's calling, please?
10 Thank you for pointing that out.
11 I understand your point but ...

B Listen to Part One of the dialogue. What is the purpose of the meeting?

THE MEETING

Senior members of the management of Chambers Hotel, Mexico City are holding a meeting in the Manager's office. Present are the following: Peter Mathers (General Manager), Maria Gonzalez (Head of Personnel), Johann Elias (IT Manager), Julia Hammell (General Manager's Secretary) and Pablo Martinez (Sales Director).

PART ONE

Peter Good morning. Hi.
Maria Hello, Peter. How are you?
Peter Fine, thanks.
Johann Morning, Peter
Julia Good morning.
Pablo Morning.
Peter Help yourself to tea and coffee. Okay. I think we can start now. Did you get the agenda I circulated?
Johann Yes.
Maria Yes, thank you.
Peter Atsushi Morita and Carl Reich send their apologies. Atsushi and Carl have a meeting with an important client, Tariq Al Said, that couldn't be re-arranged. I think

	some of you may know Mr Al Said. That meeting will be a real mixture of cultural backgrounds – Arab, German and Japanese. Anyway... you should also have received the minutes of the meeting last month.
Maria	There's one question I'd like to raise here, Peter.
Peter	Okay.
Maria	The new rates of overtime pay for staff. I thought we said they would come into effect on 1st October not 10th October.
Johann	That's what I thought too.
Peter	Mm ...Yes, I think you're right. I think it's just a typing error. Okay, we'll change that. Thank you for pointing that out. Anything else? No. Okay. The first item on the agenda today is bringing forward the date for implementing the changes to our software. Bookings for next month are low, as is usual for that time of year. So, it should be a relatively good time to make changes. We all know these changes will be disruptive but going with it next month might be the least disruptive time. I wanted all of us to talk this through together before making a final decision. What do you think?
Johann	When would the changes actually start?
Peter	In two weeks' time. At the beginning of the month.
Maria	Er ... That is soon.
Peter	The sooner the better. The current system keeps crashing.

C Listen to the rest of the discussion (Part Two). Why is Maria Gonzalez unhappy with Peter Mather's proposals?

PART TWO

Maria	Well ... I'm not exactly looking forward to it whenever it happens. Are we confident that it's going to work properly? The last time we went through installing updated software, it was a nightmare. Do you remember the chaos there was? Nobody knew what was happening or what to do because they didn't understand how to operate the new software. People were tearing their hair out.
Peter	Oh. It wasn't that bad, Maria. In fact ...

Johann	Can I come in here? As you know I wasn't working here when the previous changes occurred so I can't comment on that experience. However, this time nearly all the work will be carried out over one weekend and we should experience, at worst, only some minor adjustments during the following few days.
Maria	I hope you're right, Johann.
Johann	Don't worry, it'll be fine.
Maria	Nothing personal, Johann. I've every confidence in you. It's just computers I don't trust ... or rather they always seem to break down at crucial moments.
Peter	Are we agreed that the changes can happen at the start of next month?
Johann	Yes.
Maria	Okay.
Pablo	Yes, that's fine.
Peter	Now, the next item concerns Securicare Services. We have been using this company to provide security for about three months now. Reports about their effectiveness have generally been favourable. However, there have been complaints, including some from hotel guests, about some of their security people being rude and rather bossy.
Pablo	Yes, I've been in touch with Securicare already about this matter. Perhaps I could ring them again ...

D Here is a list of the points that Julia Hammell made beforehand. Which of these are actually mentioned in the meeting?

- Atsushi and Carl send their apologies
- minutes of last meeting
- agenda received?
- finish by 5pm
- new desks in offices
- the company logo
- last year's sales figures
- security firm
- new software
- date of next meeting

16.4 Comprehension

Julia Hammell was responsible for taking notes and writing the minutes. Listen to the extract again. She also attended another meeting the same day and has got confused about what exactly happened in each meeting. Correct any errors in her notes.

MINUTES OF THE MEETING date: 28 August

1 Present: Peter Mathers, Maria Gonzalez, Carl Reich, Johann Elias, Julia Hammell

Apologies for absence: Atsushi Morita

2 Approval of the minutes of the last meeting.

Problem with dates – change new pay rates to start on the 10th.

3 *Topic 1*: date for new computers.

Discussion: concern expressed by MG. AT assured the meeting that problems would be minimal – about 2 weeks.

Action to be taken: new computers installed.

Person responsible: MG.

Deadline: the end of the next month.

4 *Topic 2*: problems with cleaning staff.

Discussion: complaints about timekeeping.

Action to be taken: contact Securicare.

Person responsible: AT.

Deadline: immediately.

6 Agenda and date for next meeting: not mentioned.

Language focus

16.5 The language of meetings

A In meetings we have to give our opinion but also various other skills are practised such as interrupting, asking others to give their opinion, disagreeing, expressing reservations, seeking clarification. Match the skill (**1–8**) and the language (**a–h**).

1 interrupting
2 asking others to give their opinion
3 agreeing

4 disagreeing
5 expressing reservations
6 seeking clarification
7 delaying answering
8 getting time to think

a Mmm....well, I need to think about that.
b Can I get back to you on that? I'll need to do some checking before I can give you a firm answer.
c Sorry, I didn't quite follow that. Could you go over that point again?
d I'm not so sure about that.
e I respect your view of course. But I see the situation differently ...
f Exactly. I think we are in agreement there.
g What's your opinion on that?
h Sorry to interrupt but ...

B Which expressions from the dialogue in **16.3** are used to express the following?

1 interrupting
2 asking others to give their opinion
3 agreeing
4 expressing reservations
5 seeking clarification

Listening 2

16.6 Cross-cultural differences

i What differences are there in the way people behave in your country and in USA or in Britain? In the USA it is common for workers to use first names when speaking to their boss. Does this happen in your country? In Britain and the USA, silence in conversation can make people feel uneasy. In Japan people are not so uncomfortable when sitting together in silence. In the Arab world people stand much closer together than in Europe or Japan.

Helen Wallenberg is a British businesswoman who travels extensively on behalf of her employer, Globalcar, an international car hire company. She discusses some of the cultural differences that she has noticed when meeting foreign business contacts.

A Pre-listening

In the interview she discusses the following countries: USA, Spain, Japan, Dubai. What cultural differences do you think she will mention?

B Listen to the interview.

What does she say about the USA, France, Japan, Dubai? Did you guess correctly?

Helen	I never travelled very much before I got this job. But not long after I joined the company, things really took off and I was asked to do a lot of the overseas promotions. So, for the past five years I've been going abroad about once every few months.
Interviewer	Where?
Helen	We have offices all over the globe.
Interviewer	Your company has a lot in the Arab world, I believe.
Helen	Yes. I've been to Dubai and Qatar several times. These are Muslim countries and of course one has to be aware of expectations concerning female clothing, namely that you have to dress modestly, and the rules about no alcohol. They, I suppose, are the obvious things. What you also have to realize is that business happens slowly. People there, as in Japan too, like to get to know you personally and feel confident about you as an individual before doing business.
Interviewer	What about Europe and the States?
Helen	Well, each country has its own special way of behaving. The French for example shake hands each time they meet whereas the British generally only do so when they are introduced for the first time. Having said that, I wonder if things are changing. People travel so much nowadays and maybe these differences in behaviour are decreasing. Perhaps more important are differences in attitude. For instance, in the States people can ask quite personal questions about you and your family and you're expected to use first names almost immediately you meet.

Language focus

16.7 Modals

These words express permission, necessity, advice and obligation: *may, can, could, must, should, might, have to.*

Are the following sentences true about your culture?

You ***must*** *always arrive at meetings exactly on time. Otherwise people may think you are unprofessional.*
You ***should*** *shake hands when meeting someone for the first time.*
It is polite to shake hands with everyone when you are leaving.
You ***might*** *invite an important client to your home for dinner with your family.*
You ***may*** *sometimes talk to clients about their family and friends.*

See **Language reference** page 224 for more information on modals.

Practice

What advice would you give to someone coming to your country for business? Write two things you should do and two things you should not do.

You should 1______________________________

2______________________________

You shouldn't 1______________________________

2______________________________

Lesson summary

In this unit you have:

- practised the language of meetings
- considered cross-cultural differences in business.

Suggestions for further practice

1 If you know or work with people from other countries, ask them about cross-cultural differences. What did they think was unusual or different about your country? Are attitudes to work the same or different in their country?

2 If you are interested in advertising, you might enjoy doing the following research. Find an advertisement for a product (e.g. a particular car) in newspapers and magazines in your country and then compare it with an advertisement for the same product in the American or British newspapers (the print version or a version on the internet). Are they the same advertisement? For example, in some countries the advertisers might emphasize the smart appearance of a car but in others the car's technical qualities might be emphasized.

the changing job market

In this unit you will

- **read about changes in employment practice**
- **learn what makes a good paragraph**
- **practise another technique for building up your vocabulary**

In many countries the job market is changing. For example, low-skilled jobs, particularly in the manufacturing sector, are decreasing while jobs in the service industries, such as tourism and call centres, are increasing. This chapter will focus on two of ways in which employment has been changing: outsourcing and downsizing.

Outsourcing

17.1 Warm-up questions

- Who does the cleaning in your company? Is the work done by company employees or a cleaning firm? Does your company employ temporary staff for secretarial, security and catering work?
- Which of the following phrases would you associate with 'temps' (an abbreviation for temporary workers) and which with permanent employees?

job security	cheap labour	salary scale
flexibility	efficiency	trade union
company loyalty	cost cutting	casual labour
low motivation	stress	

- Does your company or a company you know use call centres?

i Did you know that when Americans telephone Microsoft for customer support they are likely to be talking to someone in a call centre in India? It is predicted that Indian call centres could be employing up to 200,000 people and earning $3.7 billion per year by 2008 (*Times Higher Education Supplement,* 23 March 2001). (Call centres are companies employing large numbers of people to deal with customer requests on the telephone. They are particularly popular with banking, insurance, retailing and transport services.)

You are going to read a newspaper article about 'outsourcing'. Outsourcing means that one company hires another company to carry out certain activities. The purpose of outsourcing is to cut costs and to use specialists who have the skills to carry out a particular task. Outsourcing is typically used in catering, office cleaning, security services and computing.

Does your company outsource any work? Before you read the article in **17.2**, think about the advantages and disadvantages of outsourcing from the employer's and the employee's viewpoints.

Reading 1

17.2 Skimming and scanning

1 Choose the best title for the article:
   a Can an outsider do an insider's job?
   b It makes financial sense to outsource non-essential services
   c Issues in employment.

2 Find one advantage and one disadvantage of outsourcing in the text.

Advantage	Disadvantage
____________________	____________________
____________________	____________________
____________________	____________________
____________________	____________________
____________________	____________________
____________________	____________________

Replacing full-time staff with temps can save money. But it might not make sense for British Airways to do it, warns Bill Saunders.

Rumours were circulating last week that after a less than rosy financial showing of late, British Airways is to contract out tiers of its administrative structure, getting rid of many permanent PAs and replacing them with external temps. Outsourcing, as this practice is known, has been a significant business strategy over the past 10 years for keeping down payrolls. But not everyone is convinced it is the best way to run a company. At its most extreme, the principle is very simple: decide which people are essential to an enterprise, and get rid of the rest. Administrative staff are supplied, sometimes in bulk, by outside agencies and are generally employed as temps or on short-term contracts. Virtually nobody directly employs cleaners, so why not tackle the basic tasks of office administration the same way?

Many sociologists have been unhappy about outsourcing, predicting a grey 'age of anxiety' in which nobody really works for anybody. But studies have tended to show that short-term contract workers are less anxious than their fully employed peers. Temps acquire a broad range of skills and experience, while those who stay put may have limited opportunities for learning anything new. Much of it is a question of mindset, of course. Temps are used to flexible working, but the thought that any Friday they might be replaced by outsourced staff does not do much for fully employed workers' peace of mind.

But what of the employers? While nobody disputes that outsourcing can be a valuable strategy, some are beginning to move against the trend. 'There is a time to outsource and a time to insource,' says David Hagan, a director at M&G Investment Management. 'It is a question of getting the balance right.' In his case, one of the factors in the balance is communication. As investment managers strive to become more accountable to their clients, they must have support staff who understand the business. 'Nothing must be lost in communication,' says Hagan, arguing that this can best be achieved if the individuals work permanently together.

Miranda Smyth, head of marketing at specialist legal recruiters ZMB, says that the need for good understanding makes outsourcing an entire operation very difficult. There are jobs that are best tackled by outsiders – strategic analysis, for example, which obviously benefits from a fresh set of eyes with no emotional attachment. But even apparently straightforward functions, such as typing, can be difficult for an outsider. All ZMB's documents conform to a house style, and unless the person entering it into the system understands it, the job will have to be done again. 'The fact is that an employee using their knowledge of the structure and the politics of an organisation will get the end product signed off more quickly,' says Smyth.

There are advantages for employees too. 'Keeping staff in-house,' says Hagan, 'gives people a chance to develop themselves'. Properly managed, the stability of a regular job can be as dynamic as the hurly-burly of the short-term contract. 'People have the opportunity to work in several areas, and to test the waters in something which may not immediately appeal.' The opportunity to develop new skills is, he says 'the essence of a happy workforce'. It goes without saying that well-trained and happy employees are more likely to 'add value' beyond their basic job description.

As yet the trend towards outsourcing shows no sign of abating. Perhaps David Hagan and Miranda Smyth take a more independent view because they have both had varied careers themselves. She qualified as a solicitor, and he was a research physicist. One does not have to be a rocket scientist to see the sense in their arguments.

[*Source*: 'Can an outsider do an insider's job?' by Bill Saunders, *Guardian*, 20 March 2000]

17.3 Vocabulary

The following words appear in the article in **17.2** above. Choose the best meaning:

1 tiers (*line 9*)	**a** one third **b** levels **c** most of
2 less than rosy (*line 8*)	**a** reasonably healthy **b** not very good **c** better than expected
3 keeping down (*line 15*)	**a** keeping good records **b** increasing **c** stopping from rising too quickly
4 virtually nobody (*line 23*)	**a** very few people **b** almost real **c** nobody at all
5 does not do much for (*line 40*)	**a** has a negative effect **b** has positive effect **c** has no effect

6 getting the balance right (*line 49*)
a reaching a compromise
b getting the right outcome
c saving money

7 signed off (*line 74*)
a eliminated
b written
c finished

8 it goes without saying (*line 87*)
a it is obvious
b it is silent
c it is secret

9 One does not have to be a rocket scientist (*lines 97–8*)
a it's impossible
b it's not easy
c it's not difficult

17.4 Comprehension

1 What do the following refer to in the article in **17.2**?

(*line 5*)	it
(*line 39*)	they
(*line 44*)	some

2 What has been the main reason for the popularity of outsourcing?

3 Which type of employee feels less stressed? Temporary or full-time?

4 Are these true or false statements? In which paragraph did you find the answer?

a British Airways is going to retrain many of its staff.
b Outsourcing will create more stress among the workforce.
c Typing should not be done by outsourced workers.
d A contented worker needs to develop new skills.

5 Why do you think the author states in the heading that 'it might not make sense' for British Airways to outsource?

17.5 Understanding text organization

If a text is well written, each paragraph should have a clear purpose. Paragraph one in the text introduces the topic. What are the purposes of the other five paragraphs? Choose from the following:

- to conclude
- to put the employer's viewpoint (twice)
- to provide the academic viewpoint
- to describe the advantages of outsourcing

paragraph 1: *introduction*
paragraph 2: ______________
paragraph 3: ______________
paragraph 4: ______________
paragraph 5: ______________
paragraph 6: ______________

17.6 What do you think?

Which would you prefer? To work as a full-time permanent employee or as a temporary outsourced employee? Why?

Downsizing

Downsizing is a term which is commonly used when organizations talk about the need to become more efficient and reduce costs. However, from an employee's viewpoint it simply means employing fewer people.

17.7 Warm-up questions

- Have there been any major changes in your company's organization recently?
- Have working practices changed?
- Is the labour force increasing or decreasing?
- Which of the following words do you associate with downsizing?

to promote	make redundant	payroll
lay off	salary	recession
lose	benefit	to fire
strike	to get the sack	growth
let go	commuter	to get the axe

Reading 2

17.8 Skimming and scanning

1 How many companies are named in the text?

2 Choose the best title for the text:

a South Korea's top conglomerates present restructuring plans.
b South Korean companies face big job losses.
c All change in South Korea's business community.

South Korea's top 30 conglomerates submitted their restructuring plans to an emergency economic committee on Saturday, Yonhap news agency reported.

It said the various proposals put forward by the firms, which include Hyundai, Samsung and Daewoo, highlighted the downsizing of chairmen's secretariats and greater responsibility on the management.

Industry sources said Hyundai pledged gradually to close down its composite planning office and concentrate on four or five key businesses, including the automobile and heavy industries.

Samsung said it would not close its chairman's secretariat but transfer it to another company that would take charge of management.

It also outlined plans to secure foreign capital through the Goldman Sachs fund and to launch capital ventures with foreign car manufacturers such as Ford and Volkswagen.

LG said it would transfer its chairman secretariat's function to a board of directors and dispose of financially weak sectors of its business group.

Daewoo, also planning a gradual closure of the chairman's office, will make public its complete restructuring blueprint next week.

SK said it would do away with its planning office from next year and have group chairmen register as top executives of five selected subsidiary companies.

These group chairmen will pump in extra money by selling their stocks in non-mainstream subsidiaries, Yonhap reported.

[Source: *BBC Business News*, 14 February 1998]

17.9 Vocabulary

Look at the following words in their context. Choose the word or phrase which has the closest meaning to the original:

1 conglomerates (*line 1*)
- **a** a large multinational company
- **b** a large group of companies producing a variety of products
- **c** a variety of companies

2 restructuring (*line 1*)
- **a** reorganization
- **b** review
- **c** resignation

3 highlighted (*line 5*)
- **a** pictured
- **b** emphasized
- **c** viewed

4 secretariats (*line 6*)
- **a** secretary
- **b** office staff
- **c** office furniture

5 pledged (*line 8*)
- **a** promised
- **b** agreed
- **c** considered

6 take charge of (*line 12*)
- **a** attend to
- **b** assume responsibility for
- **c** give help to

7 make public (*line 21*)
- **a** make free
- **b** announce
- **c** describe

8 blueprint (*line 21*)
- **a** document
- **b** paper
- **c** plan

9 subsidiary companies (*line 24*)
- **a** additional companies
- **b** companies owned by a parent company
- **c** supporting companies

10 stocks (*line 26*)
- **a** shares
- **b** raw materials
- **c** goods

17.10 Comprehension

Read the article in 17.8 again.

A Complete the statements with the most appropriate ending:

1 South Korea's biggest commercial organizations agreed
  a to give greater responsibility to some managers.
  b to cut the number of associated companies.
  c to redesign the structure of their organizations.

2 Unlike other conglomerates, Samsung decided to
  a reduce the chairman's responsibilities.
  b put the manager's secretary into a new office.
  c give responsibility for the chairman's office to another organization.

B Match the companies and the information provided in the text:

	Daewoo	Hyundai	Samsung	LG	SK	Ford	Volkswagen
1 downsizing secretariats	✓	✓	✓	✓	✓		
2 looking for foreign finance							
3 closing its planning office							
4 publicizing plans shortly							

17.11 Building your vocabulary

Another way of extending your range of vocabulary is to learn words not separately but in 'family' groupings. You could also add examples of word partnerships (see **Unit 3**). Fill in the gaps in the table overleaf, using a dictionary if necessary.

Noun(s)	Verb	Adjective	Word partnership
1 management/ manager	to manage	managerial	managing director
2 ____________	to compete	____________	competitive advantage
3 transfer	____________	____________	transfer funds
4 earnings	____________	earned	earned income
5 ____________	____________	registered	____________
6 ____________	to highlight	____________	

Suggestions for further practice

1 Are any English language newspapers published in your country? Do they have a business section? What are the most important issues affecting your country's economy at the moment?

2 Imagine you are going to meet a group of foreign business people who want to know about changes in the economy of your country during the past year. Prepare a short presentation. If possible, discuss your ideas with an English-speaking colleague at work.

3 As well as newspapers, radio and television, the internet is a useful source of international business news. Try some of the sites in the **Useful web addresses** section on page 239.

18 check your progress

18.1 Vocabulary

Fill in the gaps in this e-mail. You can use words from the box below.

From: Ray Smith <rsmith@mda.com>
To: David Sitorus <ho@sunrise-products.co.id>
Date: Thursday 29th April
Subject: trip to Indonesia

Dear David

I will be ___________ in Jakarta at Soekarno-Hatta Airport at 13.10 on Friday 5th May. I'm ___________ with Emirates and my flight number is EMI 7721. Can you confirm that someone will be able to ___________ me up at the airport? By the way, I will not be staying at the Hotel Borobodur as it is completely ___________. I am booked into the Hilton Hotel.

We are also ___________ you some sample materials and some technical documents by courier. You should have those by Monday midday at the latest. Please let me __________ if they do not arrive. They ___________ coming with Europe and Asia couriers and the reference number is JAK37274A.

I look ___________ to seeing you again next week. Let me know if there is ___________ you would ___________ me to bring from London.

Regards

Ray Smith

full arriving know anything travel forward sending like pick will are want flying

18.2 Questions

Ray Smith's secretary is talking to the Managing Director about Ray's travel plans. These are the answers to some questions about the travel arrangements. Write the missing questions.

MD *When is Ray leaving for Indonesia?*
Kate He's leaving on Thursday, at midday.
MD Who ________________________________?
Kate Emirate Airlines.
MD How much ____________________________?
Kate Three thousand two hundred and seventeen pounds.

MD Gosh, that's a lot. ______________________?
Kate He's staying at the Hilton Hotel.
MD How long ______________________?
Kate Eight days. He's leaving the following Saturday.
MD Who ______________________?
Kate He's meeting the Head of Overseas Marketing, David Sitorus, when he arrives, and he's meeting the Chairman of Sunrise Products on Tuesday 9th May.
MD How long ______________________?
Kate It's an eighteen-hour flight.
MD Well, ask him to come and see me as soon as he gets back.

18.3 What would you say?

a You are telephoning a colleague. You need to arrange a time for a meeting. Tomorrow at 11 am would be a good time for you. Make a suggestion.
b You want to use the photocopier but you don't know how it works. Ask someone for help.
c You are visiting another company and you would like to make a phone call. Ask the secretary for permission.
d Your computer printer is not working. There are several sheets of paper jammed inside it. Explain the problem to the technician (on the telephone).
e There is a telephone call for your colleague, but he is not at work today. Explain this to the caller and offer to take a message.
f Your colleague is on the phone. He suggests a time for a meeting (tomorrow at 11). This is okay for you, so tell him you agree.

18.4 Missing words

Complete these sentences with appropriate words which appeared in Units 15–17.

1 Ray Smith is planning a business __________ to Indonesia next month.
2 He is __________ at the Hilton Hotel in Jakarta.
3 There is a __________ leaving London at 10.30 and arriving in Dubai at 13.45 local time.
4 Please can you __________ a meeting with the Head of the Personnel Department on Friday?
5 I can't come to a meeting tomorrow but I'm __________ all day on Friday.

6 Before we start the meeting, has everyone got a copy of the agenda and the __________ of the last meeting?
7 In Britain people usually __________ hands the first time they meet someone.
8 More than 2,000 people will be __________ redundant when Fujitsu closes its plant next month.
9 Many companies are replacing __________ staff with temps.
10 IBM has announced plans to __________ the number of sales staff from 3,000 to 2,500.
11 In Britain and the USA it is important to arrive at meetings __________ time.
12 Women travelling to the Middle East know that they __________ to dress modestly.
13 I'm afraid I don't __________ with you on this point. In my opinion it is a mistake to outsource secretarial services.
14 What's the __________ of a business class ticket from London to Frankfurt, return?

18.5 Self evaluation

a Look back over the units you have studied in this coursebook. What areas of your English do you think have improved? Vocabulary? Grammar? Speaking? Listening? Reading? Pronunciation? Writing? Making telephone calls?
b If a colleague asked you for advice on learning English, what tips could you give him or her? What are the best strategies for learning and practising English in your experience?
c Which areas of English would you like to continue to improve?
d What resources could you use to continue learning?
- Buy another book
- Use the internet
- Watch TV and films in English
- Read newspapers and magazines
- Practise writing dialogues, letters and e-mails
- Find friends to talk to in English
- Find a pen friend or keypal to correspond with
- Other suggestions:

Don't stop working on your English just because you have finished this book. Set some new goals for yourself for improving your English over the next few months. Then write an action plan of things you can do to achieve these goals.

Look at the section **Taking it further** at the end of this book for more ideas about ways to study English.

Unit 1: Companies

1.2

1 Benton International Powders Ltd. 2 IT/computing and travel. 3 Multimedia Solutions Incorporated. 4 Benton International Powders Ltd. 5 Business Travel Ltd.

1.3

Company name	*Business Travel Limited*	*Multimedia Solutions Incorporated*	*Benton International Powders Ltd.*
Main area of business	*Travel*	*Website design*	*Manufacture of powder paints*
Products / Services	*Travel services for businesses: flights, hotels, briefings, meetings*	*Design and management of websites and e-commerce*	*epoxy resin powder paint*
Customers	*Shell, House of Fraser, IBM (UK)*	*financial services insurance brokering and underwriting travel services, computer retailing, vehicle leasing*	*Manufacturers of metal shelving, lampshades, vehicle components, metal garden furniture*
Location: Head office Subsidiaries	*London* *USA: NY & LA, Europe*	*Guildford* *Birmingham, Dublin, Manchester, Ed'burgh, Paris, Rome, Madrid*	*Birmingham* *Surrey and other plants (total 6)*
When did it start up?	*1989*	1993	*1979*
Number of employees	270	200+	*480*
Other information	*Profits £1.3 million last year.*		*Last year turnover exceeded £25 million; profits £4.8 million*

1.4

2 Operation and management of the rail network. 3 Broadcasting and internet. 4 Television production and broadcasting AND hotels and catering. 5 Banking. 6 Computer hardware manufacture. 7 Insurance. 8 Design of computer software. 9 Computer hardware manufacture. 10 Petroleum production. 11 Petroleum production. 12 Advertising. 13 Design of computer software. 14 Publishing. 15 Vehicle manufacture. 16 Food and soap manufacture. 17 Retailing foods and consumer products.

1.5

Suggested answers:

1	a factory	a plant	a production facility	
2	a warehouse	a distribution centre		
3	a subsidiary	an agency	a sister company	a franchise
4	the head office	a parent company	main office	
5	a department	a section	a division	a branch
6	a multinational	a conglomerate	a group of companies	

1.6

1 established; 2 groups; 3 employees; 4 subsidiary; 5 brands; 6 owns; 7 goods; 8 on; 9 areas; 10 chains; 11 Electrical; 12 number; 13 profits; 14 Office.

1.8

1 3. 2 The production division. 3 Birmingham, Leicester, Salford, Glasgow and South East London. 4 Research and Development. 5 Faversham, in Kent. 6 The development of new products, quality control, technical assistance to customers.

Unit 2: Jobs and introductions

2.2

1 b. 2 c. 3 e. 4 a. 5 f. 6 d.

2.3

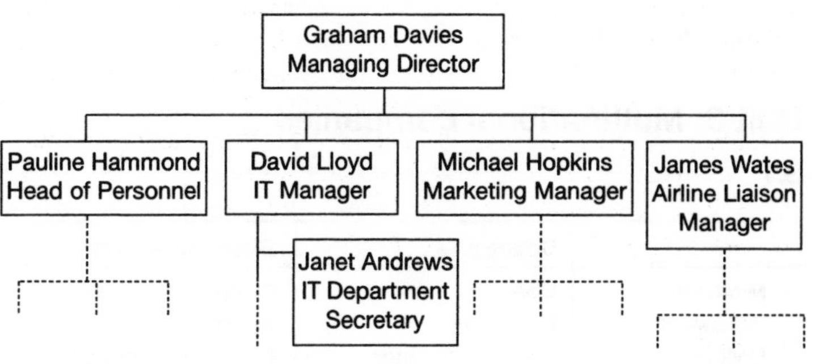

2.4

2 False. 3 True. 4 False. 5 True. 6 True. 7 False. 8 True. 9 False. 10 False.

2 **Pauline Hammond** is the Head of Personnel.
4 Jim Smith works for **the Los Angeles office of BTL.**
7 Michael Hopkins is going to have **lunch** with Jim Smith.
9 The Marketing Manager **introduced himself** to Jim.
10 Jim Smith is going to be working in London for about three **months.**

2.7

Speaker	Job	Speaker	Job
1	Personnel manager	2	E-commerce co-ordinator
3	Sales manager	4	PA to the Managing Director
5	Receptionist	6	Accountant
7	Sales representative	8	External Relations Director

2.9

1 He's the Head of the Finance Department.
2 She's an accountant with PriceWaterhouseCoopers.
3 He's from British Airways.
4 She works for the Sales Department of ICL.
5 They work for American Express in the traveller's cheque division.

2.10

1 Organizes; Authorizes.

Unit 3: Multinational companies

3.1

	Country	Business activity
Microsoft	USA	computer software
Volkswagen	Germany	automobiles
Unilever	UK & Netherlands	household products
Hitachi	Japan	electronic equipment
Barclays	UK	banking

3.2

1 Paragraph D. 2 1917.

3.3

A new company: paragraph A.
Early growth: paragraph B.
Organization: paragraph C.
Product range: paragraph D.

3.4

1 b. 2 a. 3 b. 4 a. 5 c.

3.5

Different answers are possible. Suggested answers: merged; company; consumer; goods; brands; Holland

3.7

1 axe jobs. 2 raw materials. 3 logic. 4 dabbled in. 5 scuppered. 6 agribusiness. 7 a spending spree.

3.8

Year
1885 Lever Brothers founded.
1917 Lever diversifies into foods.
1930 Merger with Margarine Unie.
1950s Moved into chemicals, packaging.
1980s Got rid of packaging companies, most of agribusiness and speciality chemicals.

1984 Bought Brooke Bond tea brand.
1996 Niall Fitzgerald became chairman.
2000 Government action to end trading agreements.

3.9

1 Company newsletter. 2 Business newspapers.
Reading 1 is from an official company history of Unilever. Reading 2 is from a BBC News report. Reading 2 is more critical of the company (*lines 27–43*) and uses more colourful expressions, e.g. 'got rid of its packaging companies' (*line 34–5*), 'spending spree' (*line 37*).

3.12

1 **a** (iv); **b** (ii); **c** (i); **d** (iii).
2 **a** General Motors; **b** General Electric; **c** Citigroup; **d** General Electric; **e** Wal-Mart.
3 Four.
4 Yes, IBM.
5 Automobiles.
6a two; UK; $51,632m; market value.

Unit 4: Job hunting

4.2

A 1 Bilingual Executive Assistant
2 Accountancy Clerk
3 Executive Trainees
4 Head of Marketing
5 Sales Executives
6 Software Support Manager

4.3

a 6. **b** 1. **c** 1, 2. **d** 4. **e** 3. **f** 2. **g** 1, 2, 6 (3, 4, 5). **h** 3. **i** 2. **j** 5. **k** 1, 2, 6.

4.4

a Patrick Kiely: Job 1. **b** Teresa Soliz: Job 1. **c** Miriam Jax: Job 4. **d** Michel Delain: Job 2. **e** David Delgado: Job 6.

4.6

1 Miriam. 2 Patrick. 3 David. 4 Miriam. 5 Teresa. 6 Michel.

a Use simple past tense ('I worked …') when talking about a period of time that is over (for example a previous job).

b Use present perfect tense ('I have worked …' or 'I have been working …') when talking about something that started in the past but is still continuing now, for example the job you are doing at the moment.

4.7

decided /id/; worked /t/; started /id/; finished /d/; ended /id/.

4.8

1 Patrick is feeling unhappy. Roberto notices he looks 'down in the dumps'.
2 Patrick's job application was unsuccessful. (c)
3 He is going to apply for the job of Bilingual Executive Assistant.

4.9

1 False. 2 True. 3 False. 4 False. 5 True. 6 False. 7 False.

4.10

1 c. 2 f. 3 d. 4 e. 5 a. 6 b.

4.11

1 Top right-hand corner of the letter.
2 At the bottom.
3 Top left, below your own address.
4 'Dear Sir', 'Dear Madam', 'Dear Sir or Madam' at the beginning. 'Yours faithfully' at the end.

4.12

He's leaving for London on Tuesday but he hasn't sorted out all the arrangements; the e-mail system is giving trouble; he doesn't know how to use it properly.

4.13

1 False. 2 True. 3 False. 4 True. 5 True. 6 True. 7 False. 8 True.

1 Pierre is **not** going to have a drink with Silvia.
3 Pierre **doesn't have a secretary**.
7 Pierre's last assistant worked for him for **only three weeks**.

4.14

A 1 e. 2 d. 3 b. 4 a. 5 c.

B Suggested answers:
To Mike: Why don't you ask the travel section to take care of them for you?
To Alicia: I think you should look for another one.
To Alexandra: If I were you, I'd complain to personnel.
To Paul: Have you tried calling IT support?
To Julie: You shouldn't buy so many new clothes.

Unit 5: Letters and CVs

5.2

Appropriate: **a, c, f, h, i, k.**
Not appropriate: **b, d, e, g, j, l.**

5.3

1 In South Ealing, in London.
2 Web Designer with West London College of Higher Education.
3 Degree in IT with Business Studies (and courses in graphic design and usability design).
4 E-commerce consultant.
5 17 May.
6 Personnel Manager.
7 Multimedia Solutions Incorporated.
8 Yes – suitable qualifications and experience.
9 Yes, it seems quite effective but see the ideas in the rest of Unit 5.

5.4

Do's: **2, 3, 4, 5, 6, 7, 9, 11, 13, 15, 16.**
Don'ts: **1, 8, 10, 12, 14.**

5.5

1 Not mentioned.
2 None mentioned.
3 None mentioned.
4 Financial consultancy and planning advice on pensions, life assurance, savings, etc.
5 Yes – 'long term prospects'.
6 Not stated (probably yes).
7 Yes, although nothing specifically mentioned.
8 Probably – 'posts throughout our European network'.
9 Not stated. Almost certainly not.
10 It sells financial products and services.
11 50–100.
12 Yes.

5.8

1 In Madrid.
2 Three.
3 St Joseph's College.
4 No information.
5 No information.
6 No information.

7 Yes.
8 Calle Prim 19, 4th Floor, 28004 Madrid.
9 National Gallery of Ireland, Comlink Computers.
10 Spanish, Maths, Economics, Physics, English and Art.
11 Spanish.
12 Advising customers and small businesses on their IT requirements. Sales, delivery and installation of PCs. Answering technical queries and dealing with IT problems.
13 The latest.

Unit 6: A job interview

6.2

1 Wanted to travel and work abroad, and also wanted to join his partner in Spain.
2 Working hard on his Spanish. Taking some other courses. Applying for jobs.
3 Feels fairly settled in Spain at the moment.

6.3

1 True. 2 False. 3 False. 4 True. 5 True. 6 False.

2 His girlfriend is Spanish.
3 He has had a number of job interviews.
5 Not completely clear – he has been working on his Spanish and has done some other courses.
6 He left the Bank of Ireland because he wanted to work abroad and his girlfriend was offered a job in Madrid.

6.4

1 decided. 2 felt. 3 have you been doing. 4 said / have been working. 5 I have been applying. 6 I've had / have turned down.

6.6

1 True. 2 False. 3 True. 4 False. 5 True.

6.7

1 a for/with. b in. c on. d down. e for. f back. g – h about.
2 a for. b about/in. c from. d on. e at/together.
3 a to turn down. b different from. c to take on. d to look at.

6.9

1 Five. 2 Patrick. 3 Teresa. 4 More relaxed? Patrick. More ambitious? Teresa. Had better Spanish? Teresa. Better English? Patrick. Was better qualified? Neither. They were both well qualified for the job.

6.10

1 d. 2 a. 3 b. 4 c.

Unit 7: Check your progress

7.1

1 Companies: multinational, firm
2 Job titles: Managing Director, Accountant
3 Job hunting: application form, advertisement
4 Describing people: ambitious, punctual

7.2

1 subsidiary. 2 established. 3 manages. 4 deals with. 5 like. 6 involved. 7 including. 8 merged. 9 how. 10 information. 11 for. 12 ran. 13 forward. 14 CV. 15 did. 16 offered. 17 seemed.

7.3

Listen to Part Two of the recording for suggested answers.

7.4

1 f. 2 d. 3 g. 4 e. 5 a. 6 b. 7 c.

Unit 8: Finance

8.1

Bill Gates has approximately $58.7 billion. The Nikkei, FTSE 100 and Wall Street are connected with stock markets.
1 stock markets. 2 unemployment. 3 interest rates.

8.3

Country	Currency	Price of a Hamburger Local currency	Dollars
Japan	Yen	Y294	2.78
European Union	Euro	€2.56	2.37
Brazil	Real	Real 2.95	1.65
Russia	Rouble	R39.50	1.39
United Kingdom	Sterling	£1.90	3.00
China	Yuan	Y 9.90	1.20
USA	Dollar	$2.51	2.51
Taiwan	New Dollar	NT $70.00	2.29
Indonesia	Rupiah	Rp 14,500	1.83

[Source: *Economist*, 27 April 2000]

8.4

a 0.5 cents. **b** 6. **c** 12. **d** 3 per cent. **e** 2 per cent. **f** 2.5 per cent. **g** 1,000. **h** 500. **i** rapid. **j** 5,000. **k** $1^1/_2$. **l** one.

8.5

1 three point five per cent.
2 twenty two thousand.
3 ten point five.
4 two dollars seventy eight cents.
5 two hundred and ninety four yen.
6 one pound ninety.
7 nine million seven hundred and eighty four thousand five hundred and ninety six.
8 five million four hundred and eighty three thousand four hundred and ninety five.

8.6

1 exceeded. 2 flagship. 3 launched. 4 light-hearted. 5 converts. 6 expensive. 7 data.

a False. **b** True. **c** Yes according to the index.

8.7

A
1 harder, hardest
2 dearer, dearest
3 more efficient, most efficient
4 better, best (*irregular*)
5 luckier, luckiest
6 more ambitious, most ambitious
7 more interesting, most interesting
8 more expensive, most expensive
9 cheaper, cheapest
10 costlier, costliest

B
1 biggest, best, more happy, more satisfied
2 longer, largest, younger

8.8

1 A city trader.

2 Some did not believe it. Others soon realized there had been a mistake.

8.9

1 b. 2 a. 3 b. 4 a. 5 a. 6 a. 7 c. 8 b. 9 b. 10 a.

8.10

a True. **b** False. **c** False. **d** False. **e** False. **f** True.

8.11

1 d. 2 c. 3 b. 4 a.

Unit 9: Using the telephone

9.2

Christos can't speak to Jim Smith because Jim's line is busy – he is talking to someone else on the telephone already.

9.3

2 His phone number is 85983 *not* 85993.
3 His company's name is Multimedia Solutions Incorporated *not* Corporation.
4 He will be in his office this morning *not* this afternoon (he will be out all afternoon).
5 He wanted to be called back.

9.4

1c. 2a. 3b. 4a.

9.5

a five five nine nine zero nine two one
b seven eight four six two two five four
c zero four six six eight seven seven seven
d eight five seven four zero zero two one
e eight five nine three zero nine zero zero
f three three six four zero nine eight six

9.7

	Message 1	Message 2	Message 3	Message 4
Name	Racquel Boutier	Liam Dwyer	Paul Delgado	Yasuko Kitamura
Date	4th May	6th May	7th May	8th May
Dept./ Company	Anglo-Spanish Travel Services	marketing department	SP Computers	Japan Tech Ltd
Tel no.	00 34 93 345 6488	extension 2931	094 3345 9704 extension 896	020 743526

Message 1
Hello, Mr Smith. This is Racquel Boutier. That's B-O-U-T-I-E-R . I work for a company called Anglo-Spanish Travel Services. I don't know if you are aware, but we are your agents in Spain. Liam Dwyer from your marketing department told me that you might be able to give us some ideas about the companies you used for your website. I must say, your site looks really impressive. Do you think I could come and meet you for about an hour? I am coming to London next weekend and I could come in any time on Friday afternoon, Monday or Tuesday morning. Could you let me know if that would be convenient? My phone number is 00 34 93 345 6488. My email address is Racquel.Boutier@ASDS.com
This message was left at 12.15 on Monday, 4 May

Message 2
Hi, Jim, this is Liam Dwyer from the marketing department. I'm trying to set up a meeting for next week about the new website and I want to know when you can make it. Can you let me know whether Wednesday late morning or Thursday afternoon anytime would be possible? You can call me back on extension 2931.
This message was left at 10.50 am on Wednesday, 6 May

Message 3
Hello, I am Paul Delgado from SP Computers. You left a message saying you wanted to speak to Pierre Blisset. Unfortunately Pierre is on vacation at the moment. Perhaps I could help. You can call me on 094 3345 9704 extension 896. My name is Delgado, spelt D-E-L-G-A-D-O. Thank you.
This message was left at 11 am on Thursday, 7 May

Message 4
My name is Yasuko Kitamura. I am the Deputy Sales Manager at Japan Tech Ltd. Could you please ring me on 020 743526? Thank you.
This message was left at 11.15 on Friday, 8 May

9.8

1 f. **2** d. **3** e. **4** c. **5** g. **6** a. **7** b.

9.10

b A delay

9.11

1 False. 2 True. 3 False. 4 True. 5 True. 6 False. 7 False.

9.12

PA Multimedia Solutions Incorporated, Development Section, good morning.

Jim Oh hello, I'd **like** to speak to Christos Georgiou.

PA He's on the other line at the moment. I'm his PA. Can I ask who's **calling**?

Jim Yes, **this** is Jim Smith from Business Travel Limited. I'm **returning** his call from this morning.

PA Oh yes, Mr Smith. **Hold** on just a second, I think he's just finished.

Christos Hello Jim, sorry to **keep** you waiting.

Jim No problem. What's up?

Christos **It's** about the new version of your website. We had some problems with the changes you asked for last week, but it's all **sorted** out now. However, we are behind schedule and we are not **going** to be able to deliver next week.

Jim Well, when do you think you will **be** able to deliver?

Christos We only need two extra days. It'll be **ready** for installation by Tuesday of the week after next.

Jim As long as we get it on the Tuesday there should be no problem. Are you sure there **won't** be any more delays?

Christos Yes, I'm sure.

Jim Okay, that's fine. But if anything else does come up, please let me **know** as early as possible.

Christos Of course. If we have any more problems, **I'll** let you know immediately.

Jim Thanks a lot. I'll give you a **call** at the end of next week anyway.

Christos Fine. **I'll** speak to you then. Have a good weekend.

Jim Bye.

9.13

a 2, 3. **b** 1, 4. **c** I'll give you a hand if you like. **d** Will you check the ones from the finance department? **e** 3.

1 c. 2 d. 3 b. 4 a.

9.14

1 b. 2 c. 3 a. 4 a. 5 c.

9.15

Listen to the recording for suggested answers.

Unit 10: E-commerce

10.1

software	computing program, e.g. Word, Excel
hardware	physical components of computing, e.g. disks
PC	personal computer
telemarketing	selling via the telephone
e-commerce	electronic business, e.g. via the web
network	system of interconnected PCs
search engine	program which searches through a database

10.2

1 search engine.
2 hardware.
3 the network.
4 software.

10.3

A It has caused great changes.
B1 100 times cheaper.
B2 Advantages: reduce paper records, store vast amounts of information, speed up the process of handling information, data can be more easily sorted and accessed, easier and faster communication between business people, customer can have access to information previously not so easily available, greater cost efficiency.
Disadvantages: fewer bank branches and fewer employees to deal with customers.

10.4

A 1 e. 2 c. 3 a. 4 b. 5 d.

B 1 paper records.
2 information technology.
3 radical changes.
4 service industries.
5 essential information.

10.5

B im'portant, 'clever, ad'vertisement, 'total, a'fford, 'borrow, 'easy, ex'change, in'crease, 'special, ad'vise

10.6

1 E-zines. The message is targeted at a specific audience.
2 classified ads.
3 banner ads.

10.7

B Introduction 1 is probably better because the speaker introduces himself to the audience, and gives a clear description of content of his presentation. However, it is formal and less friendly than Introduction 2.

C
1. Introduce yourself, the purpose of the presentation and how things will be organized. Memorize the first few words.
2. Signal each of the points.
3. Brief summary, thank the audience and answer questions.

10.8

1, 4, 6 = concluding.
2 = starting a new point.
3 = introductions.
4, 5 = referring to a previous point.

10.9

1. To start with ... If you have any questions ...
2. He does follow Paolo's advice. Some critics might feel that using 'secondly ... thirdly ... fourthly...' at the start of each new point is a rather dull and simple way of organizing his talk. However, it is correct English. This is Paolo's first presentation and he prefers to play safe.

Unit 11: Socializing

11.1

1. Dialogue 2.
2. Dialogue 1.
3. Dialogue 1: How about meeting; That would be great.
   Dialogue 2: We were wondering if ...; It's good of you to offer.

11.4

1. Julio da Silva.
2. Anna Smith.
3. Mexico City.
4. His card.
5. To buy him a drink.

11.5

A Several answers are possible. Here are some suggestions.

a How was your weekend?
Did you watch the football yesterday?

b How about getting together for a drink one night this week?
Have you played much lately?
We must have a game sometime.
c That's very kind of you
d Hello, Peter. How are things in the IT section?
e Excuse me. Are you Mr Andrews ? I'm ... from MS Development.
Was the journey alright?
Did you have a pleasant flight?
Great weather we are having at the moment.
I'm afraid the weather hasn't been very good recently.

B a 1. b 3. c 4. d 5. e 6.

11.6

1 f. 2 d. 3 i. 4 h. 5 g. 6 c. 7 a. 8 e. 9 b.

1 got the green light.
2 red tape.
3 put on hold.
4 in the pipeline.
5 on the blink.
6 started the ball rolling.
7 tied up all day.
8 in the red.
9 a long shot.

11.7

A curry: India.
pâté: France.
spaghetti bolognaise: Italy.
borscht: Russia.
taco: Mexico.
couscous: Tunisia.
sushi: Japan.

B 1 curry. 2 spaghetti bolognaise.

11.8

What would you like to drink? A pint of Guinness, please.
What kind of wine would you like? A dry white wine, please.
This is on me/It's my round. Thank you very much.
Cheers! Cheers!
Another one before you go? I'd better not. I'm driving. Thanks all the same.

11.9

A *Suggested answer*: Thanks very much for offering. But really I just can't drink any more. I have an important meeting early tomorrow morning.
B Oh, how interesting!
C

Asking questions politely	Answer: Yes	Answer: No
1 Excuse me, could you...?	Certainly.	
2 Is it all right to...?		Sorry. I'm afraid ...
3 Do you mind if ...?	Please do.	
4 Sorry to disturb you. Can I ...?	Yes, of course.	
5 Could I have a ..., please?	Here you are.	
6 May I ...?	Yes.	
7 Would you like some coffee?	That would be lovely. Thank you.	
8 Could you tell me... please?		Sorry.

a Would you like to put your coat there?
b Can I offer you a cup of coffee?
c How do you spell your name, please?
d What company are you from, please?
e Can I help you?
f Is it all right to smoke a cigarette in here? / Could you tell me where the smoking area is, please?

11.10

B 1 The first version is more polite.
2 The second version is more polite.
3 The first version is more polite.

Unit 12: Making contact

12.2

1 Business Travel Limited
2 He is trying to find out what sort of support he can get from specialized companies to expand the capabilities of his company's website.
3 His business card and some brochures.
4 a Probably not.
b Yes, probably.
c Probably not.
d Yes, probably.

12.3

1 False.
2 True.
3 True.
4 False. Mike gave Jim his business card and a brochure about *his* company.
5 False. Mike Saunders's company has already set up interactive sites with full e-commerce capability for a number of clients.
6 True.
7 False. Mike suggested that Jim should look at some websites designed by *his* company.

12.6

Recep Project Personnel, good morning.

Mike Oh good morning, I want to talk to someone about getting some IT consultants in, on a temporary basis.

Recep I'll put you **through** to our IT department. Hold on a minute.

Celia IT recruitment. Celia Robins **speaking**.

Mike Oh, good morning. My name is Mike Saunders, I work with a company called Multimedia Solutions. I don't think we have used your agency before.

Celia How can I **help** you, Mr Saunders?

Mike We need to recruit extra web designers for a new contract. The project will probably **take/last** about one and a half to two months.

Celia Right. How **many** people are we talking about exactly?

Mike Five. We need people with **experience** in e-commerce, using Dreamweaver and Oracle database. Do you have anyone like that?

Celia Yes, that should be no problem. When do you **need** them for?

Mike As soon as **possible**. Say next week? I know that is short notice but we need to get them in pretty urgently.

Celia Okay. We do have some suitable people, I need to check if they are **available** for starting next week. I could fax or email some CVs over to you this afternoon.

Mike That would be great. Can you give me some **idea** about cost?

Celia If you need people for more than a month, around £50 an hour.

Mike Right. Well if you have **suitable** people that would be fine.

Celia Okay, well **leave** it with me and as I say I should be able to send you the details this afternoon.

Mike Okay, I'll **give** you my email. It's M dot Saunders S-A-U-N-D-E-R-S at M-S-I dot co dot U-K. And the phone number is 020 7648 6868.

Celia Fine. I'll be in **touch** this afternoon.

12.7

1 a. 2 c. 3 b. 4 d. 5 e. 6 f.

12.8

1 able to/can do.
2 capable of/can be/up to.
3 experience of/have already.
4 be possible/can guarantee.

12.10

1 Business travel.
2 Organizing travel – flights, hotels, etc. for other companies.
3 The Western Credit Group.
4 IT advisor.
5 Interesting, although they didn't agree with everything the speaker said.
6 It isn't clearly stated but probably to get some information and advice on setting up e-commerce.

12.11

A *This is what you might normally do when you meet someone at a conference or a reception in an English-speaking country, but of course there are different possibilities*:
1 Tell them what you think of the conference/the reception/the seminar *or* Talk about something neutral.
2 Introduce yourself.
3 Find out what field they work in.
4 Ask who they work for.
5 Discuss the possibility of meeting.
6 Arrange a meeting.

B 1 They talked about what they thought of the talk.
2 Geoff asked Peter what field he worked in.
3 Peter answered then he asked Geoff the same.
Geoff gave the name of his company and explained about his job.
5 Geoff gave Peter his card.
6 Peter gave Geoff his card and suggested a meeting.
7 Geoff agreed.

Unit 13: The energy business

13.2

1 Organization of Petroleum Exporting Countries.

2 No. There are alternatives available but it is likely to be a long time before it is replaced as the most important source of energy.

13.3

1 b. 2 c. 3 b. 4 c. 5 b. 6 a. 7 b. 8 b. 9 a. 10 a.

13.4

1 **a** World's daily consumption of oil.
b OPEC's oil reserves are sufficient to last for 80 years.
c The 11 members of OPEC.
d OPEC increased production of oil in order to prevent prices rocketing and causing instability in the world economy.

2 **a** True. **b** True. **c** False – but it does have a very strong influence. **d** False. **e** True.

3 Oil can be found on all the continents of the world, the largest **deposits** being in the Gulf states. Although it is a **limited** resource, OPEC at least believes it has enough for at least another 80 years. However, the oil companies are nonetheless investigating **alternative** sources of energy. OPEC is the key figure in the oil business and produces about **half** of the world's production – its share may well increase in the future. OPEC tends to favour a policy of **market stability** and will increase supply if for any reason, e.g. **war**, supplies to the world markets are reduced. While it continues to be a comparatively **cheap** source of energy it will continue to play a vital role in the political economy of the world.

4 **a** North Atlantic Free Trade Area. **b** World Trade Organization. **c** European Community. **d** Financial Times Stock Exchange. **e** Association of South East Asian Nations. **f** International Monetary Fund. **g** Pan African Congress.

13.6

1 Three.
2 It will never recover its once-dominant position.

13.7

1 **a** Coal. **b** The belief that more accidents are inevitable. **c** Motor manufacturers.
2 **a** Probably true. **b** True. **c** False. **d** False. **e** True.

13.8

1 the Northern countries.
2 oil reserves.
3 coal.
4 coal's.

5 nuclear power.
6 renewable fuels.
7 people living in an eastern European county during the Soviet era.

13.9

A 1 f. 2 c. 3 d. 4 e. 5 g. 6 a. 7 b.

B 1 a. 2 c. 3 a. 4 a.

Unit 14: Check your progress

14.1

Finance: application form. Currencies: gold. Companies: FTSE100. Energy: fluctuations.

14.2

c, d, e, b, g, f, h, a.

14.3

Information technology has radically **changed** many industries, especially banking. Banks can **store** more information, use **less** paper, and process transactions more **quickly** and more cheaply. As a result, customers can check their **accounts**, pay bills and **withdraw** money without ever **entering** a bank.

14.4

a in the red. b tied up. c put on hold. d on the blink.

Unit 15: Making arrangements

15.1

1 Jakarta, Indonesia.
2 Before 8 May.
3 Business negotiations with Sunrise Products PTE.
4 The chairman and other key people in Sunrise Products PTE.
5 Hotel Borobodur Intercontinental.

15.2

1 d. 2 a. 3 b. 4 e. 5 f. 6 c. 7 g. 8 h.

15.4

BUSINESS TRAVEL LIMITED
Flight request form

Name of passenger (s) ***Mr Ray SMITH***
Number of passengers: Adults: ***1*** Children: ***0***
Flying from ***London*** To ***Jakarta*** Single or return ***Return***
Date of travel ***4 May 2001***
Date of return ***13 May 2001***
Preferred airline ***Emirates?***
Preferred route / stopovers ***none***
Class: First / Business / Economy ***business***
Hotel booking required? ***Yes – Hotel Borobodur Intercontinental***
Car hire, pick up, other services ***none***

15.6

1 None.
2 It was full.
3 Hilton Hotel.
4 **d** BTL will mail the ticket to Kate.
5 **d** BTL will send a bill to be paid later.

Ticket for Mr Ray Smith

Thursday **4th** May	Depart London **Heathrow** Airport	Flight EMI 7721	**12.30**
	Arrive Dubai International		21.45
	Depart Dubai International	Flight EMI 2190	23.00
Friday 5th May	Arrive Jakarta Soekarno-Hatta		**13.10**
Saturday 13th May	Depart Jakarta Soekarno-Hatta	Flight EMI 2191	**08.00**
	Arrive Dubai International		14.05
	Depart Dubai International	Flight EMI 7720	15.20
	Arrive London **Heathrow** Airport		**20.00**
Special meals:	normal meals / vegetarian / vegan / other (please specify)		

Hotel **Hilton** International. 5th May – 13th May (8 nights).
Type of room: **single** / double / suite
Invoice to: **International Plastics** Account Number IP23Z
Tickets: courier / **first class post** / customer collects / pick up at airport

15.7

1 Ray Smith is going to Indonesia on 4 May.
2 His plane leaves from Heathrow Airport.
3 It takes off at 12.30.
4 He is staying there for eight nights.
5 He is staying in Hotel Hilton International.

6 On Monday 8 May, David Sitorus is showing him around Sunrise Products' plants.
7 He is meeting the chairman of Sunrise Products on Monday 8 May.
8 He is flying back to the UK on Saturday 13 May.
9 His flight arrives back in the UK at 8 p.m.
10 Someone from Sunrise Products is meeting him at the airport in Jakarta.

15.8

The meeting will be on Wednesday 3 May at 10.30 a.m.

15.9

A
1 It's too late. Ray Smith is leaving for Indonesia.
2 She is interviewing someone.
3 Helen has a meeting in Birmingham.
4 In France with his children – he has the day off.
5 An appointment with a software supplier
6 Probably in Ray Smith's office.

C 1 b. 2 e. 3 h. 4 d. 5 a. 6 c. 7 f. 8 g.

Unit 16: Meetings

16.2

A 1 e. 2 a. 3 c. 4 f. 5 g. 6 d. 7 b.

B 1 circulate/agenda.
2 items.
3 minutes.
4 apologies.

16.3

A 2, 3, 7, 8, 10, 11.

B Bringing forward the date for changes to hotel's software.

C The last time the company installed new software, it was a nightmare.

D *Atsushi and Carl send their apologies.*
Minutes of last meeting.
Security firm.
New software.

16.4

1 Carl Reich was not present.
Apologies for absence came from Carl Reich and Atsushi Morita.
2 New pay rates to start on 1st not 10th.
3 The first topic discussed was the implementation of new software *not* the date for new computers.
It was Johann Elias, not AT, who assured the meeting that problems would be minimal – about two weeks.
Person responsible is Johann Elias, not MG.
The deadline is the start of next month, not the end.
4 The second topic concerns problems with security staff who have been rude and rather bossy.
Action to be taken: Pablo Martinez will phone the company.
AT are not the initials of anyone present at the meeting.
No deadline was given for action on the second topic.

16.5

A 1 h. 2 g. 3 f. 4 e. 5 d. 6 c. 7 a & b. 8 a & b.
B 1 Can I come in here?
2 What do you think?
3 That's what I thought too.
4 Well... I'm not exactly looking forward to it.
5 When would the changes actually start?

16.6

Dubai – women should dress modestly. Dubai and Japan – business happens slowly, good personal relations are very important. France – people shake hands frequently. USA – people use first names more readily.

Unit 17: The changing job market

17.1

Some words are clearly and easily associated with temps or permanent workers. For example, temporary workers: flexibility, cheap labour, motivation, cost-cutting, casual labour; permanent workers: job security, company loyalty. However, others, e.g. stress, are a matter of opinion.

17.2

1 **a** is best but **b** is also possible.
2 *Possible Advantages*: workers less anxious; workers gain a broad range of skills and experience.

Possible Disadvantages: workers can easily lose their jobs; communication and understanding of company practices may not be so good with temporary staff; workers do not get the opportunity to develop themselves.

17.3

1 b. 2 b. 3 c. 4 a. 5 a. 6 b. 7 c. 8 a. 9 c.

17.4

1 it = replace full-time staff with temps; they = temps; some = employers.
2 Keeping down payrolls.
3 temporary
4 **a** False (paragraph 1). **b** True for full-time workers (paragraph 2). **c** False (paragraph 4). **d** True (paragraph 5).
5 Because the disadvantages of outsourcing may be too great.

17.5

Paragraph 1: introduction
Paragraph 2: academic viewpoint
Paragraph 3: employer's viewpoint
Paragraph 4: employer's viewpoint
Paragraph 5: advantages of outsourcing
Paragraph 6: conclusion

17.7

make redundant / lay off / recession / lose / to fire / strike / to get the sack / let go / to get the axe.

17.8

1 Nine, including Yonhap News Agency.
2 South Korea's top conglomerates present restructuring plans.

17.9

1 b. 2 a. 3 b. 4 b. 5 a. 6 b. 7 b. 8 c. 9 b. 10 a.

17.10

A 1 c. 2 c.

B 2 Samsung. 3 Hyundai, SK. 4 Daewoo.

17.11

2 competition, to compete, competitive, competitive advantage
3 transfer, to transfer, transferred, transfer funds

4 earnings, to earn, earned, earned income
5 register, to register, registered, registered company
6 highlight, to highlight, highlighted

Unit 18: Check your progress

18.1

From: Ray Smith <rsmith@mda.com>
To: David Sitorus <ho@sunrise-products.co.id>
Date: Thursday 29th April
Subject: trip to Indonesia

Dear David

I will be **arriving** in Jakarta at Soekarno-Hatta Airport at 13.10 on Friday 5th May. I'm **flying** with Emirates and my flight number is EMI 7721. Can you confirm that someone will be able to **pick** me up at the airport? By the way, I will not be staying at the Hotel Borobodur as it is completely **full**. I am booked into the Hilton Hotel.
We are also **sending** you some sample materials and some technical documents by courier. You should have those by Monday midday at the latest. Please let me **know** if they do not arrive. They **are** coming with Europe and Asia couriers and the reference number is JAK37274A.
I look **forward** to seeing you again next week. Let me know if there is **anything** you would **like** me to bring from London.

Regards

Ray Smith

18.2

Who is he flying with?
How much did it cost? (Also possible: How much does it cost? How much will it cost? How much is it costing? How much was the ticket?)
Where is he staying?
How long is he staying?
Who is he meeting?
How long is the flight?

18.3

Possible answers:
a How about tomorrow at 11 am?
b Excuse me, could you tell me how the photocopier works, please?
c May I use your phone to make a quick call to the office?
d I'm having trouble with my printer.
e I'm sorry. He's not here today. Can I take a message?
f Tomorrow at 11 will be fine.

18.4

1 trip
2 staying
3 flight (plane)
4 arrange (organize, fix, fix up, set up)
5 free (available)
6 minutes
7 shake
8 made
9 permanent
10 cut, reduce
11 on
12 have
13 agree
14 price (cost)

1 Tenses

	present	present perfect	past	past perfect
simple	Sales increase.	Sales have increased.	Sales increased.	Sales had increased.
continuous	Sales are increasing.	Sales have been increasing.	Sales were increasing.	Sales had been increasing.

future	Prices are going to increase. Prices will increase. Prices are falling from tomorrow.

Present simple

- You use this tense when talking about habitual actions (not a specific occasion) or when talking generally.
  Examples: She reads the *Financial Times* every morning.
  He visits the gym twice a week.
  Unilever employs about 290,000 people world-wide.
- You can use the present simple to discuss the future when talking about programmes and timetables.
  Examples: The plane leaves at 4.30 pm on Wednesday.
  The courses start next month.

Present continuous

- You use this tense to talk about actions that are not finished or that someone is still in the process of doing.
  Examples: Faisal is working in the marketing department till the end of August.
  I'm still reading that report on the new marketing plan.
- You can use the present continuous to talk about future arrangements.
  Examples: The company is opening another plant in La Paz in February next year.
- Some verbs are not usually used in the present continuous form.
  Examples:

verbs of thinking:	*know realize remember forget*
verbs of feeling or emotions:	*like hate want prefer*
verbs of the senses:	*hear see smell*
verbs of possession:	*belong own possess*

Present perfect

We use the present perfect when talking about an action which in some way connects the present to the past.

- It is used to talk about something that began in the past and continues in the present.
  Example: He has worked in the Barcelona office since May 2000. (i.e. *He began in May 2000 and is still working there.*)

- It is used when talking about something that happened at an unspecified time in the past and which has a result in the present.
  Example: Oh no! I've left my diary at home. (*Result: I do not have my diary now.*)

for and *since*

We use *for* to describe the length of an action and *since* to indicate when it started.

Examples: I have known Ryuichi *for 8* years.
I have known Ryuichi *since* 1996.

just, yet and *already*

These words are often used with the present perfect.

Examples: John has *just* left the building.
Have you spoken to Pierre *yet*?
Martha has *already* gone home.

NB One of the small differences between British and American English concerns the use of the present perfect. Americans often use the simple past with *just/yet/already* instead of the present perfect.

British English	**American English**
John has just left the building.	John just left the building.
Have you spoken to Pierre yet?	Did you speak to Pierre yet?
Martha has already gone home.	Martha went home already.

Simple past

We use this tense to refer to a completed action in the past.

Examples: The price of ICI shares rose by 10% last year.
Did you go to the meeting yesterday?

Past continuous

This tense is used to talk about an action in the past that we were in the middle of doing.

Example: When we met her last year, I was still training to become an accountant.

Past perfect

This tense is used to talk about past events that occurred before other past events.

Examples: After they had finished the project, they went home.
It had been a difficult time. The company had reorganized and in the process many jobs had been lost.

NB The past perfect is often used in reported speech.

Examples: She phoned yesterday. → She said that she had phoned yesterday.
Profits rose sharply. → The newspaper reported that profits had risen sharply.

Past perfect continuous

This tense is used to talk about an action that happened over a period of time and continued up to a certain time in the past.

Example: The business had been doing very well until the winter of 2000.

Compare the present perfect continuous and the past perfect continuous:

He looks tired. He has been working late again.
He looked tired. He had been working late again.

Future

As well as *will* we can use *going to* and the present continuous to express future meaning.

- We can use *will* when making predictions or general statements about the future.
  Example: By the end of the year 2003, the population of Britain will be about 61 million.
- We can use the present continuous to talk about future arrangements.
  Example: We're meeting at 6 pm this evening.
- We can use *going to* + infinitive to emphasize intentions.
  Example: I'm going to discuss the problem with him at the first opportunity tomorrow morning.

2 Modals

I You He She We They	can may might must ought to should	check the share price every day. book the tickets on the internet.

Modals are used often in English and express a large variety of ideas, such as ability, possibility, certainty, permission and obligation.
Remember:

- Whether we use *I*, *you*, *we*, *he*, *she* or *they*, the form of the modal verb does not change.
  Examples: Abdulah was ill on Wednesday so he couldn't come to the meeting.
  Company employees can purchase goods at a 10% discount.
- *do/does* are not used in questions or in negatives.
  Examples: May I speak to the manager, please?
  You must not smoke anywhere inside the building.
- Most modals (except *ought to*) are followed by the infinitive without *to*.
  Examples: He looks ill. He should go home.
  You ought to ask Charles Guilbert in the Finance department for advice on this matter.

3 *If...* sentences

Examples: If you pay by cash, you'll get a 5% discount on your purchase.
If the government raised company taxes, it would probably result in higher unemployment.
If I had known that, I wouldn't have signed the contract.

These sentences consist of an *if*-clause (*If you pay by cash*) and a main clause (*you'll get a 5% discount on your purchase*). There are a number of possible combinations of verb forms. The most common are:

- **Type 1**
  Form: *If* + present simple, *will*
  We use the first type to talk about the results of something that may happen in the future.
  Example: If you post the parcel this afternoon, it will arrive tomorrow morning.
- **Type 2**
  Form: *If* + past, *would*
  We use the second type to talk about something that probably won't happen.
  Example: If I won the lottery, I would buy a boat and sail around the world.
- **Type 3**
  Form: *If* + past perfect, *would have*

We use the third type to talk about something that is an impossibility now.

Example: If the employers had not agreed to a pay rise, the transport workers would have gone on strike.

4 Passive

Active: *Information technology has radically changed the way many industries work.*

Passive: *The way many industries work has been radically changed by information technology.*

Active: *Mr Ling will lead the project team.*

Passive: *The project team will be led by Mr Ling.*

In these sentences, the meaning is the same but the emphasis is different. In the active sentences, the emphasis is on the thing (or person) doing the action. In the passive sentences, the emphasis is on the thing (or person) affected by the action. The passive is often used in formal written language to achieve an impersonal tone.

Form: subject + *to be* + past participle

Examples:

Present simple
Most of the components are imported from Taiwan.

Present continuous
A new office block is being built in the suburbs.

Present perfect
The ship has not been badly damaged.

Simple past
Chambers Ltd, an electrical goods company, was established in 1950 by Peter Chambers.

Past continuous
Your report was being read by Martin when I arrived at the office.

Past perfect
The parcel had been delivered by courier while I was out of the office.

Will and other modal verbs (*can*, *could*, *ought to*, etc.) use *be* + the past participle:

The goods will be sent to you by courier next Monday.
Purchases can be paid in cash or by credit card.

5 Relative clauses

	defining		non-defining	
	people	**things**	**people**	**things**
subject	who, that	which, that	who	which
object	who, that, *whom	which, that	who, *whom	which
possessive	whose	whose	whose	whose

*Used in formal writing but is now considered old-fashioned and is not often used in speech or informal writing.

There are two types of relative clause: the defining relative clause and the non-defining relative clause.

i The defining relative clause provides essential information and tells us exactly which person or thing is being referred to.
Examples: The company which produced these components has closed down.
Employers who treat their employees fairly are always respected.

NB Commas are not used to separate the relative clause and the main clause. It is possible to leave out *who*, *that* or *which* when they are the object of a relative clause, e.g. Some of the people (that) we met at the exhibition were very interested in our product.

ii The non-defining relative clause provides extra, non-essential information.
Examples: Anita Roddick, who started the Body Shop organization about 25 years ago, has written a new book on her approach to business.
Maria Carlucci, who runs the fashion department, is on vacation at the moment.

NB Commas are usually used to separate the relative clause and the main clause. *That* is not used in non-defining relative clauses.

6 Reported speech

Direct speech: 'I haven't seen Melissa for ages.'
Reported speech: He said he hadn't seen Melissa for ages.

In moving from direct to reported speech certain changes may occur. If the reporting verb is in the past (e.g. *asked, said*), then usually the verb in the reported clause moves one step further back in the past. Thus,

present → past
present perfect → past perfect
past → past perfect

However, if the reporting verb is in the present, then the tense in the reported clause needn't be changed:
Direct speech: *'Oil prices are rising'*
Reported speech: *He says that oil prices are rising.*

7 Articles: *the, a/an*

Some of the most common uses of *the* are:

- when talking about something / someone that is unique, e.g. *the president of Mexico, the* Wall Street Journal, *the best swimmer in the world*
- when talking about a particular person / thing or when it is obvious who / what is meant, e.g. *I spoke to the manager earlier today. She said the office closes at 5 pm.*
- hotels, e.g. *the Hilton*

Some of the most common uses of *a / an* are:

- when referring to a single thing, e.g. *Could you recommend a good hotel in Lima?*
- when referring to a job, e.g. *She's a teacher. He's an accountant.*

No article

We do not use *the* or *a / an*:

- when making generalizations referring to plural nouns (e.g. *Computers are expensive to buy.*) or uncountable nouns (e.g. *Everybody needs money.*)
- with most proper nouns (names), e.g. *Faisal Ali, Maria Gonzalez*

8 Phrasal verbs

Examples:

I've been *looking for* another job.
Please *switch off* all the computers before you leave.
The missing documents *turned up* two days later.

A phrasal verb is a combination of a verb (*look*, *make*, *put*, *switch*, *cut*, etc.) with one or two particles (adverbs or prepositions such as *on, off, away, forward, to* etc.).

Sometimes the meaning of the verb can be guessed easily if you know the meaning of its parts:

He *got off* the plane.
Please *take* your coat *off*.

More often though, phrasal verbs are idioms. You can't easily guess the meaning of the whole expression just by knowing what its parts mean.

The plane *took off*.
I'm really *looking forward* to my holiday
She left the job because she couldn't *get on with* her boss.

In terms of grammar there are three groups of phrasal verbs:

i **Intransitive verbs.** These have no object and the adverb always comes directly after the verb.

Examples:

The plane *took off*.
The meeting *went on* for hours.
The number of customers has *fallen off* recently.

ii **Transitive inseparable verbs.** The preposition in these verbs always comes after the verb and before the object (even if the object is a preposition).

Examples:

He wasn't looking forward to the meeting.
He wasn't looking forward to it.

iii **Transitive separable verbs.** The particle in these phrasal verbs can come before or after the object.

Examples:

Don't forget to *turn* the computer *off* before you leave.
Don't forget to *turn off* the computer before you leave.
He *gave up* his job last month.
He *gave* his job *up* last month.

If the object is a pronoun (such as *it, them, you, this, him, her, us*), the particle must follow the pronoun, it can't come before it:

He didn't like his job so he *gave* it *up*.
Can you check the computers, please? I'm not sure if I *turned* them *off*.

Note that some phrasal verbs can be both transitive and intransitive, with different meanings:

The plane *took off* an hour late. (*intransitive*)
She *took* her coat *off*. (*transitive, separable*)

Here are some common *intransitive* phrasal verbs:

take off	My plane takes off at 13.45.
check in	You must check in at least two hours before departure.
go on	The meeting went on for over three hours.
drop off	Profits have dropped off sharply in the last six months.
break down	Sorry I'm late. My car broke down.

Here are some common *inseparable* phrasal verbs:

look forward to	I'm really looking forward to my holiday.
run into	I ran into an old friend of yours at a conference last week.
get on with	Can we get on with the meeting? I have to leave by 5 today.
take care of	There was a problem with the fax machine but the technician took care of it.
look after	Jane Myers, the personnel manager, looks after all issues related to staff training and promotion.
carry on with	Let's have lunch now and then we can carry on with our discussions afterwards.

Here are some common *separable* phrasal verbs:

switch on	It's better to switch the monitor on before the PC.
switch off	If you switch the lights off, we will be able to see the presentation more clearly.
turn on	Turn on the answerphone before you leave the office.
turn off	It has been estimated that turning off all the computers in the office at night could save us $10,000 a year.
set up	Can you set up a meeting with David and Sally for some time next week?
take over	There had been rumours that Sabena would be taken over by Virgin Atlantic Airlines.
put off	We'll have to put off the meeting until next month because Juan has gone into hospital.

9 *Verb + ing or verb + to + infinitive?*

You will often hear or read sentences where one verb is followed by another verb.

Sometimes the second verb will take an *-ing* form and sometimes it will take the form of *to + infinitive*.

Examples:

He *risked losing* a lot of money if the plan had failed.
She *mentioned seeing* him at the trade fair in Leipzig last month.

We *agreed to meet* again in two weeks' time.
The management *wanted to introduce* new pay scales for the employees.

Verbs usually followed by the *-ing* form include:

admit	appreciate	resist	can't help
delay	deny	dislike	can't stand
finish	practise	stop	miss
suggest			

Verbs usually followed by *to + infinitive* include:

agree	ask	can't afford	choose
decide	expect	neglect	happen
hope	manage	promise	plan
refuse	seem	want	would like

Some verbs (for example, *begin, hate, like, prefer, start, continue, intend*) can be followed by either the *-ing* form or *to + infinitive* and often there is no great difference in meaning:

Examples:

He began working at 9 am and didn't finish till 2 pm.
He began to work at 9 am and didn't finish till 2 pm.

I like watching football on the television.
I like to watch football on the television.

Phonemic symbols

A good English dictionary can help with understanding pronunciation. This is especially important if you are teaching yourself. It is very helpful therefore to be able to use the phonemic alphabet – these are symbols used in dictionaries to explain the pronunciation of words.

Vowels and dipthongs

ɪ	sit	/ sɪt /	**ɪə**	ear	/ ɪə /
i:	see	/ si: /	**eɪ**	page	/ peɪdʒ /
ʊ	look	/ lʊk /	**ʊə**	pure	/ pjʊə /
u:	two	/ tu: /	**ɔɪ**	boy	/ bɔɪ /
e	egg	/ eg /	**əʊ**	no	/ nəʊ /
ə	about	/ əbaʊt /	**eə**	there	/ ðeə /
ɜ:	learn	/ lɜ:n /	**aɪ**	eye	/ aɪ /
ɔ:	short	/ ʃɔ:t /	**aʊ**	now	/ naʊ /
æ	hat	/ hæt /			
ʌ	cup	/ kʌp /			
ɑ:	arm	/ ɑ:m /			
ɒ	got	/ gɒt /			

Consonants

p	pen	/ pen /	**s**	so	/ səʊ /
b	bee	/ bi: /	**z**	zoo	/ zu: /
t	tea	/ ti: /	**ʃ**	she	/ ʃi: /
d	dog	/ dɒg /	**ʒ**	pleasure	/ pleʒə /
k	cat	/ kæt /	**h**	house	/ haʊs /
g	got	/ gɒt /	**m**	me	/ mi: /

tʃ	chair	/ tʃeə /	n	no	/ nəʊ /
dʒ	just	/ dʒʌst /	ŋ	long	/ lɒŋ /
f	five	/ faɪv /	l	leg	/ leg /
v	very	/ verɪ /	r	right	/ rɑɪt /
θ	thin	/ θɪn /	j	yes	/ jes /
ð	this	/ ðɪs /	w	we	/ wiː /

Stress

When we speak, the emphasis we give to a particular part of a word is called **stress**. For example, the stress in *<u>nu</u>mber* is on the first syllable. In the word *ad<u>vise</u>*, it is on the second syllable.

Dictionaries usually indicate the pronunciation of a word using phonemic symbols, e.g. *computer* /kəmpjuːtə/. However, if you do not know phonemic symbols, you can still work out the stress. Normally, there is a ˈ symbol before the stressed part, e.g. *number* /ˈnʌmbə/, *advise* /ədˈvaɪz/.

Dictionaries

1 British English dictionary
http://www.cup.cam.ac.uk/elt/dictionary

2 American English dictionary
http://www.m-w.com/home.htm

3 A dictionary of financial vocabulary
http://Investorwords.com

Newspapers, magazines and news organizations

4 *The Financial Times* newspaper
http://www.ft.com

5 *The Economist*
http://www.economist.com

6 *The Wall Street Journal*
http://www.wsj.com

7 *Business Week*
http://www.businessweek.com

8 *Fortune* magazine
http://www.fortune.com
The website of *Fortune* magazine produces interesting lists, such as the 'America's most admired companies', 'the 100 fastest growing companies', 'the most powerful women'.

9 *BBC Business news*
http://www.bbc.co.uk/worldservice/business/index.shtml
World business news to read or listen to.

10 Netscape Business news
http://cnn.netscape.cnn.com/news

Learning English – General English and Business English Sites

11 BBC learning English
http://www.bbc.co.uk/worldservice/learningenglish
Includes information on English for work

12 The British Council

http://www.britishcouncil.org

13 Dave Sperling's ESL café. Lots of useful pages for all aspects of learning English and links to many other sites
http://www.eslcafe.com/
Includes resources for learning business English
http://eslcafe.com/search/Business_English/index.htm

Other useful websites

Sites with links to business information
14 http://www.niss.ac.uk/cr/business.html
15 http://globaledge.msu.edu/index.asp

Job search sites. You can read job advertisements and also view CVs of people looking for new jobs
16 http://www.SuperJobSearch.com/html/profiles.html
17 http://www.superstaff.com/
18 http://www.elmundo.es/empleo/

Sites which look at differences between British English and American English
19 http://www.scit.wlv.ac.uk/~jphb/american.html

Help with writing business letters, job applications and CVs
20 http://www.ruthvilmi.net/hut/help/writing_instructions/
21 http://www.businessenglishtraining.com
22 http://owl.english.purdue.edu/handouts/index2.html
23 http://www1.umn.edu/ohr/ecep/resume/

Learning business communication skills
24 http://business.englishclub.com

Tips for visitors to the UK including cultural information. Intended for visitors from the USA but useful for anyone
25 http://www.london-daily.co.uk/guide/gd-tips.htm

Information about finance, including a dictionary of financial terms
26 http://www.investopedia.com

Company reports
27 http://www.areport.com

glossary of grammatical terms and punctuation

Article *Adjective* *Verb* *Adverb* *Comma* *Modal verb*

When a large American motor manufacturer (General Motors) first introduced its new car, the *Chevy Nova* into South America, it didn't realize that 'no va' means 'it won't go' in Spanish. Not surprisingly, sales were low. When the company finally worked out what had happened it renamed the car in its Spanish-speaking countries as the *Caribe*.

Phrasal verb *Italics* *Pronoun* *Noun* *Preposition*

Capital letters *Apostrophe* *Question mark*

Do you want to know how to become successful in business? Paul Getty was one of the richest people in the world and made his fortune in the oil business. When asked for advice on how to become rich he said, 'You've got to get up early, go to bed late and above all strike oil'. By this he meant you must work hard and be lucky!

Exclamation mark *Quotation marks* *Full stop (Br) / Period (Am)*

adjective: a word which gives information about a noun, *e.g. large, new, black, richest*

adverb: a word which gives information about a verb, an adjective, an adverb or a phrase, *e.g. surprisingly, finally, quickly*

apostrophe: the symbol used to indicate where a letter has been omitted, or to indicate the possessive form of a noun, *e.g. you've, don't, Paul Getty's company*

article: In English 'a' or 'an' is known as the indefinite article and 'the' as the definite article, *e.g. a company, an investment, the Chevy Nova*

brackets/parentheses [( )]: these are used to give extra information.

capital letter: large form of a letter, used at the beginning of a sentence or for names, *e.g. Paul Getty, BBC*

comma [,]: symbol used to separate words in a sentence to indicate a pause or to separate items in a list, *e.g. He visited Jakarta, Singapore, Kuala Lumpur and Bangkok.*

exclamation mark [!]: symbol used to indicate surprise or shock, *e.g. Look out!*

full stop/period [.]: symbol used at the end of sentences.

italics: a style of printing in which the characters are slanted. Used for emphasis, *e.g. These examples are in italics.*

modal verb: verbs such as *can, may*. These are used with other verbs to describe ideas such as possibility and intention, *e.g. These letters should be sent off today. The contract might be late.*

noun: a word that names an object, a place, a person or an abstract idea, *e.g. car, office, secretaries, investment*

phrasal verb: a verb made up of two parts, a verb plus either an adverb or a preposition. The meaning may be different from that of its separate parts, *e.g. work out, get up, take over, put through*

preposition: a word that usually comes before a noun or pronoun connecting it to another word, *e.g. to, from, in, by, over*

pronoun: a word used instead of a noun or noun phrase, *e.g. it, they, he*

question mark [?]: symbol used to indicate a question, *e.g. What did you say?*

quotation marks [' ' / " "]: symbols used at the start and end of a word or phrase to indicate that someone has spoken or written it, *e.g. Paul Getty said 'You've got to get up early ...'*

verb: a word that describes an action or a condition, *e.g. introduced, realizes, feel, employs*

index

Sophie King (www.sophieking.info) is the author of five romantic fiction novels published by Hodder & Stoughton as well as four by Janey Fraser by Random House. Her novel *The Wedding Party* was shortlisted for Love Story of the Year by the Romantic Novelists' Association in 2010 and her recent novel, *After the Honeymoon*, has received wide praise. She has also had hundreds of romantic short stories published in women's magazines, such as *Woman's Weekly* and *My Weekly*, and is a past winner of the Elizabeth Goudge Award and the Vera Brittain Cup (short story category). Janey runs workshops at the Winchester Writers' Conference and at the Matera Women's Fiction Festival in Italy, as well as being a guest speaker at numerous events including the Chipping Norton Literary Festival, the Guildford Literary Festival and the Glasgow Literary Festival. As a creative writing tutor, she keeps in touch with the needs of aspiring writers and is the author of *How To Write Short Stories for Magazines – and Get Published*; *How To Write Your First Novel*; and *How To Write Your Life Story in Ten Easy Steps*. She is also a Royal Literary Fund Fellow at Exeter University.

Also published by Constable & Robinson

Masterclasses in Creative Writing

365 Ways to Get You Writing

Get Writing Children's Fiction

The Five-Minute Writer

How To Write Your First Novel

How To Write Comedy

How To Write Short Stories for Magazines

HOW TO WRITE ROMANTIC FICTION

Sophie King

ROBINSON

First published in Great Britain in 2014 by Robinson

A CIP catalogue record for this book
is available from the British Library.

ISBN 978-1-84528-581-4 (hardback)
ISBN: 978-1-84528-582-1 (ebook)

Typeset in the UK by Basement Press, Glaisdale
Printed and bound in Great Britain

Robinson
is an imprint of
Constable & Robinson Ltd
100 Victoria Embankment
London EC4Y 0DY

An Hachette UK Company
www.hachette.co.uk

www.constablerobinson.com

CONTENTS

Acknowledgements

I would like to thank the team at Constable & Robinson; my agent Teresa Chris; my students; my husband (a great model for a hero!); and all my friends at the Romantic Novelists' Association.

INTRODUCTION: WHY YOU NEED THIS BOOK

Writing romantic fiction has never been so popular. Or so frustrating!

Thousands of men and women all over the world are trying to get published in one of the most competitive writing fields available. And although – thanks to self-publishing – it's possible for almost anyone to get a book in print or online, it's still hard to get sales that will guarantee a steady income.

Love, as a great aunt of mine used to say with a steely look in her good eye, is all very well. But you still need something to live on. The same is true for romantic fiction. So how do you crack the nut?

I have to be honest here. There are so many self-help books out there that they almost rival the novel market. But there are very few that are dedicated to writing romantic fiction.

Please don't think I'm blowing my own trumpet but (as Sophie King and Janey Fraser) I have had nine romantic comedies published by mainline publishers over the last nine years. One was shortlisted for Love Story of the Year by the Romantic Novelists' Association.

It wasn't easy. Before that, I wrote several other books that didn't get published because I was still learning my trade.

Some of you will have read my other writing guides such as *How To Write Your First Novel* and *How To Write Short Stories and Get Published.* They contained general advice on how to structure a plot and create real-life characters.

This book, however, will concentrate on the nuts and bolts of hearts, champagne and, dare I say it, the bedroom. Should you close the boudoir door when describing a passionate scene? Or should you leave it wide open? All will be revealed within these pages.

This book will cover short fiction as well as novels. Over the last twelve or so years, I've had hundreds of stories published in magazines such as *Woman's Weekly*, *My Weekly* and *People's Friend*. I'm also a past winner of the Elizabeth Goudge Award and the Vera Brittain Cup. So I know that sex in short stories is not usually as graphic as it can be in novels – something I didn't realize when I first set out. Romance, too, is handled in a different way.

As a speaker and workshop leader, I've shared some of my experiences at Skyros Writing Labs, the Winchester Writers' Conference, the Matera Women's Fiction Festival in Italy, Lisa Clifford's renowned course in Florence, the Guildford Literary Festival, the Chipping Norton Festival, the Scilly Isles Writing Course, Oxford University, the North London Literary Festival and the Glasgow Literary Festival. Love and romance featured heavily in all of them – especially when there was a touch of heavy breathing from one delegate who nodded off in the front row!

Comedy, as you might already have guessed, is vital to any healthy relationship, whether it's the marital variety or the reader/author type. My book will help you make the reader laugh and, in so doing, engage with your characters.

It also goes without saying that true love never runs smoothly. So expect a few tears – as well as advice on how to make your reader reach for the tissue box. That is, after all, an essential ingredient.

Romance, in my book, should be practical too. You'll find plenty of practicality in the exercises at the end of each chapter – as well as tips from other authors including the famous Katie Fforde.

So are you ready? Love means taking a chance in life. But if you don't try it, you'll never know. Meanwhile – forgive the pun – forget Mr Right: this is all about Mr and Ms Write.

1
WHAT EXACTLY IS ROMANTIC FICTION?

'I don't write romance,' declared a friend when I was trying to persuade her to come to a talk at the Romantic Novelists' Association. 'I write about real life.'

I shot her a wry look. 'But the main characters in your last book fell in love at the end.'

She shrugged. 'That's not romance.'

Really? It's amazing how many writers, whether published or not, assume that romance has to be pink lace and Barbara Cartland. Perhaps it's because they're worried about not being taken seriously. Or because they're embarrassed about reactions from friends and family. So they go into denial.

In fact, romantic fiction is a very broad term. It might be of the *Fifty Shades* variety. Or it could involve a simple, shy kiss at the end.

If there's one thing I've learned through writing my romantic fiction, it's not to be ashamed of your genre. Where would we be without love in life? Exactly. So why not write about it – and be proud of it too?

If you're not proud of what you are doing, your lack of self-confidence will come out in your writing. So the first step when writing romantic fiction is to puff out your chest and stand up for yourself. If nothing else, it's a great topic when someone at a party asks what you do . . .

Don't be fooled, however. Modern romantic fiction demands feisty characters: not wimps (unless they undergo a transformation into the Incredible Hulk). Nor is it a soft option. (No pun intended.) To write in this genre, you need lots of twists in the plot to keep the reader spellbound.

Nowadays, there are all kinds of love to write about. In fact, the field has never been wider. Gay relationships are no longer taboo. Nor is incest: I recently read a Jodi Picoult-style book about a brother and sister, which I initially started with reservations but found myself unable to put down. (I should add here that the above themes are less acceptable in short stories than novels, depending on the magazine's guidelines.)

Even the traditional man/woman love affair is not what it was. Step-parenting; working away from home; and online dating are merely three contemporary factors that have altered romantic fiction beyond all recognition in the last few years.

It might be funny from beginning to end. Or it might be serious. It could involve one couple or several. It might be a time-slip romance or a historical or a contemporary one.

How exciting! All you need to decide is which one *you're* going to write. There's no doubt that it helps if your novel pitch makes this clear. Not sure? Then try the following.

EXERCISES

- Make a list of five romantic fiction books you've enjoyed.
- Write down at least three bullet points, explaining briefly why they 'did it for you'.
- Now pretend *you* are the novelist and write an opening line or paragraph for the same book without referring to the text. Do this quite quickly without thinking too much. Spend no more than ten minutes on each.
- Do the same for each of the five books. Then read your paragraphs out loud. Which one sends shivers down your spine? Which one made you want to go on? Which one had chemistry? And which one was downright boring?
- Pick the one you like most and give it a second date. Write another paragraph and see where it takes you.

- Make a list of five other novels you've enjoyed in different genres. They might be crime or sci-fi or time slips. In each one, was there any romance? If so, how was the story different from those on your previous list of romantic fiction? Was the romance a by-product of the plot? How did the other elements complement the love story?

Note: There are no 'rights' or 'wrongs' for the above exercises, but they will help you see that romantic fiction is a broader beast than it might appear to be on the surface.

SUMMING UP

Any story that contains love could be said to be romantic fiction. But some are more romance-heavy than others.

EXPERT TIPS

Romantic fiction can cover all kinds of elements like adventure and history. It's not just Mills & Boon. However, like any other kind of genre, it needs a good, strong plot.

Teresa Chris, literary agent

Although I write pretty racy stuff, I lead a very normal life, and people can be surprised that I'm the author of 'that sort' of novel. I never apologize. I'm proud of what I write, and I think my sexy writing celebrates sensuality and women's sexual desires. I get teased sometimes, but I think that most of the mums at the school gate appreciate my raunchy imagination and several of them have told me that they've enjoyed my books.

Electra Shepherd, author of numerous books including *Man or Machine*, www.electrashepherd.com

A problem with romantic fiction as a genre is that it encompasses so many types of writing. At one end of a very broad spectrum are utterly predictable scenarios, peopled by characters from central casting, created for women who generally don't read very much. This is escapism, pure and simple; and the cardboard cut-out lovers and join-the-dots plotting are all part of the experience. At the other end of the spectrum is romance in literary fiction: sophisticated character-driven stories where the outcome is up for grabs.

When I was a neuropsychology researcher (can't get much more intellectual than that . . .), I used to buy a Mars bar and a copy of *Women's Weekly* ('famed for its knitting') every Thursday and consume them both, in an orgy of self-indulgence, on the bus home to my dismal Clapham Junction flat. More recently I read *Fifty Shades* with that same sense of embarrassment and rather cloying enjoyment. But I *raced* through *The Time Traveller's Wife* with my brain firing on all cylinders. Yes, it's a romance, but it's so much more besides!

The only characteristic these two types of romance share is the motivation of their main protagonists to get together, get it on, and live happily ever after. In *Woman's Weekly*, they might succeed; in literary fiction, who knows?

And the main difference between the two, to my mind, is the uniqueness of the characters and, bound up with this, the believability of their motivation. Whatever else you might think of Bella and Edward in the *Twilight* series, or Ana and Christian in *Fifty Shades*, they bear very little resemblance to real people – in how they look, think or behave.

By contrast, the idiosyncratic characters of literary fiction follow their unique passions and so end up clashing in interesting and surprising ways. Indeed, if they're well drawn by an author who knows what she's doing, they can't help it. And for me that makes for a more satisfying, albeit less indulgent, reading experience.

Debbie Taylor, Editor of *Mslexia: For Women Who Write*

2
HOW TO FIND A GREAT ROMANTIC FICTION IDEA FOR YOUR NOVEL

If you want to get noticed by an agent, a competition judge or a magazine fiction editor, you need an idea that stands out from the crowd. So how do you go about that?

Finding the Angle

Personally, I try to see things from a different angle. I wrote a short magazine story about a recently divorced mum who was dating again. Nothing new there. But I tackled it from the perspective of her teenage son who was 'testing' out prospective stepdads by setting them challenges. It was accepted by return of email.

I do think that part of that success was down to luck. The fiction editor happened to be looking for a story about women starting again. However, if my story had hit her screen a day later, someone else might have got in there first. But I also believe that 'changing your eye' can help you give a unique take on an old subject.

Let's take the old story of a teenage daughter falling in love with a boy of whom her mother doesn't approve. How could we make it different? We might start by thinking it through from each character's viewpoint, beginning with the mother.

What was her own love life like in the past? You might consider flashbacks, showing us something important such as a relationship that went wrong.

Through glimpses back to the mother's early romances, you could show why the mother doesn't approve of her daughter's relationship. This way, we can encourage readers to change emotions (great for keeping your audience on its toes) and make them more sympathetic to the supposedly difficult older woman.

While we're at it, why not bring in the parents of the boy with whom the teenage girl has fallen in love? Could there be some link between the girl's mother and the boy's father? Or, if that's too cheesy, how about a link between the girl's mother and the boy's mother? Could they once have been in love with the same man?

The more you start to think about it, the more ideas begin to flow. Here's another thought. What about the grandmother? Was she responsible for breaking off the mother's teenage relationship? Could she now offer advice to the young girl: her granddaughter?

EXERCISE

Take a look at some of the following age-old love stories. How could you rewrite them so they stand out? Jot down a few ideas such as the following and see if they take you anywhere:

- granny reunited with first love;
- warring couple patch up their differences;
- forbidden love (one might be married or there could be cultural differences);
- age difference in love;
- obsessive love.

Getting Ideas from Friends and Family

There's nothing like friends and family – especially when it comes to finding the Great Romantic Fiction Idea.

'He's got the wrong end of the stick,' wailed a friend down the phone the other day. 'He thinks I like him. I used to – but that was when he didn't like me. Now I've gone off him but he won't stop emailing me.'

Great. Just what we want for a romantic fiction plot. Or, at least, part of it.

'Now he wants to take me skydiving because he thinks it will impress me, even though I know he's scared of heights,' continued the friend. 'I'd actually like to go but not with him. What do you think I should do? Hello? Are you listening?'

Actually, I'm afraid my concentration was wavering slightly. Like all writers, I was jotting down notes while trying to think of some good advice for my 'always-unlucky-in-love' friend.

She might not know it but, unwittingly, she's given me an idea for a short story that might extend to a novel. Of course, I'll disguise it heavily because it wouldn't be right to plunder her life. Maybe I'll reverse the sexes so it's a male character being pursued by a woman who wasn't interested in him a few weeks ago. And perhaps I'll change the skydiving to white-water rafting. But either way, there's a romantic fiction story there, just waiting to burst out. And it's all thanks to my friend . . .

Most writers will swear on their granny's wedding ring that they don't write about real people. In fact, it's a very dangerous thing to do from a legal point of view. But it's impossible, as a writer, to go through life without making real-life observations or taking in real-life situations.

The trick is to disguise them, as described above. You could also amplify the situation. To be honest, my friend didn't really get an offer to go skydiving. Her would-be boyfriend actually suggested bowling. But the former has far more potential for things to go wrong; just like white-water rafting.

If you don't feel able to use your friends' love lives, re-examine your own. It doesn't matter how far back you go – or how far you imagine into the future. Is there something in your romantic history that might make an idea or a plot pusher?

Without giving too much away, here's a brief list of things that have happened to me. (Note to my children: look away now!)

- Falling in love at sixteen. Being forced to break it off by my mother who was worried it might interfere with my school work.
- Being bridesmaid at an old boyfriend's wedding.

- Marrying the best man from my own wedding, thirty years later.
- Bumping into an old boyfriend from my teenage days, many years later – and not recognizing him. (He came up to me at a conference.)

Each of these could be part of a novel idea or a short story in its own right, providing I can create warm characters with lots of twists.

Sourcing Ideas from Problem Pages

This is a great source of romantic fiction ideas. Sometimes, the answer can be more of a plot-trigger than the reader's question itself. One of my favourite Sunday-night occupations is to go through the weekend papers and tear out some 'What Shall I Do?' letters. (It drives my husband mad if the feature he's reading continues on the other side of the missing page!) Then I store them in a shoebox or file for future reference if I get stuck for a plot.

The great thing about problem pages is that you can use real-life events without losing friends or family. However, you might still want to adapt them. Below is a selection of dilemmas from my shoebox:

- Unmarried woman in love with sister's new boyfriend.
- Man who sent a loving email to his boss instead of his girlfriend. (The former thinks he's interested.)
- Teenager who's fallen for her stepbrother but hates her stepfather.
- Woman whose neighbour undresses every night, without drawing the curtains.
- Mother who invites a divorced friend over the weekend because she feels sorry for her – only to find that the friend makes an open play for her husband.

Turning a Scenario into a Short Story or Novel

All of these scenarios might make a short story or a novel. Let's go through a couple of them and see how.

Unmarried woman in love with sister's new boyfriend

Bit close to the bone, isn't it? Not exactly incest but nevertheless, a bit of a taboo subject. Sisters aren't meant to fall in love with their sibling's other half – but it does happen. It's what I call a 'biggie'. In other words, a meaty problem that might not be resolved in 1,000 to 2,000 words, which is the average length for a magazine short story.

If I was writing this, I would try to get inside the characters' bones. I might start by asking myself the following questions:

- How old is the unmarried sister?
- Why is she still single?
- Does she like her sister?
- Did one of them hurt the other in the past?
- What is the boyfriend like?
- Is he tempted by the other sister?
- Whose point of view should I tell the story from?

Already, an idea is forming in my mind. I think I'd tell it from the point of view of all three characters. The first chapter would be from the single sister; the second from the boyfriend who was thinking of breaking it off; the third from the second sister who finds herself pregnant.

I'd then start to write and see where the characters took me. But you can tell from the brief outline above that there is plenty of scope for action.

Man who sent a loving email to his boss instead of his girlfriend

I'm rather intrigued by this one; partly because it's quite plausible. Most people, at some point, have sent an email or text to the wrong person. And there's no denying that office romances are responsible for wrecking all too many marriages.

But what if we turned this on its head? Supposing the girlfriend sent an 'I don't like you any more' email to her long-term boyfriend.

Perhaps the male boss picks it up because he's going through his employee's inbox. What if the boss decides to play Cupid and tries to get the young couple back together? Then he meets the girl in question and falls for her, himself?

I think this is a short story, rather than a novel. It hasn't got quite enough to flesh out a whole novel, unless you use it as part of a bigger plot. But it's got just enough of a twist to make an unusual Valentine's story. In fact, I might just write it myself. Mind you, I'd have to create a surprise at the end and I'm not quite sure what that is, yet. That doesn't matter, at this stage, as you'll see in Chapter 4 on plot.

Using News Items for Ideas

Local papers are a great source of romantic ideas. They tend to have the sort of detail that brings warmth to a novel or short story. My favourite are the golden wedding reports that tell the reader how a couple met or give their recipe for a loving relationship.

As I'm writing this, I've got an idea. What if you started a novel with a news item about three couples celebrating a big anniversary? Supposing they all got married in the same year, in 1940. Then you could go back in time to when they met. The story could be told from the point of view of each couple (either the man or the woman). Unknown to them, the couples' paths cross every now and then. Maybe the woman from the first pair used to know the brother of the man from the second. They survive tragedies in the Second World War and all kinds of ups and downs, so the reader is hooked by their lives. But each partner has a secret from their other half, which isn't revealed until they all finally meet at an award ceremony for long-married couples run by the local paper.

Don't pinch this idea! I might write about it myself. But – hand on heart – I didn't think about it until I started writing this section of the chapter. It just goes to show what the mind can come up with.

Getting Ideas from Fantasies

We might not like to admit it, but most of us have fantasies. Don't you remember daydreaming as a teenager about the boy on the bus or someone at college? I certainly do!

However, as we get older, we're taught that fantasies are 'wrong'. Problem pages often carry anguished letters from readers who feel 'guilty' if they pretend they're in bed with someone else.

I'm not going to get into this moral minefield! But I do think that fantasizing about your own life can help you kick-start a great romantic idea. So let's see, shall we? Start by drawing the curtains and having some quiet time to yourself. Close your eyes and let your mind go. Release all the strains of the world around you (you might need to put your children in front of the television for this). Imagine there is a knock on the door. Who is coming in . . . ?

Then write it down. It might not necessarily be an idea in its own right but it could be part of one. The main thing is that you've allowed your brain to have a free rein. The more you do it, the easier it gets. Here's an example from one of my students:

> I imagine being an actress in a television series I watch regularly. Every now and then, I close my study door and pretend I am her. It gives me ideas for my novel. Somehow it frees up my mind to be someone else. She does things I would never do.

Recording Your Dreams

Dreams can be a great source for romantic fiction ideas. Keep a pad of paper and pen by your bed and write them down as soon as you wake up. Take a look at them later in the day and see if they might make a story or part of one.

Some authors swear by banging their head on the pillow before they go to sleep and asking an unknown force to give them a plot for their current manuscript. I don't go that far. But I often wake up at 5 a.m. to find ideas pouring into my head as though someone is unleashing them. That's where the pen, paper – and torch – come in handy.

Generating Ideas with Statistics

The other day I read an article that claimed that 50 per cent of all couples still think about their first loves. Even more interestingly, 30 per cent fancied the partner of their sibling or friend. Now I don't know if that's true (how do these people do their research?), but it did make me start thinking about a plot for either a short story or novel.

- What sort of situations could encourage a woman to fall for her sister's husband or fiancé? A hospital scene, perhaps, where one needs support?
- What might make a man search for a former love? A divorce – or the need to find out an unresolved secret?

EXERCISE

Do some research into the statistics of love. Use it to write down three ideas for a short story or novel. Make a file of surveys about love. You never know when it will come in useful.

Not sure where to start? Try searching 'love statistics' online. I came up with the following site which had lots of interesting facts and figures: http://facts.randomhistory.com/2009/08/04_love.html. For example, apples are often used as a symbol of love because they are one of the most long-lasting fruits. There must be a story there . . .

Talking and Listening to People

Writers are generally chatty souls although, personally, I need peace and quiet when writing. If you're stuck for a romantic fiction idea, your ears are one of your best tools. Listen to conversations on trains and buses. Avoid the Quiet Carriage and tune into someone's mobile phone conversation.

Yes, I know it's a bit naughty. But who said writers were good? The other day, on a train, I heard a man telling his friend that he was going out with an older woman and a younger one at the same time. He couldn't make up his mind which one he really liked. When he'd finished, an elderly man tapped him on the shoulder. 'Hope you don't mind me saying so,' he declared with a twinkle in his eye. 'But in my view, there's nothing to beat an older woman.'

We all roared with laughter. To our disappointment, the conversation ended there – partly because the man on the phone promptly got off, perhaps out of embarrassment. But it made me think about a short story about a commuter who became an agony uncle on the 7.31 from Eastbourne. Or a novel where I could take four people in one carriage and follow their love lives.

Asking your friends

I belong to a small gym group. We joke that we exercise our mouths as much as our limbs. But if I'm ever stuck for a plot, all I have to do is ask 'the girls' and someone is bound to know someone who's had a colourful love life. And yes, of course I would change the details.

Finding a Title

Every now and then, writers come up with a cracking title – before they even know what the novel is about. It can be a good way of thinking of an idea.

Spend some time browsing through bookshops or online to find a title that jumps out at you. Then ask yourself:

- Why does it grab you?
- Does it have a universal appeal?
- Does it speak to you?
- Is it funny?
- Does it have two meanings?

Now invent a list of titles that might catch someone else's attention. To get you going, here are a few that I've made up:

- The Confirmed Bachelor
- Someone for Me
- My Friend Sam
- Single Again

By the way, it doesn't matter if a title has been used before. However, you might find yourself in hot water if you have the same name as the original author.

EXERCISES

- Make a list of five events that have happened in your love life or your friends. Write a brief outline for one of them, taking care to change details. Ask yourself if there's enough meat for a novel or if it is a short story instead.
- Find five problem-page letters from newspapers or magazines. Take one and write a brief short story/novel outline.
- Find a news or radio item that has a whiff of romance. Write a brief outline for a short story or novel.
- Take a bus or train and listen out for conversations. Write a story outline.
- Get a group of friends together and chat. What kind of story evolves?
- Fantasize about being someone else – or getting together with someone else. Does it give you an idea for a novel or short story?
- Keep a daily dream diary. It might help you dream up that great story.
- Make a list of titles to grab a reader.

Are You Up for a Challenge?

It's all very well talking about how to find an idea, but how can we then expand it so it becomes a number one bestseller? I'm going to show you how through taking one idea and building on it; adding character, dialogue and, of course, plot.

I'm hoping that you will help me through adding to it at home with the exercises I'll be providing. But first we need an idea with plenty of scope. I'm going to plunge right in now and take one of the titles from my previous list to kick us off. Yes. You've guessed it. It's 'Single Again'. Why? Because it leaves the way open for lots of characters in search of a new relationship. Almost anything could happen. However, I might change the title once I get into the plot. I've learned over the years that as a writer you often need to alter your original ideas once you're more familiar with both characters and story.

In the following chapters, I'm going to help you develop all the other strands that are needed for a novel – and we'll be using 'Single Again' as an example. Exciting!

SUMMING UP

- Some great romantic fiction ideas just come to you in a flash. Others have to be worked on.
- Learn to turn familiar stories round so they have a fresh slant.
- Listen to your friends' stories.
- Keep an ear out on the bus or train or any busy place.
- Talk to people.
- Read problem-page letters.
- Learn to love your fantasies.
- Write down your dreams.
- Check out statistics.
- Titles can lead to great ideas.

EXPERT TIPS

A good idea needs to jump out at the reader from the first sentence.

Matt Bates, Fiction Buyer, WHSmith

I remember someone saying to me, 'How can I write about what I know? Nothing really romantic has ever happened to me.'

It made me stop and think a bit. How often have you heard the phrase . . . write about what you know? Boring! But without using some knowledge of the surroundings and events, it will never ring true.

You can use your imagination to create the romance but set it in a familiar place or even somewhere you have researched. Guide books, travel brochures can all help. Add your hero and heroine and you have the beginnings of a story. I often look at people in films and on television and imagine them into my stories. You have a person there to describe and fall in love with . . . just a little. And surely, your female part of this can be a tiny bit of you? Young or old . . . it doesn't matter.

If you can't imagine some sort of romantic element, then you're not a writer. It's a matter of using both what you know and imagination.

Chrissie Loveday, author of *For the Sake of Love,*
http://www.chrissieloveday.com

We all know that all good things come in twos, so if I was going to give romance writers two pieces of advice it would be these:

1. Be original and ordinary: falling in love, out of love, keeping in love, hiding from love – this all happens to us on a daily basis. Writers need to capture the ordinary and make it original.
2. It's all about the tension, that's what keeps our hearts beating and readers turning the pages faster.

Kimberley Young, Publishing Director, Harper Collins

3
HOW TO FIND A GREAT ROMANTIC FICTION IDEA FOR YOUR SHORT STORY

What's the difference between an idea for a short story and one for a novel? In my view, it's a bit like a river.

Picture a short story as one stream with maybe a little one running off towards the end – or alongside it all the way. A novel is a river with lots of little streams going off in different directions although, somehow, they all join up at the end.

The streams and the rivers and their tributaries are all problems; necessary for making the novel or short story flow. The trick is to pick the type of problems that work best for novels or short stories, depending on what you want to write.

I love writing both! In my experience, an idea that's best suited to a short story is one that can be wrapped up neatly in a few pages (about 1,000–2000 words). An idea for a novel, however, needs to be able to do more miles per hour. It has to have the potential to lead to more issues and greater character conflict that will take it through to 100,000 words plus.

Sometimes, you might start writing what you think is a short story, only to find that it's really a novel bursting to get out. This happened to one of my students who came to me for advice when her historical short story had been rejected by magazines. I suspected that the problem her heroine was facing was a slow-burner. It couldn't be easily sorted in a page or two. I encouraged her to write more of it and, within six months, it had grown into a novel. I then showed it to my agent who is currently very interested.

So how could this help you?

Below is a list of ideas. Some might work best for short stories and some for novels. A few might work for both. We're going to go through them together and work out which boxes they tick.

Girl starts dating online and meets friend of her brother. He doesn't know it's her because she hasn't given her real name

I think this might make the beginning of either a short story or a novel. Why? Because you could think of a twist within a page or two. For instance, the brother's friend might know it was her all along. He'd always fancied her but was worried she might reject him. So he encouraged her brother to persuade her to date online.

Alternatively, this could make a novel if you brought in a subplot. Supposing you took three characters, all of whom started dating online on the same day (including the girl who meets the friend of her brother). You could then follow their stories.

Unhappily-married woman gets stuck on a train when it breaks down. She starts talking to the man next to her and discovers an instant rapport. At the end of the journey, he asks for her number. She isn't the type to be unfaithful but something tells her that if she doesn't take this chance, she might always regret it.

This isn't the sort of problem that can easily be sorted in one to two pages. It's a massive river that is going to need lots of ups and downs before things work out – if indeed they ever do. So I'd definitely say this was novel material.

A woman receives a bunch of flowers without a note. Her family want to know who they're from. Who knows? After all, her husband hasn't sent her flowers for years.

This sort of idea doesn't have the stamina to make a novel. It would be difficult to tease a reader along for 100,000 words. Granted, it might well make a plot-pusher in a novel: in other words a scene that pushes the plot along. But I see this as a short story. In fact, it's the basis of a short story that I wrote for a woman's magazine. I'm not going to tell you what happens because we're going to be analysing the plot later on!

So where do we get ideas for short stories from? The main answers can be found in the previous chapter, but they include:

- real life;
- listening to people;
- news stories;
- radio;
- pictures;
- friends and family;
- looking at things in a slightly different way.

I got the idea for the flowers story through using the last method. Out of the blue, one day I received a bouquet that didn't seem to have the sender's name on it. In fact, it was right down at the bottom of the box but for a minute my husband looked rather worried. So did I. I felt slightly spooked to think I might have an unknown admirer. Or could it be that the flowers had been meant for someone else? After all, my name was misspelled on the box and so was the address. In fact, it was from a friend who wanted to thank me for something I had done for her. But it did make me wonder what chain of events might have occurred if I hadn't found out who the sender was.

Writing Serials

Serials are notoriously difficult to crack. They need a plot that can entertain the reader for an average of 9,000 to 20,000 words. But they also need a story that isn't going to take longer than that to tie up the threads.

However, they can be perfect for an idea that falls between the short story and the novel!

Unlike a short story, which is usually just sent in to a magazine on spec (see Chapter 15), a serial is generally commissioned by an editor before it's written. Each magazine has its own guidelines on the kind of ideas for which it's looking. It's wise to study these first before you send in an idea for a serial and also before you write a short story.

You can generally find these guidelines on the magazine website or you can contact the magazine directly.

EXERCISES

- Make a list of romantic short-story ideas and work out a rough plot. If you find the story insists on going on and on – or if there's no easy way to sort out the problem – you might have a novel on your hands.
- Read a selection of women's magazine short stories and analyse the plot. See if you can work out why they are better suited as short stories instead of novels.
- Do the same with a magazine serial.

SUMMING UP

A romantic short story generally focuses on one idea rather than several. That idea can be a serious one. But if it's too complicated, it will need more than 2,000 words to work it out.

You can still use similar sources to find your idea, e.g. news items, word of mouth, etc.

4
HOW TO PLOT YOUR ROMANTIC NOVEL

What comes first? Character or plot? It's a question that everyone asks – and it's very understandable. Should your hunky hero take precedence when you're starting your romantic fiction novel? Or should you start thinking about what he's going to *do* before describing his pecs, his passion for curry and his fear of marriage?

In my view, the two are tied so tightly that it's very difficult to tell them apart. However, if I was pushed, I'd say that I imagine it visually as giving birth to twins. One comes first but then the other is very close behind. They remain entwined together for the rest of the novel, breathing each other in. A well-written character will give you ideas for the story through his personality. If our hero loves curry for example, he might find his true love in the local curry house.

But I also have to admit that, in my head, the first-born 'twin' is actually the plot. I personally need a glimmer of an idea before I can start matching it with a cast of characters.

A romantic fiction idea also needs to be much more challenging than it was a few years ago. It's not enough to have a storyline that goes like this:

- boy meets girl;
- problem;
- boy marries girl.

Today's romantic fiction is far more adventurous and braver. It might have several problems along the way that reflect today's life. Here are some examples:

- career v. love conflict;
- travel v. love;
- previous relationships gone wrong (is your heroine or hero still grappling with old baggage?);
- stepchildren;
- single parents;
- single grandparents (old people fall in love too!);
- confusion over gender issues (is your hero really gay?);
- living together v. marriage;
- being together apart (living in separate houses).

And much more! You might like to add to the list yourself.

The good news is that all this will broaden the plot – which means you're less likely to be stuck for things to write about.

How to Begin

Take your idea. Allow it to simmer for some weeks. While this is happening, make notes. Do not be alarmed if other ideas occur to you while doing different things. However, always make sure you have a pen and paper to hand. Using a bare wrist to write notes on, recording on a Dictaphone or leaving yourself a message on the answerphone are some of my own favourite desperate measures! Many writers just type a note or record a memo on their mobile.

Above is my recipe for starting a novel. The simmering process is crucial. If you plunge straight in, you might find that the idea is forced. It's far better to get to know it in your head and imagine the various directions it could go in.

So let's start with 'Single Again'. I'm going to take a piece of paper (please do the same) and write down the title in the middle of a sheet of blank paper. Now draw a circle round it and then add spider legs. Along each leg, write down one thought that comes to you when looking at the title.

Here are my 'line legs':

- Who is single?
- Is something preventing him or her from having a relationship?
- Secret?
- Children?
- Problem?
- More than one main character?

I'm not sure of the answers myself yet but that's because we've just begun. I'm going to mull it over for a bit because I find that ideas often come to me when I'm doing something else like walking the dog or – as I'm doing at the moment – sitting in an airport. (Scientists have a phrase, 'the Inspiration Paradox', for the fact that you get inspiration when your mind is engaged on something else. It's all to do with the left- and right-hand brain but since I've never been very good at science, I'll skip the explanation.)

In the meantime, I'm going to think of a place where characters might meet. This is always a good starting point for a plot. It means you can bring together lots of people and – crucially for the story – give them different quests and problems in life.

The 'P' word is essential for a plot. Without a 'problem', there won't be enough for the reader to turn the page. We've all read books in which not enough happens. Yours is going to be different. It *has* to, if it's to succeed in a competitive world like romantic fiction.

One problem, however, is not enough. Your readers will start to fidget or, even worse, give up if you make them wait until the end of your novel until you solve the difficulty. Yet if you do it halfway through and then spend the rest of the novel describing places and people without making anything big happen, you stand a fair chance of losing your audience.

The trick is to think of a plot where there is potential for lots of problems. In my previous novels, I have covered the following:

- *The School Run*: about a group of parents on the school run.
- *Mums@Home*: about a group of parents who join a parenting support website.

- *The Supper Club*: about a group of friends who start eating at each other's houses once a month.
- *Second Time Lucky*: about a group of strangers who buy flats in a converted old house.
- *The Wedding Party*: about a group of wedding guests due to go to a wedding in nine months time.
- *The Playgroup*: about a group of parents (and a teacher) who meet through school.
- *The Au Pair*: about a mum who starts an au pair business.
- *Happy Families*: about parents (and a glamorous gran) who go to parenting classes.
- *After the Honeymoon*: about parents who go on honeymoon (along with teenage kids).

Each one of these has a centre that unites the characters – either a place or an organization. So what are we going to choose for 'our' novel, the one we're going to write together in this book?

As you're not sitting beside me, I'm going to make a unilateral decision. I mentioned a few lines ago that I'm sitting in the airport. I'm actually in a café, having breakfast, before a very early flight. As I look up from my laptop, I can see a middle-aged woman serving behind the bar who seems very chatty and smiley. But then she turns to one side and her expression looks anxious. She's also checking her watch.

Interesting.

Behind me is a young man who is talking urgently on the phone. I'm trying hard to hear what he's saying but all I can hear are the words, 'I need a week. Please.'

Also interesting.

In a minute, I'm going to pick up my bags and make my way to the gate. I could bump into anyone on the way, including that young girl who is carrying a folder marked 'Single Holidays with a Difference'. Either she's going on a holiday or maybe she's organizing one.

Even more interesting. Especially as she's not actually there. I've simply imagined her.

I've now got the beginnings of an idea. Three people. At an airport. What could happen to their lives in a week? Are they single; about to be single; or about to find their true love?

There are quite a few love meanings associated with airports too:

- arrivals;
- departures;
- security;
- checking in.

And there's the potential for drama:

- emergency on the plane;
- emergency at the airport;
- unexpected meetings;
- urgent messages on the Tannoy;
- delayed planes;
- excitement of the unknown at the other end.

All in all, it sounds quite promising . . . However, I'm not going to make up my mind yet. Instead, I'm jotting it all down in my ideas book and then I'm going to do something else, like board the plane. It might give me an idea on how to start the very first chapter.

I'm also going to change the title at this stage. (I did warn that I might!) Instead of 'Single Again', it's going to be 'Love is in the Air'. Now my plot is clearer, I like the double meaning that my title suggests. Love is in the atmosphere but it could also refer to love on the plane. It also suggests mystery and romance.

To Plan or Not to Plan

I'm often asked, as indeed are all authors, whether one should plan or not. When I first started writing novels years ago, I sat down and forced myself to imagine what might happen in every chapter.

Then I wrote down a plan and made myself stick to it.

That novel didn't get published.

However, I have other friends who can't write a word without having a precise plan at their elbow by the keyboard. And some of those are always in the bestseller list.

Personally, I think it depends on your personality. If you're a very methodical person, you might feel safer starting off with a blueprint. Nothing wrong with that. But I would urge you to be flexible. If you start writing a scene that you planned a few months ago but now doesn't feel quite right, listen to that inner voice.

It may well be that the novel is taking its own direction. You've become more familiar with the characters and the story than you were before you started writing the body of the text. As a result, your hand is itching to make your story go in a different direction.

So allow it to breathe! If you don't, it might come out all stilted.

However, you might be one of those writers who just start without any idea of where they're going. Sometimes this works. And sometimes it doesn't. Personally, I think this is like getting into a car and driving without a map or satnav. You might find a lovely place to visit. Or you could end up in the back of the beyond. Actually, I have a friend who did this and found her perfect cottage along with her husband. But that's another story.

The third type of planning is a mixture of both. You'll have a theme. You'll also have some ideas written down; you have a vague idea of the characters who will 'people' them; you know that something important needs to happen in each chapter although you're not sure what. Then you start writing and allow the characters and the theme to direct you.

'How?' asked a student recently.

Well, it helps if you start thinking like the character. Imagine you are in the place that your character is in. Ask yourself what kind of problem your character is facing and how they might react. Then, without over-thinking, allow yourself to write. After all, we start to walk, talk and eat without thinking too much. We also fall in love without thinking it through properly – which is, come to think of it, something that might happen to one of our heroines.

Using Mindmaps for Planning

Whether you are a detailed planner or a partial planner, I believe it's crucial to have a notebook to write down your various ideas and notes while writing your novel.

Personally, I also find tree diagrams useful, both while writing a novel and after it's finished. Basically, this is like a mindmap: a visual way of seeing what you plan to write or have already written. It can remind you of what you've written and it might also help you spot lengthy periods of inaction or too much action.

You can do a mindmap for a chapter or for the whole novel. Start by drawing a vertical line – the trunk – down the middle of a sheet of A4 paper. Then draw branches off this trunk, starting from the bottom right and going up to the top. After that, go down the left hand side.

If you're doing this for a chapter or a short story, treat each branch as a paragraph. Write down one line that sums up the first paragraph and then write it along the first branch. Then the second. And so on.

If you're drawing a tree diagram for a novel, treat each branch as a chapter. Write down one line that sums up the first chapter and write it on the first branch. Then the second. And so on.

Finally, on the trunk down the middle, write one line that sums up the chapter or the novel.

We're going to do this with our story as we go along. At the moment, I'm just going to write the following on our main trunk: 'Three People Find Love in Airport'.

Meanwhile, you might like to start drawing your own tree diagram at home.

There are also lots of other ways to record your plot. Here are some suggestions:

- Scrivener or other similar computer program;
- notice board;
- index cards;
- the inside of your head.

Establishing a Subplot

'There were three of us in this marriage.' It's a royal line that will haunt many of us for years to come. But it's also worth its weight in gold when it comes to romantic fiction. In fact, why stop at three?

One pair of star-crossed lovers with a problem might not be enough to hold the reader's interest. Personally, I like to have three main characters, each with their own story, in order to move the plot along. This way, you are never stuck for things to happen. I tend to focus on one character in the first chapter; a second in the second chapter; and a third in the third. Before long, the reader finds they are all connected, through a job or place or situation.

This is known as multi-character viewpoint. Each one is a sort of subplot for the others. However, if this sounds too complicated, you might prefer just one subplot – in other words, a story that is connected to the main story but runs alongside it.

For instance, if I chose to concentrate on just one main character for 'Love Is in the Air', I might pick the young girl in charge of the singles group. For the subplot, I could follow the story of her widowed mother who has started to see a man in her yoga-for-the-over-fifties group. She hasn't told her daughter because she thinks she might disapprove. But now her daughter has gone away for work, she decides to ring him up!

Subplots are best divided from the main story through chapters or through a device such as a row of stars, indicating a line break. They are useful because they provide variety for the reader and also widen the possibility for plot. They also cast a wider net. If a reader isn't grabbed by the main story, they might continue because of their interest in the subplot.

Needing a Prologue?

A prologue is usually a short piece of text that whets the reader's appetite. It often points to something that has happened or might happen in the past or future. Sometimes it's a bit of a teaser: designed to make the reader read on. Often it's used to set the scene.

I actually think there might be a place for a prologue in 'Love Is in the Air'. The shorter and punchier the better. See it as a taster; something that whets your reader's appetite with lots of unanswered questions.

It might go like this:

> 4.10 a.m. at Stansted airport. There's a feeling that the day is about to begin. The check-in desks are beginning to open and, on the other side of security, the morning papers are being delivered; crisp and fresh like buns out of the oven.
>
> A woman waits by the security scanning machines. Her bag is being re-checked and she wonders if she's left her tweezers inside again.
>
> A young man keeps checking his phone in case a message has popped up in the last thirty seconds.
>
> And the manageress of the coffee shop is trying to forget what happened the night before.
>
> The Destination board shows the date. January 15.
>
> In a week's time, life will have changed. For everyone.

I think I'd read this. Wouldn't you? In fact, I'm going to suggest using it as the prologue for our novel.

Using Flashbacks

Many loves are rooted in the past: romantic fiction is no exception. Your hero and heroine might have history together many years earlier. Or one of them could still be haunted by something that happened in the past.

Flashbacks are a useful way of showing the emotions that this event involved instead of just telling the reader. Let's go back to our middle-aged woman behind the bar. When she looks anxious, perhaps her mind is going back to a special day, an anniversary perhaps.

However, you don't want the flashback to interfere too much with the current narrative. So keep it quite short – maybe two or three paragraphs – in order not to take the reader away from the main story. I also think it's sometimes a good idea to divide it from the main text with a device such as a row of stars to show the reader there's been a 'gear shift'. Some novelists use italics to show flashbacks, which can be useful although not all editors like this. Alternatively, if the flashback plays a crucial role in the main story, you might devote an entire chapter to it.

Another option is a subtle integration of a flashback without the use of stars or italics. For instance, the man checking his phone might recall a character from the past.

> As he listened to the answerphone message, the high voice at the other end reminded him of a girl he used to date when he'd been a teenager. She had been demanding too, he recalled.

The reference is slight enough for us to stay in the present scene but is nevertheless a reminder of something that was important some time ago.

Here's an example of a longer – but still short – flashback in 'Love Is in the Air'. I've called our character Dilly because I rather like names ending in 'y' or 'ie'. They sound warmer. However, I might change this later on when I get to know her better.

> Dilly forced herself to smile at the young boy as he paid for his latte while checking his mobile phone at the same time. Then she turned away to hide the tears that were pricking her eyes. He looked so young .The same age as John when she'd married him. Normally, she blocked out the memories but today, they kept nagging her. It was always the same. January 15. Their wedding anniversary.

> They'd only known each other two weeks before he'd popped the question. She'd been so surprised that she'd said 'Yes.'
>
> 'You will?' John whispered. 'Really?'
>
> And then, before she knew it, the whole thing had begun to snowball until it was too late to change her mind.
>
> Dilly shivered as she turned back to the bar to fill the coffee percolator. Young people nowadays were much more careful. Take this young girl in front of her now with a clipboard. She didn't look the type to get married in three months and stick it for thirty-odd years.
>
> 'May I help you?' she said, plastering that smile back onto her face.

You'll see that in the above example I've just given a glimpse of Dilly's past. The main story is right now, in the airport. But it makes us realize that there is more to this woman than meets the eye.

Following Plot Rules

Although I'm not a great planner, I do believe that there are certain plot rules to follow. So here goes.

Grabbing your reader

Your romantic fiction novel should engage the reader at 'Hello'. However, at the same time, it doesn't always work to start with a crisis before the reader has had a chance to engage with the character. Let's imagine that the young woman in charge of the singles group loses her passport in the second line.

> Susie reached into the bottom of her bag and gasped. Her passport had disappeared.

We probably feel sorry for her. Indeed, we'd be callous not to. But we'd feel more sympathy for her if we'd already had half a page or a page, telling us a bit more about her. Let's imagine the novel starts like this.

'Gd luck on yr first day'.

Susie glanced at Mum's text which had just popped up on her phone and tried to quell the butterflies that were bouncing round her stomach. Mum wanted her to succeed in her new job almost more than she did herself.

It wasn't great when you were twenty-five and you still didn't really know what you wanted to do in life. Looking after a group of Singles definitely wasn't her ideal job. But as Mum had said when the employment agency had rung, nothing ventured nothing gained.

Besides, it might help her forget James . . .

'Right!' She beamed at the small group of hopeful faces round her. 'We're all here now and our gate number is up on the board. Everyone got their passport?'

Susie waited, trying to be patient while a very tall, thin woman went through every single compartment in her handbag before finally finding hers. Thank goodness for that. The last thing she needed on her first day was for someone to lose their documents.

'Great. I'll just get mine and . . .'

Susie froze as she went to unzip her shoulder bag. It was already open even though she could swear she'd closed it after security. A cold sweat trickled down her back. Her purse wasn't there. And nor was her passport.

I feel much sorrier for Susie in the second version. Don't you? By starting to build up her character as well as the plot (who exactly is James?), we've created someone we care about. Therefore there's more impact when Susie runs into trouble.

Keeping the pace moving

Another plot rule is to include at least one big event per chapter. That way, you should keep the reader's attention and the pace moving. Sometimes, when I've told a student that in my opinion, not enough happens in their first chapter, they will tell me that the action starts in the second or third chapter instead. That's far too late! Susie's passport loss is an obstacle but I'm not sure I'd call it a really big event. What else could happen to her in the first chapter?

Here's a list of my own thoughts. See if you can add a few more.

- Someone in the group has a panic attack on the plane.
- Susie isn't allowed on the plane because of her lost passport.
- Someone in the group mislays their boarding pass.
- A new person joins the group at the last minute – James's former girlfriend.

I know which one I'd go for! Imagine having to lead a group of singles that included your ex-boyfriend's ex! Especially if she doesn't know who you are. Even better if you don't know who she is either!

I did, at one stage, think about making this character (as yet unnamed) James's former wife or even current wife, from whom he is separated. However, I chose not to in case that made the reader lose empathy with Susie. Romantic fiction readers can be quite a moral bunch. Some might think that Susie shouldn't get involved with a man who isn't yet divorced. Obviously, not everyone would think that but, in my view, it isn't worth taking the risk. We want to gain readers, not lose them. I remember being very sensitive about these issues myself, as a reader, when I was going through a divorce. In fact, I would abandon a book if I felt a main character wasn't playing fair.

Ending each chapter with a cliffhanger

In other words, add another event at the end that makes the reader desperate to know what happens next. Personally, I think that James's ex-wife's arrival does that nicely . . .

Being aware of the time

I don't mean the number of hours you're putting in – although that's important too. I'm talking about the time structure in your novel. My first published novel, *The School Run*, was set over one week. This made it quite easy to write the book. I divided it up into seven sections, e.g. Monday, Tuesday, Wednesday and so on. Within each section (rather like Part 1, Part 2, etc.), I had seven sections, each reflecting the various characters' viewpoints.

This blueprint makes it easier to plan so I suggest doing the same with 'Love Is in the Air'. Under 'Monday', for instance, we could have different chapters, each focusing on a different viewpoint.

The advantage of setting our novel over one week is that it increases the tension. We want to know what happens to Susie during her tour. We know that the young man with the phone has begged someone to give him a week. And we could also go back to Dilly, behind the bar, and slip in the fact that she only has a week before she makes a big decision. We don't know what that decision is yet – but that's part of keeping the reader guessing.

I find it useful to write down anything to do with time in my notebook containing character names and plot ideas. If my novel is set over one week, I will put aside seven pages and use them to record what happens on them. That way, it's easier to remember who fell in love with whom on which date!

It should also eliminate confusion. If Susie decides she'll return James's call in three days' time, we need to make sure it's not four. Believe me, that's very easy to do!

Getting the ending right

The ending in a romantic novel or short story needs to be quite clear. On the whole, agents and publishers prefer endings where the reader knows what happens to the main characters. They usually like happy conclusions too where the good characters have their problems resolved and the not-so-nice ones get their just deserts.

Don't panic if the ending doesn't come to you immediately. I usually begin to get a feel for it about three-quarters of the way through a novel. By then, my characters will have become real people and will 'give' me suggestions. You will find this too – I promise! If you don't, it might mean that your characters aren't vivid enough or their problems aren't right. But if you go back and address that, you will come up with a good story and a great ending.

It's also important to be realistic. Don't be tempted to wrap up the story by creating an ending that's implausible. If you have found you've dug yourself into a hole when it comes to plot and you don't know how to resolve it, you might need to go back and rework it. Similarly, don't rush the ending just because you want to get it over and done with, or because time is running out. A reader can tell if you've done this. And so can an agent or publisher.

EXERCISES

Make a list of big events that could stir up your own romantic novel (a different one from 'Single Again'/'Love Is in the Air'). Here are some to kick you off:

- Hero gets girl pregnant when drunk: has to do the right thing, even though he secretly holds a candle for her best friend.
- Single-mother heroine turns down date because she wants to concentrate on the children.
- Young man is about to suggest moving in with girlfriend when he spots her with someone else.

Also make a list of ordinary events that happen to us as part of life. See if you could slot them into your novel to pep it up. Think about:

- birthdays;
- wedding anniversaries;
- engagement parties;
- dates;
- Man flu;
- first shared holiday.

SUMMING UP

- Plots don't have to be planned with great precision before you write. The characters will suggest ways in which the story can go forward. For instance, Susie is keen to do well on the first day of her new job. This might make you, as a writer, tempted to make something go wrong.
- However, it is essential to check the plot is smooth and consistent. Some writers do this as they go along. Others, like me, prefer to wait until the end when they have got the story straight. See Chapter 14 on good writing practice and revision.
- Consider telling the story from the point of view of more than one character to move the plot along.
- Make sure something big happens in each chapter.
- Include at least one major event in each chapter.
- End the chapter on a cliffhanger.
- Be on the lookout for news or stories that could help you with the above.
- Don't panic if the ending doesn't come to mind before you start writing.
- Make sure the ending is clear and not open ended.

EXPERT TIPS

Don't tell us too much before the story gets going. Slip in the back-story as you go along.

Katie Fforde, author of several novels including *A French Affair* and *The Perfect Match*, www.katiefforde.com

Pace is everything. Make them laugh, make them cry but make them wait. Start your story with something that hits the reader between the eyes but *not* the back-story. For example, if you tell us your heroine is the daughter of an earl who is out to reclaim her inheritance in the first couple of sentences, you've taken the wind out of your story before you've really started. The reader needs enough information to get them interested but not enough to allow them to second guess the twists in the plot. However, this doesn't mean rushing the story either.

Know when to add in detail and when not to. As a general rule of thumb there tends to be more description in the first third of the book. Once you've described a room or place to your readers you don't have to do it again as they have a mental image in their head. Vary the location of the scenes.

Carefully decide what the reader needs to know at a certain point and what to keep from them until later. Remember, a story isn't just about what happens but in what order.

The writing has to be tight, tight, tight to keep the story motoring along and keep readers interested so cut ruthlessly anything that doesn't enhance the story. That includes 40 per cent of the speech tags. If there are two people talking the syntax and expressions should show you who's saying what.

Warning signs of a drop in pace:

The pace can drop dramatically if the main protagonists are apart, doing their own thing, for chapter after chapter. A character can be very busy with all sorts of things, which have nothing whatsoever to do with the plot.

All the characters are getting on just fine: in real life that's what we aim for but in a story it's dull. Throw in a few fireworks in the form of jealousies, thwarted ambitions, dark secrets that have to remain hidden, etc. And please, please, please don't have your characters re-telling each other things the reader already knows.

Are secondary characters taking over? I don't buy the excuse, 'but the character just took on a life of their own'. No they didn't.

You lost sight of the story. However, if you do find a secondary character taking too much of your attention then ask yourself if they might be better playing a different part in your story.

Look again:

See if you can add some twists and turns into your plot or characters. Is there too much narrative? If there is, look at ways of adding in dialogue to speed things up – this also can help you in the show-not-tell department. Is there a lot of sitting about? Are there unnecessary passages? Only scenes that add to the plot are allowed.

Possible remedies:

If major surgery is needed then bite the bullet. Cut ruthlessly and rewrite.

You could try a plot graft and add something in but beware that this can sometimes be more difficult than the major surgery option – think dropping a stitch in a Fair Isle knitting pattern and trying to weave it back in. If your story dies on the operating table then don't despair. Nothing is wasted so don't discard or delete anything as it might rise, phoenix-like, in another book.

And cut, cut, cut!

Jean Fullerton, author of numerous novels including *Call Nurse Millie* and *All Change for Nurse Millie*, www.jeanfullerton.com

What is plot? Every book I own on plots and plotting says something different. So, the way I see it is this: A romance novel is driven by emotional tension. Emotional tension is caused by internal and external conflict. The writer must work out where to weave emotional tension into the story, in order to make the reader keep turning the pages. I believe that when readers say that they like a good story, they actually mean that they like a good plot!

Gina Rossi, author of *Life After 6 Tequilas* and *The Wild Heart*

As conflict is the driving force of any story put your hero and heroine between a rock and a hard place with no easy solutions. How? By giving them goals/ambitions that place them on opposing sides while powerful attraction draws them emotionally and physically closer.

Jane Jackson, author of *Devil's Prize* and *Eye of the Wind*, www.janejackson.net

If you find yourself thinking, even for a moment, 'Don't worry, it gets interesting on page xx . . .', throw out pages 1–xx and take it from there.

Jo Beverley, author of *A Shocking Delight*, www.jobev.com

5
HOW TO PLOT YOUR SHORT STORY

The idea behind plotting a short story is similar to that of a novel, but on a smaller scale. So instead of a series of problems to solve, the character might have one or two.

The pace, however, needs to be much brisker. When I write short stories, I try to move the plot along every three or four paragraphs. I do this by making the main character do something different or maybe by bringing on another character. Something might be discovered or something lost; someone might arrive at a new place or leave an old.

The most important thing is to keep the pace flowing faster than you would in a novel. After all, you have less time. Your readership is also different. Many people buy magazines for a features article or a line on the cover. They might not normally read short stories but they're reading yours because it's part of the magazine. Your goal is therefore to keep them reading: you have to weave a spell like an enchantress.

In order to do this, you need to up the ante: in other words, bring in events that will increase the tension. These could be normal events in everyday lives, such as:

- leaving something behind;
- being ill;
- getting a parking ticket.

However, try seeing them with a different eye:

- leaving behind an object on a train, which had been given to your heroine by a past love; she has to get it back – but how?

- stepping in for a work colleague who is poorly and can't go to a function – your heroine goes instead and meets someone;
- she doesn't have the right change for the parking meter so goes into a shop to change a note and bumps into someone she hasn't seen for a long time, getting a parking ticket as a result.

All these are ideas that have the possibility for a story, but are also resolvable in 1,000 words.

Analysing a Short Story

Below is the short story I mentioned earlier, about a woman who received a bouquet of flowers. Go through it with a red pen or highlighter and mark the changes where the story moves on. I'm not holding this up as an example of how to do it. Indeed, the story may not be to your taste. But I hope it shows that you can't afford, as a short-story writer, to write a story that lags.

> WHO, ON EARTH, COULD SEND ME FLOWERS?
>
> The doorbell rang just as I was putting on supper. It was Mike's favourite; cod mornay, although he probably wouldn't notice. Nowadays, he's so busy with work that he doesn't seem to notice anything. I know it's a cliché but he just doesn't understand me any more.
>
> The doorbell rang again. 'Will someone get that please?' I called out irritated. Honestly! You'd think that with two hulking teenagers in the front room, not to mention a husband who was sprawled out in front of the television exhausted after a day in the office, someone would bother answering the door.
>
> 'Aileen, Ben,' I called out, stirring the cheese sauce. It smelt good, even though I said it myself. Of course, it would be wolfed down in minutes even though it had taken me ages to make. And then Aileen and Ben would beat a hasty retreat back

to the telly or MSN, with me calling after them to take their plates to the dishwasher.

If I sound like a bit of a martyr, let me put you right. I AM a martyr. And, yes I know, it's all my own fault. As my next-door neighbour and best friend Eileen constantly tells me, I do too much for them, like many mums. The trouble is that I've got used to it. And they've got used to me doing it. So when I ask them to help out, they'll say 'OK, in a minute.' Frankly, it's quicker to do it myself. As for Mike, well he's always so tired that I feel guilty asking him to do anything.

This time, however, it sounded like my husband had actually made it to the front door. I could hear surprised noises and my neighbour Eileen's voice. Turning off the cheese sauce and taking off my pinny, I went out to see what the fuss was all about.

Eileen was holding the most beautiful bouquet of flowers I had ever seen. There were freesias, roses, gypsophila, lilies and almost everything else I can think about. 'I found them by my front door when I got back from work,' said Eileen. 'The courier company must have left them by mistake because they're quite clearly addressed to you.'

'To me?' I gasped. 'Who are they from?'

I glanced at Mike. If I'd harboured any fanciful thoughts that he might have sent them to me, they were instantly dispelled by the surprised look on his face. 'What does the card say?' he asked, delving into the beautiful display. But there wasn't one.

'Oooh,' said Eileen, her eyes sparkling. 'You must have a secret admirer!'

I could see Mike didn't like the idea of that at all. Part of me felt quite pleased. I mean, when was the last time he had sent me flowers? 'Why don't you ring the courier company and find out who placed the order,' he said in a strange voice.

'Good idea.' I handed him the phone book. 'Go ahead.'

It took him a while to work out that the business numbers were at the front of the telephone book, which shows how often he looks up a number for himself. Eileen and I left him to it while I returned to the cheese sauce which was now a bit black looking. Mike came in, a few minutes later, with a frown on his face. 'The girl said she wasn't allowed to say who placed the order but apparently the customer gave specific instructions that there wasn't any message.'

'Blimey, Mum,' said Aileen, who was riveted enough to tear herself away from *Big Brother* to see the drama that was now taking place in her very own kitchen. 'Have you got a boyfriend?'

'Don't be silly,' I said crossly. But even so, I couldn't help going red. Mike was looking at me with a very strange expression. 'Maybe it's my mother,' I said lamely. 'A sort of early birthday present.'

'Your birthday isn't for three months,' said Ben, dipping his finger into the cheese sauce.

'Well, I don't know.' I tried again, thinking hard. 'Perhaps I've won them. You know I'm always entering competitions.'

'They'd have definitely left a message if you had,' said Mike, who was in advertising. 'They'd want as much promotion as possible.'

'What about your new boss?' asked Eileen, a touch too helpfully I thought. 'You said he had a bit of a roving eye.'

'I didn't know that, Mum,' said Aileen sharply.

I went red again. 'He doesn't really. Only for the younger women anyway. Whoops. Looks like this cheese sauce is ready now. Do you want to stay for supper, Eileen? There's more than enough.'

She patted me on the shoulder. 'I don't think so, love. Looks like you've got more on your plate already! Wish someone would send me flowers like that. I feel quite jealous.'

There was no shortage of conversation at the table, that night. Everyone was talking about who could have sent Mum such a fabulous bouquet of flowers. And for the first time in ages, Mike actually cleared the table while I arranged them in a vase – well, three vases actually. They clearly cost a fortune.

'Are you sure you don't know who sent them?' he said for the millionth time.

And that's when I snapped. 'Why do you keep asking? At least it shows that someone cares about me.'

He went pale. 'Don't be silly. You know how much I love you.'

'Do I? You never talk to me at the end of the day because you're so tired. I wait on you all hand and foot even though I work as well. And the kids don't lift a finger.'

Mike nodded. 'You're right. Well, it will all change from now on. By the way, love, where do you keep the dishwasher tablets?'

Amazingly, he was right. It did all change. Mike drew up a rota for the kids so they learned to tidy their rooms, clean the kitchen and help with the vacuuming. That weekend, he took me out to a film, followed by dinner. And the week after that, I got a big bunch of flowers, this time with a message.

'To show you that I love you. Mike. PS. Now you don't need to buy yourself flowers any more.'

'How did you guess?' I gasped.

He put his arms round me and gave me a big lovely warm hug. 'Because I understand you better than you think, you daft thing!'

I wasn't buying that one. 'Eileen told you, didn't she?'

He had the grace to look embarrassed. 'No. But next time you buy yourself flowers, it might be a good idea to hide the receipt!'

Hopefully, you have spotted all the places where the story moves on. These include the sections beginning:

- The doorbell rang again.
- If I sound like a bit of a martyr . . .
- 'To me?' I gasped.
- 'Blimey, Mum,' said Aileen . . .
- 'How did you guess?'

Adding Flashbacks and Prologues

There generally isn't enough space within a short story to write lengthy flashbacks or prologues. But it can be done, providing it's tightly written. Remember, longer flashbacks can be signposted clearly with a device such as a row of stars to show that the character is thinking back or that the story is going back in time.

Using Multi-Character Viewpoint

You might not think it's possible to write a short story from the point of view of more than one character. But it is – even though you won't have so long to write the individual stories. I recently wrote a romantic short story where three characters reflected on their honeymoons. From a plot point of view, it moved the pace along although I was careful to divide each character's viewpoint with a row of stars to show a line break.

SUMMING UP

- A short-story plot needs to move along at a brisk pace. People fall in or out of love within paragraphs rather than chapters. However, there is still room for flashbacks.
- As with novels, the characters should be strong enough to give you ideas on where the plot is going.
- Don't make your plot so difficult that you run out of space to solve it.
- Short-story editors like historical romantic fiction as well as contemporary settings.

EXPERT TIP

What makes a good romantic short story? That's a big question with so many obvious answers: a strong storyline, super characters and a satisfying ending are the usual sound if predictable answers. For me it goes beyond those.

I try to concentrate on the enigmatic way a story can simply draw you in, wrap itself around you and keep your attention to the exclusion of all else. It should sweep you along to a conclusion that you couldn't predict but can't imagine it ending any other way either. There's no simple instruction for making that happen as each story has its own backbone.

With some writers it may be the way they make narrative feel as if they are inside that person observing through their eyes. Or it might be such convincing dialogue that it feels like a very real conversation with that person. With others, it might mean simply touching the emotional or hilarious nerve of a theme. A really good story tackles both light and shade as in real life.

Advice in a nutshell: find the backbone of your writing – work out what you do best and construct the body of your story from that.

Liz Smith, Fiction Editor, *My Weekly*

6
DEVELOPING CHARACTER

How to Create Your Ideal Hero and Heroine (not to mention all the other people involved)

We've already worked out that you need a great plot with lots of twists and turns to make your romantic novel work. But that's not enough on its own. You also need characters with whom you can identify – and who will each play a vital role in your story.

I've just finished reading a book by a well-known author and feel rather dissatisfied, to be honest. The story was there and there were plenty of characters, but I didn't warm to any of them. Nor did the author give us much of a background to the characters, which might have explained why they acted as they did. So for me, it didn't work.

A character isn't just a person who plays a walk-on role in a story. It's someone whom you like or dislike. It's a person whom you can picture in your head. You can hear them speak. And you want them to be able to solve the problems that come up. There should also be a curiosity or a burning desire to find out more about their background and what makes them tick.

Your task is almost harder in a romantic novel, where you need your hero or heroine to show passion; either in love or anger or both.

So how exactly can you do this? Let's start with a bit of personal research. Think back to the first time that you fell in love. What was the person like? Write down everything you remember about the following:

- Looks
- Personality
- Voice
- Walk

- Character traits
- Star sign
- Family
- Job (school?)
- Likes and dislikes
- How you met
- Kiss
- Smell
- Romantic effect on you

To make you feel less embarrassed, I'm going to do the exercise with you. In fact, I'm going to delve back into my teenage years and describe what stood out about my very first boyfriend. It was all quite innocent but I was certain, at the time, that this was the Real Thing. As they say, you never forget your first love. So this is what I remember about X . . .

- Looks: Fair. Blue eyes. Pale eyelashes. Tall. Lanky.
- Personality: Quiet sense of humour. Liked rock music. Books. The sea. Dogs. Walking.
- Voice: Deep. Sounded older than he was.
- Walk: Lollop! Long strides.
- Character traits: Always late for dates. Never rang when he promised.
- Star sign: Leo.
- Family: Mother who didn't like me.
- Job (school?): School.
- Likes and dislikes: Liked geography. Disliked cities.
- How you met: His mother (who knew mine) asked him to come round to our house to borrow something.
- Kiss: A surprise! I didn't expect it.
- Smell: I can still recall his spicy aftershave!
- Romantic effect on you: Made me feel special. Kept pinching myself. Did that really just happen?

How Can We Use Our First Loves for Our Characters?

For a start, I'd definitely change some details. It might not do for our first loves to recognize themselves in print. But at the same time, we need to keep our original love in mind because it will help us to create a real person.

Let's take the young man who is on the phone at the airport in 'Love Is in the Air'. I've already suggested that he's looking rather nervous and that he's asked for an extra week.

Now we need to get into his character.

What's his name? What does he do for a job? It can help to give your hero or heroine a career with which you're familiar. My background is in journalism so I'm going to imagine he's a journalist who has a new editor. He's been told to come up with a great feature for Valentine's Day or else he's out of a job. So he's booked a flight to Paris, the City of Love, in the hope of coming across a story.

Already I can feel another plot strand unravelling in my head. Maybe he spots Susie, the girl who is gathering together her single clients. She's waiting for a Chris Wilson who hasn't turned up yet. By some amazing coincidence, our anxious young man has the same name. He eavesdrops on the group, realizes they're a singles group and decided to masquerade as Chris Wilson. (Further on in the novel, Susie realizes that his passport details don't match her list so he is rumbled. But we'll deal with that later. At the moment, he can still get through Passport Control because he's already booked on the same flight with his real details.)

I think we might be getting somewhere. But there's a problem. At the moment, the story is in danger of taking over from the character. I still need to know what our journalist looks like, what his personality is, what he likes and dislikes and all the other things we've mentioned in the previous paragraphs.

This is where my first love is going to come in, although with a few changes. Chris Wilson is going to be blond with hair that's in need of a bit of a trim. (He was going to get it done before leaving but ran out of time. Why? This could be significant so I'm going to make a note of this in my jottings book.) Chris is always late for everything; a reaction to his family's military background.

Chris is quite short for a man: about five foot six. He's very aware of this because girls tend to like taller men. What he lacks in stature, however, he makes up for in charm. Our hero has a deep voice and a way of speaking to people that makes them feel special. Does he have a girlfriend? I'm not sure yet so I'm going to make a note to check this out when I know him better.

He's twenty-nine and he has a Significant Birthday coming up. (When? Valentine's Day? Maybe but we won't tell the reader this as it could be a twist.) Chris loves dogs, flying, Italian food and the sea. He hates cities, especially Paris, which has a special significance for him. (What? Not sure yet. Another one for our jottings book. Perhaps he had a bad holiday there with his parents? Maybe they told him they were splitting up then?)

Right. Now I'm going to write a few opening paragraphs about him, using some of the character details above.

'Right, everyone! We've just got to wait for a Chris Wilson and then we can go to the Departure Gate.'

Chris Wilson? But that was *his* name!

Turning round from his seat at the table, Chris's eye fell on the tall, pretty girl with the bouncy ponytail who was urgently scanning other customers in the bar area. She had a file in front of her, marked 'Romantic Singles Trip to Paris', and was sitting with a group of five girls and two men, each of whom had a heart-shaped sticker attached to their jackets or coats. Immediately, he felt that tingle running down his spine. The one he always got when he smelt a good story.

'Did he know we were meant to be meeting here?' he overheard one of the women ask, bossily.

'Yes'. The ponytail girl checked her phone in the same anxious way that he'd been checking his own earlier.

'I think we should go without him or he'll make us miss the flight.'

This was the bossy woman again. Already Chris had decided he didn't like her. She reminded him of his new editor. Talk about controlling! 'I want you to go to Paris for Valentine's Day,' she'd informed him tartly in the office yesterday. 'Find a story with a difference. Yes, I know you've got the day off but I don't care. We need something good. So make sure you come back with it.'

So he'd had to cancel the romantic dinner he'd planned for Rosie and got the jolly features secretary to book a return weekend flight. As for the story, he only hoped he would find something when he got there. A couple who'd just got engaged perhaps? Or maybe he could do a 'vox pop', the journalist term for interviewing people on the spot, and asking them what Valentine's Day meant to them.

None of the ideas were that original but now, through some amazing stroke of luck, it looked as though something else had just fallen into his lap!

Getting up, he put on his coat while using the action as a pretext for getting a better look at the pretty girl's file. Under the title 'Romantic Singles Trip to Paris' was the copy of an advert.

Fed up with Valentine's Day?
Want to meet like-minded souls?
Then get away with a weekend to Paris! Meet friends and maybe find your soulmate at the same time.

Chris almost laughed out loud. How cheesy! But at the same time, wasn't this exactly the story he'd been looking for? As Rosie had said when he left this morning, he was always good at spotting opportunities. 'Even if they don't fit in with other people's lives,' she'd added caustically.

Rosie . . . For a minute, Chris's heart missed a beat. Then he gathered himself. He couldn't think about her now. Not until he'd got his life straight. And that included making sure that he kept his job with the new editor.

'Excuse me.' The table of faces swung towards him. It was an effect that his deep voice often had on people; something that Chris had discovered as a gawky teenager. For some reason, it seemed to make up for his shortish height. 'Did you say you were waiting for Chris Wilson?'

The girl with the ponytail nodded. She had a rather sweet upturned nose and – how unusual – one eye that was blue while the other was green. 'That's me.' He gesticulated to his table. 'I didn't notice you when I came in.'

He held his breath. None of this was a lie. Chris prided himself on never telling lies; something that made him different from many of his journalist contemporaries. But if other people wanted to make assumptions, well, that was up to them.

'About time,' snapped the plump woman. 'They've called our Gate. We're going to have to rush now.'

Chris gave her the full benefit of his smile: something else that had always come naturally to him since childhood. 'A sunny disposition' was how his childhood reports had described him, along with 'often late for class; slow in maths; vivid imagination'.

'I'm terribly sorry,' he said. 'Let me help you with your hand luggage.'

The plump woman's face melted and it was all Chris could do not to make notes. A weekend away, posing as a Singles hopeful. If he could get away with it, it could be one hell of a story. Just as long as he could shut out the memory of the last time he'd been to Paris . . .

EXERCISE

Hopefully, I've managed to weave in quite a lot about Chris's character along with plot. Interestingly, the idea about Rosie came to me when I was writing. But you'll see that I've kept their relationship quite vague, on purpose. That way, the reader will want to know more. Now I'd like you to write a couple of paragraphs that show Chris getting onto the plane with the others and talking during the journey. Try to combine both character and plot. The following pointers might help:

- Does Chris like flying?
- Whom does he sit next to?
- What do they talk about?
- Does Chris read during the journey?
- Could you use the flight to get him to think back to the last time he was in Paris?
- What are the other characters like? Think in terms of thumbnail sketches at this stage.

Don't Expect to Know Your Characters Immediately

You might have noticed, a few pages ago, that I asked myself some questions in brackets and wrote the words 'Don't know yet'. This is because you can't, as the author, be expected to know exactly how something is going to turn out – or what a character is like – right at the beginning of the novel.

So I write myself a reminder to go more deeply into this bit when I do know. Personally, I find it easier to do this on screen, rather than on a scrap of paper that might get lost. Usually, I use a key word like TAKE IN or CHECK or DON'T KNOW. I always write it in caps. Then, at the end of my first draft, I do a search for these words in capitals so that I can add the extra detail.

By then, I will know far more about my character and, as a result, have more ideas about what he or she will do. For instance, I made a note to myself about Chris's birthday. If it was on Valentine's Day, he might have the same issues that other people have if their birthday coincides with the most important romantic day of the year. He might be able to hide the fact that he doesn't have any Valentine cards because he's going to receive lots of cards anyway. Or he might not get so many birthday cards because his friends are preoccupied with the significance of the day for themselves. I feel that Chris is quite a sensitive soul under that 'must get a story' journalist facade. So perhaps it's the latter.

I don't know yet because it takes time to know a character, just as it takes time to know someone in real life. If you think back to some of your best friends, you understand their characters far better now than you did when you first met them. The same goes for fictional characters. So for the time being, we must be content with letting them develop in a slow-burn way. We must allow ourselves to enjoy creating them rather than rushing in and forcing ourselves to cast them into an unchangeable mould.

This is why revision is so important. It allows us to go back to the beginning when we know our characters inside out. Then we can drop in the little nuances we've learned about our people to make them more fully rounded people.

What Do Your Characters Look Like?

When I'm writing, I have a vague idea of what my characters look like but I must admit that they are a bit hazy. That's why I cut out pictures from weekend supplements that are as close to my mental image as possible. Then I pin them to a large cork board near my desk and look at them while writing. It helps me to describe the angle of their nose or their long neck.

I also like to ask myself the following questions:

- What do they enjoy doing?
- What is their biggest fear/ambition/worst nightmare?
- What was school like for them?
- What colours do they like to wear or refuse to wear – and why?

HELPFUL HINT

Give your character a signature smell. You could use it as a plot-pusher too. One day your heroine doesn't wear it. What has happened in her life to stop her putting it on? What if she suddenly goes off it? Does it mean she's pregnant? (Many women dislike certain smells when they are expecting.)

How could smell 'bring out' your hero's character? I recently heard about a man who has several girlfriends on the go and gives them each the same fragrance so he doesn't get caught out if one smells perfume on him.

Understanding that Characters Have Flaws

We all like to think we're perfect. But at the same time, we're very aware this isn't possible. We have flaws with which we might have been born or we develop along the way as a result of an incident.

Yet strangely, many authors, when starting off, create heroes or heroines that are doll-perfect. They have blond hair and blue eyes and they never put a foot wrong.

Or they might go the other way and create a baddie who is rotten through and through.

Such a shame, because they're missing out on a great way to create a more interesting person who, in turn, will push the plot along.

The most interesting characters have a mixture of good points and bad. They might be contradictory (perhaps Susie likes chocolate but only treats herself on Fridays). The reasons behind these character traits can be equally vital. Maybe Chris hates having his hair cut because it reminds him of his military father who insisted he had short hair as a child. That in turn led to him being teased at school.

EXERCISE

What good/bad/contradictory points can you give your characters? You can start by thinking about your own – and then adding some that belong to others whom you know. Be careful, of course, that they aren't too recognizable. Here's my list to start you off.

- generous to others but mean to self;
- shy inside but outgoing on the surface;
- limited cook;
- fussy;
- caring;
- over-punctual;
- walks too fast;
- self-critical;
- generous;
- easily hurt.

Now add your own. You might like to write down the very opposite of certain characteristics. That can be quite an eye-opener.

Understanding that People Change

How often have we said that someone has changed? Perhaps you feel hurt by the alteration in their character. Maybe it annoys you. Perhaps it will change your attitude to that person. Maybe you don't want to see that person again because of it.

Great! We can use that in our characters. Let's take Dilly, the middle-aged woman at the bar. Perhaps she left her husband recently because he changed. Or maybe *she* changed. What happened to precipitate that change?

Perhaps she found a new job/new man/felt lonely when the children left home/got fed up with her husband's gambling habits or lack of conversation.

Perhaps a friend of hers left her husband and this made our heroine wonder if she ought to do the same. Dilly isn't normally the kind of woman who's influenced by someone else. But maybe she went to see a clairvoyant for fun. She was told that another life lay out there, waiting for her. But she had to leave her husband first. Something inside Dilly told her that if she didn't seize the opportunity, she might never have it again. So for the first time in her life, she does something out of character.

Can you see how closely character is entwined with plot here? Of course, I'm presuming that Dilly and her husband are divorced. But maybe he died . . .

Establishing a Character's Entourage and Background

Characters don't exist on their own. Even if they live on their own, they generally have families. They have to have a roof over their heads or maybe they are sleeping rough. They had a childhood of some sort and they generally went to school. They also have friends (and if not, why not?).

Let's think about Dilly again. We could make a list of bullet points about her:

- Family (Does she have children? How old? How old was she when she married her husband?)
- Home (Does she still live in the family home? Did she leave a comfortable semi-detached house and is now renting?)
- Childhood (Did she grow up in the town or country? Were her parents kind or neglectful? Did they expect too much or little of her? Does she have brothers or sisters? Might they play a part in the novel?)
- School (Was Dilly clever? Could she have gone to university? Did she give up the chance in order to marry her husband young? Would she like to go to university now?)
- Friends (Who are her friends? Does she have a best one?)

EXERCISE

Write down a list of points that help establish the background and entourage of the main characters in our novel: Chris and Susie.

Deciding How Many Characters You Should Have

My editor doesn't believe in 'crowding' the reader. If you have too many important characters in the first chapter, you run the risk of muddling the reader. They won't know whom to focus on and loyalties can become divided. Far better to bring in one main character to begin with: usually one to whom the reader will warm. At the same time, show the character's weaknesses. The aim is to make your reader empathize with that person but, at the same time, be aware of their faults. You might bring a second main character into the first chapter but perhaps they should have a smaller role. This can get bigger as the novel goes on. Then maybe a third . . .

I tend to write books now with three main characters and a cast of smaller ones. If you find the smaller ones getting bigger in your head, it might mean that they need a bigger role. For instance, the bossy plump girl in the group is already assuming slightly bigger proportions in my mind than I intended. It might be that she plays a pivotal role later in the novel. Perhaps she interferes in a relationship. Maybe she happens to know Chris's girlfriend through a work connection. I'm not sure yet but I'm going to jot down various possibilities as I go along.

Using Pictures to Aid Characterization

It's not always easy to visualize your characters clearly. I've already mentioned the value of searching for magazine pictures that remind me of my imagined characters and then storing them in a box or pinning them on a board.

Just by looking at them, you can describe the way their eyebrows arch or imagine what they are saying. Maybe you will think about what they have just been doing or are going to be doing. Their faces will indicate if they are kind or mean. Whether they are hurt or have hurt someone. Whether they are in love or not. Let your imagination run riot!

Creating a Baddy

The most interesting baddies in romantic fiction are the ones that turn out to be not-so-bad after all. Think Darcy in *Bridget Jones's Diary*! The trick with baddies is to give them a reason for behaving badly. Maybe they've been hurt in the past. Or perhaps they need a good woman (or man) to help them see the errors of their ways . . .

In other words, make sure your baddy isn't two-dimensional. There is usually a reason behind everyone's 'unforgiveable' behaviour. It might be jealousy/fear/hurt/lack of parental support, etc.

Similarly, if you feel your hero is rather bland or boring, why not turn him on his head. Perhaps that beige exterior is a hidden foil for someone who is actually rather unpleasant.

In fact, this might work for 'Love Is in the Air'. Supposing Susie, the tour guide, works with a French guide in Paris. He seems very charming but our journalist is rightly suspicious. He's determined to prove that this creep isn't what he seems.

Shag, Marry or Die

If you don't know this game, you're in for a treat. In fact, I'll make a confession here. I sometimes play Shag, Marry or Die while going round art galleries in the portrait section. Naturally, I only do it for character research! The idea is that you look at a picture of someone and ask yourself if you would shag them, marry them or rather die than do either.

It's very funny and – most importantly for this book – can give you some good ideas while writing sex scenes. Just pretend you've got a picture of a small, mean-looking bloke with bird-like eyes. Rather die than shag or marry? Think again. Perhaps he's not so mean when someone shows him love. Maybe he blossoms and those eyes become soft. So what if he's short? Small men often have a great sense of humour. Besides, he'd be a great contrast to your tall heroine who has had her fill of lanky hunks who can't commit.

Already, my Shag, Marry or Die game has given me an idea for a character and part of a plot. Tall, beautiful model falls for seemingly unattractive man with great sense of humour.

EXERCISE

Imagine you could have a night of unbridled passion with anyone you wanted. Write about it in the first person. Then put it into the third person, from the point of view of one of the 'Love Is in the Air' characters – or a different character entirely. Do the same with a magazine picture.

EXPERT TIP

What don't I like? Heroines who have pets with silly names that are meant to show the owner's quirkiness! What DO I like? A feisty heroine with a problem that she (mainly) solves on her own rather than being saved. Romance may be the essential theme but, at the same time, it needs other elements to give it depth. The days of a silly girl with not much of a job, looking for love, are over.

Gillian Holmes, Editor, Arrow, Random House

Creating Characters for Short Stories

Don't be fooled: characters in short stories also need enough depth for the reader to identify with them. The problem is that you don't have so much room to create them. So how do you go about it?

One great tip is to imagine your character standing in front of one of those fairground mirrors that exaggerate your features. I'm not suggesting you have a character with a huge nose or an elongated neck! But it does pay to have one or two features that make your hero or heroine stand out.

It might be:

- eyes where one is a different colour from the other (you'll notice I did that with Susie);
- frequent blinking while speaking;
- a large pair of glasses;
- hair that changes colour every week;
- a sing-song voice.

Can you add any more?

Characters in short stories also need a back-story/family/home/job in order to be believable. But if they're not central to the story, you can just refer to them in passing.

Dialogue is also essential in making each character stand out (see Chapter 10). So too, is internal thought (also see Chapter 10).

Personally, I don't think it's a good idea to have more than two main characters per short story. Otherwise you could muddle your reader and make it hard for them to pick the one they're rooting for. But I do sometimes have one or, at the most two, subsidiary walk-ons, providing they have a job in the plot. For instance, in my short story 'Who, on Earth, Has Sent Me Flowers?', we get a glimpse of the heroine's teenagers even though the main characters are the woman herself and her husband.

Otherwise, follow the advice given in the earlier part of this chapter, especially the part about cutting out pictures. It really does make a difference to look at an image of someone on a board. It's rather like having a swatch on the wall. You forget it's there but every time you walk past it, you decide if you like it or what you could change about it.

EXERCISES

- Cut out pictures from magazines that remind you of your characters.
- Take a character from 'Love Is in the Air' and write a paragraph about the following:
  - Likes and dislikes
  - Previous relationships
  - Fears
  - Dreams
  - Ambitions
  - Dress sense
- Get up and walk around like one of the characters. How do you walk? How do you talk?
- Imagine you are one of the characters about to board the flight. How do you feel? Whom do you sit next to? Are you scared of flying? Do you love it?
- Imagine you are another one of the characters in 'Love Is in the Air'. Something is about to go wrong in your life. What might that be and how would you react?
- Now pretend the same character is in for a lovely surprise. What might that be and how would you react?
- Think about all the love rats you've encountered in life. What made them behave badly? What might make them nicer people?

SUMMING UP

- Characters need to be made of flesh and blood. It's up to you to create an all-round person.
- Think like that character and imagine what they would do in a situation.
- Make sure your characters stand out from each other.

- Don't introduce too many at the same time.
- Ensure they have flaws.
- At the same time, make some of them likeable.
- Are the unlikeable characters difficult because of something that has happened to them in the past?
- How does the plot make your characters change during the novel?
- Can you change the 'who loves whom' dimension?

EXPERT TIPS

Perhaps the most important element to include in your romantic story is emotion. It encourages the reader to feel empathy for your characters and their situations and makes them want to read on.

Bring emotion into your story through description and action (facial expressions/behaviour/physical reactions), through dialogue (what they say and how they say it) and especially through internal thought.

Think about an emotion and anything that's affecting it. Do you see it as a colour? What season of the year? What food? What piece of music? What situation might provoke it?

Choose one emotion and write about a character experiencing it.

Rosanna Ley, author of *Bay of Secrets* and *The Villa*, www.rosannaley.co.uk

Be careful if your characters dwell on the past, especially early in the book. Yes, their past is important, and yes you might feel the reader needs to know, but the reader is interested in the now. Imagine the curtain rising on a play with characters on stage, but they are frozen as someone begins a long narrative of the story so far. Reveal the past only as it impacts the present. If the present is interesting, the reader will wait for the past to be revealed.

Jo Beverley

For me, everything comes from character. It's where I begin and end. Once I have my main character, I put them in a situation and ask 'what is the worst thing that can happen to them?'. Then I have their motivation, their goal. From there comes the story.

Sophie Duffy, author of *The Generation Game* and *This Holey Life*, www.sophieduffy.com

As a woman and a writer, it isn't too hard to get inside a romantic heroine's head. And we can describe what a hero looks like in terms of height and hair and eyes and physique. But for authenticity I feel it helps to see the world as our hero would see it. If, like me, you are five-zero in your stockinged feet, and your hero is six-two, find a step-stool and take it around the house with you and stand on it in various places so you can see the world through his eyes. Do you now reach straight out, or down, for a door handle? Can you see over next door's fence from the kitchen window now you are higher up? What is it really like looking down on the top of someone's head? – can you smell shampoo or days' old cooking? If you kiss the top of someone's head does it tickle your lips? And what about men's usually bigger-than-women's feet? I once bought a pair of size thirteen trainers from a charity shop and tried to walk about in them, and I found they do not fit on a stair tread the way my size fives do!

Linda Mitchelmore, author of *Emma: There's No Turning Back* and *To Turn Full Circle* as well as short stories, http://lindashortstories.wordpress.com

By definition, every romantic novel needs a 'to die for' hero. But that can lead to problems. Perfection can be boring. Speaking personally, I like my hero to have at least one flaw or, maybe, something in his past that he needs to keep hidden –

like Mr Rochester and his mad wife in the attic. Or Mr Darcy with his insufferable pride – although his rudeness at the beginning of *Pride and Prejudice* would not get past an editor today. My ultimate hero has always been Rhett Butler. Ever since I read *Gone with the Wind* when I was thirteen, no other man (real or fictional!) has ever quite measured up.

Modern heroes, however, are different. To quote from *The Craft of Writing Romance* by Jean Saunders: 'I want my reader to fall in love with my hero, therefore he has to be charismatic. He has to be the strongest character in the book. But he doesn't have to be portrayed as perfect in every way.'

Whatever type of romantic fiction you're writing, whether it's Mills & Boon or Classic Romance, you must be in love with your hero. If you're not, the reader won't be either.

Tricia Maw, author of *No More Secrets*

Make your characters interesting. Interesting is always more interesting than beautiful. Readers are not *all* tall, dark, handsome, even tempered and rich – so give them someone human, or they won't empathize.

Gina Rossi

Put yourself right into the character's mind. Write diary entries for him/her.

Lynne Connolly, author of *Fascinating Rhythm*, www.lynneconnolly.com

Wounds from the past can give us an insight into who our characters are. I love a good scar story! Marks on bodies explain or clarify our protagonists.

Lisa Clifford, author of *The Promise*, www.lisacliffordwriter.com, who also runs writing courses in Florence, Italy, www.the-art-of-writing.com

7
FINDING THE ROMANTIC VIEWPOINT

When I first started writing novels, I'd never heard of the term 'viewpoint'. I certainly didn't appreciate the difference it could make to my writing. Then, one day, after nearly six years of trying to get a novel published, an editor rang me up. She'd seen my recent novel and said she wanted to give me some advice. To my surprise, she asked me into her office, sat me down and explained that viewpoint simply means 'whose eyes are you looking through?'.

Viewpoint is really important in romantic fiction. It's a means of getting into a character's emotions and also showing how others react.

Here's an example of how not to do it.

> Katie pushed open the door in a hurry. To her horror, it flew open and banged the wall. 'Be careful what you're doing,' said a voice. Shocked by her own bad manners, she started to apologize. A wave of pain shot through Robert. Oh dear, thought Katie, as she took in this tall man with a rather floppy fringe and moody eyes. She'd done it now.
>
> Robert hadn't meant to snap but his foot was hurting. How silly of the girl to open the door like that. Yet now, as he looked at her stricken expression, he wished he'd kept his mouth shut. How could he make it up to her? She wasn't to know he'd just had an operation. Katie tried to pretend it hadn't happened but it was obvious that she'd injured his leg. What a great way to start an interview!

Nothing wrong with this, you might think. But in fact, I'm deliberately going back and forth between viewpoints within each paragraph. We start off by identifying with poor old Katie who is running late for her interview. But just as we're getting into her character, we are told that a wave of pain shot through Robert. The only way that Katie would know that is if she sees him wince with pain. But there's no description of that. Therefore, we presume that the writer wants us to enter Robert's head. Yet in the next sentence, we are back inside Katie's head again. Muddling, isn't it? It also waters down the impact that Katie could have on us if the writing concentrated on her alone.

In the second paragraph, the same thing happens. The author jumps in and out of Katie and Robert's heads like a game of ping-pong. The result? We get the gist of the plot (I reckon something's going to brew between those two) but we don't identify fully with either character.

I'm going to rewrite those paragraphs now, so they look like this:

> Katie pushed open the door in a hurry. To her horror, it flew open and banged the wall. 'Be careful what you're doing,' said a voice. Shocked by her own bad manners, she started to apologize. Oh dear, thought Katie, as she took in this tall man with a rather floppy fringe and moody eyes. She'd done it now. He was hopping around in pain. What a great way to start an interview!
>
> Robert hadn't meant to snap but his foot was hurting. How silly of the girl to open the door like that. Yet now, as he looked at her stricken expression, he wished he'd kept his mouth shut. How could he make it up to her? She wasn't to know he'd just had an operation.

This way, the division between feelings is clearer. The first paragraph deals with Katie and the second with Robert. We are allowed to concentrate on one character's feelings at a time. In other words, we're looking at Katie's viewpoint first and then that of Robert.

However, in romantic fiction, there are usually several paragraphs devoted to one viewpoint and then a row of stars or a line break or a new chapter to show that another viewpoint has started. Again, several paragraphs will be used to display this viewpoint.

Here's an example from my latest Janey Fraser novel, *After the Honeymoon*. It concentrates on a character called Rosie. You'll see that although other 'people' are mentioned, we see them all through Rosie's eyes.

> Rosie woke, blissfully aware of the lovely warm Mediterranean sun streaming in through the half-open white wooden shutters. If she opened her eyes just enough, she could see it dancing off the glittering aquamarine sea outside, in little sparkly lines. It was going to be a scorcher, she thought, sleepily stretching out like one of the stray cats who would, no doubt, be lazily licking themselves on the terrace outside while waiting for breakfast.
>
> Even after sixteen years of living in Siphalonia, she still found herself counting her lucky stars. Paradise! That's what the wide-eyed tourists called it – at least the ones who were adventurous enough to stray off the beaten track and find them.
>
> You could see why. Long, sandy beaches with clean fine white sand that you could run your fingers through. Whitewashed cottages with terracotta roofs, nestling next to each other like cloves studded on an apple, on different levels, leading up to the mountains above. Purple flowers eagerly clambering up the sun-scorched, cracked white walls. A secret recipe for a special type of moussaka that melted in your mouth followed by sticky, addictive baklavas (or as one of the more elderly guests kept calling them, 'balaclavas'). Locals with gappy teeth and wrinkled leathery skins who grinned at strangers.
>
> But Rosie was under no delusions. It took at least two generations to be fully accepted here. Jack's children might just make it, if they were lucky.
>
> Jack. Oh God. Rosie sat upright in bed, stark naked in the liberating knowledge that her bedroom was built in such a way

that no one could see her through the window. Perhaps it wasn't a good idea after all, to leave him. Running her hands through her short curls, bleached over the years by the sun, she suddenly panicked now that the time had come. Was she mad to leave Jack for three whole days on his own in charge of the Villa Rosa?

It wasn't too late to change her mind.

'I can do it, Mum,' he had insisted when the subject had first been raised, weeks ago. 'Don't you trust me?'

Yes. She did. Jack wasn't like the fifteen-year-old boys you read about in the English newspapers from home that the guests left behind. He was reliable. Solid. Practical. Older than he looked with a wise head on his young shoulders. Much taller than she was, which wasn't difficult given that she was barely five foot two. He'd had to grow up fast. They both had.

But every now and then, her son made the odd slip up like that booking last year which he'd forgotten to write down. 'It won't happen again, Mum,' he'd assured her. And it hadn't. At least, as far as she knew.

Now Rosie slipped into her pretty cotton rosebud dressing gown that her friend Gemma had sent her for Christmas (they were both suckers for Cath Kidston) and padded across the room to turn off the noisy air conditioning. She needed to keep an eye on the bills but a/c was an essential at night when it could get unbearably stuffy. Glancing in the mirror, with its bright blue driftwood frame decorated with shells, she tilted her head to one side, looking at what her old drama teacher had described as her 'delicate elfin features and mischievous eyes' which had earned her the role of Puck one year in the school play.

School! That seemed so long ago. As did England. Now, opening the shutters, she leaned onto the window sill and gazed out across the water. It was a view that never failed to enthral her. That was the thing about the sea. It was always changing. Today, there was a large white liner on the horizon and, closer to the shore, a fishing boat returning with the morning catch. Greco's perhaps. 'The Siphalonian' with its jaunty red and white bow and little cabin beneath.

Rosie felt a small smile creeping across her face along with a tremor of misgiving as a tall, lean, tanned man with the hint of a beard, wearing shorts and nothing on top, leaped easily out onto the shore, hauling the boat in.

It wasn't Jack she needed to worry about. It was Greco with his broad chest and mass of curly black hairs sweeping down to his navel.

'You're going to Athens?' he had exclaimed when, the previous month, she'd casually mentioned she needed to visit suppliers. 'It so happens I have some business there myself. I will go with you, yes?' He'd laid a hand lightly on her arm as he did to any woman under ninety. 'A beautiful woman like you should not travel alone.'

Of course, she had laughed him off, pointing out that she'd been independent for a very long time and was quite used to looking after herself, thank you. Anyway, she'd added with a slight edge suggesting she didn't fully believe his story, what kind of business did he have out there himself?

'You think I am just a fisherman?' he had replied, his eyes twinkling. 'I will surprise you, Rosie. Just you wait and see. Besides, it will be good to have some time alone together, will it not?' His face grew serious. 'Away from the island and all those prying eyes.'

He had a point.

What had got into her, Rosie asked herself, now stepping into her shower and shuddering as the cold water spurted out, suggesting that the hot had run out again. Greco of all people! When she'd arrived, all those years ago, pregnant with Jack, she had been warned, almost immediately, by Cara who had run the villa at the time.

> 'That Greco, he bad boy.' The old woman, whose command of the English language had been shaped by visitors to the island, had waggled her short brown index finger. 'You do not fall for his charms, yes?'
>
> Back then, Rosie wasn't falling for anyone's charms. She'd already made one grave misjudgement and look where that had got her.

In *After the Honeymoon*, I have one viewpoint per chapter. In total, I have three main viewpoints in the novel. The first chapter is from Emma's point of view; the second from Winston's; and the third from Rosie's. Then the fourth chapter is from Emma's viewpoint and so on.

It means that the reader gets to see each character through another character's eyes, which can create a more rounded person. It also helps to push the plot along because there is always something happening! Very useful in romantic fiction . . .

Using the Authorial Voice

Using the authorial voice is an alternative to this way of writing. Some books are written from the authorial point of view; in other words, the author is telling the story in such a way that the narrator is a character in their own right.

The fairy-story format is a good example of this: 'Once upon a time, there were two children called Hansel and Gretel', and so on.

The voice of the storyteller is always there in the background. At the same time, we might see inside Hansel's head in one line and then Gretel's head in the next.

The downside of this, however, is that you don't really form a close bond with a particular character. In my view, bonds and loyalties are crucial in romantic fiction: they help woo the reader into rooting for the hero or heroine.

Using Tricks and Tips to Help with Viewpoint

The trick with viewpoint is to imagine that you are the character. It's their eyes that you're looking through. Be brave! Get up and walk around. Act it out even if (like me) you shrink at the thought of getting on stage. Find a time and a spot where no one is around and be either Chris Wilson the journalist or Dilly behind the bar or Susie in charge of the singles group. What are they feeling? What are they seeing? It's amazing how deep you can go if you pretend to be someone else.

Also try writing in the first person to get into that person's skin and then change it back into the third. Let's imagine that Susie has succeeded in rounding up her group and they're now all on the plane, waiting for take-off.

> Susie leant back in her seat and closed her eyes. She could have done without that late arrival who seemed very cocky. Her heart sank. She'd seen his type before on the last trip with a pushy know-it-all who had made her life very difficult.

This says what I want it to, I suppose. But it doesn't really get into her character. So I'm going to rewrite it in the first person.

> Leaning back in my seat, I closed my eyes, pretending to be asleep. I needed quiet time; a space to calm down after that worry over the late arrival. Still, at least Chris Wilson had arrived. I shuddered as I recalled the woman from the last trip who'd turned up after the final call and then demanded a full refund from 'Single Holidays', claiming she'd been given the wrong departure time. Did my boss believe me? To be honest, I'm not sure.
>
> Barry looked as though he might cause trouble too. A real cocky type. I knew his sort. They're usually embarrassed about being on a Singles holiday so they put on an act of bravado. Still, I reminded myself, wasn't that just what I was doing?

I hadn't expected to write that last bit. But somehow, getting into the first person made it easier. However, 'Love Is in the Air' is written in the third person so I'm now going to turn it back, while keeping the flavour of the first.

> Leaning back in her seat, Susie closed her eyes, pretending to be asleep. She needed quiet time; a space to calm down after her missing passport (that had turned up at the bottom of her bag) and that worry over the late arrival. Still at least Chris Wilson had arrived. Susie shuddered as she recalled the woman from the last trip who'd turned up after the final call and then demanded a full refund from 'Single Holidays', claiming she'd been given the wrong time. Did her boss believe her? Susie still wasn't sure.
>
> Barry looked as though he might cause trouble too. A real cocky type. Susie knew his sort. They were usually embarrassed about being on a Singles holiday so they put on an act of bravado. Still, she reminded herself, wasn't that just what *she* was doing?

I feel happier about the last paragraph than the first. It seems to get further under the character's skin even though it took a bit of work to get there.

Challenges of Using the First Person in Romantic Fiction

If 'I' is your main character, it stands to reason that it's not easy to write about what is going on in another character's head. After all, if we could read other people's minds, we'd all be millionaires!

However, as a novelist, you have to get into someone else's head, even if you are using the first person. If you don't, you stand to write a very one-dimensional novel, which is just as bad as a one-sided relationship. Why? Because the thoughts and reasoning behind one character won't be enough to get you through 100,000 words.

Luckily, there are ways of getting round this.

Getting the main character to imagine the life of another

Make your 'I' character pretend that they are imagining what another character is doing. For instance, if we were writing 'Love Is in the Air' in the first person from Susie's point of view, we might describe Chris like this:

> I could just imagine the sort of person he was. Divorced maybe or unable to commit to a long relationship. He'd live in an untidy one bedroom flat in Acton and go jogging every evening. Bet he works in advertising – those yellow socks are a dead give-away – and he probably sinks Jägerbombs with his mates after work. They've all got married now (going down like flies, as he'd say) and the time has come for him to start thinking about the future. He's probably got a mother who keeps ringing and saying, 'Have you met anyone nice yet?'

I've got quite a good picture of Chris from this. But the joy of the first person is that the 'I' character may have the wrong end of the stick. Chris Wilson might not be like this at all. It will all lead to confusion, which, in romantic fiction, is exactly what we want!

Using Dialogue

An 'I' character will need to talk and interact with other characters. That in turn will tell us what they are like. Let's go back to Susie in the first person again.

> 'What do you think of Chris Wilson?' asked the girl on my left with the name Michelle pinned on her Singles badge.
>
> I was a bit taken aback to be honest. A group organizer is meant to do just that. Organize and not cast judgements. At least not to other people.
>
> 'He seems very pleasant,' I said casually, crossing my fingers mentally.

Michelle leant towards me in a conspiratorial manner. 'Well I think there's something a bit odd about him. He keeps looking at us all and making notes.'

I began to feel a bit uneasy.

'And he hasn't brought any luggage for the hold, you know. Only carry-on.' Michelle's pencilled-in eyebrows rose in disbelief. 'How can you fit everything you need for a week into a small bag? An Arsenal one at that?'

Right. So now we know the following about Chris through dialogue between two different people:

- he is an Arsenal supporter;
- he travels light;
- he makes notes;
- he's observant.

We also know a bit more about Michelle. She's:

- nosy;
- quick to criticize;
- has pencilled-in eyebrows.

All useful stuff if your viewpoint is in the first person because it helps you get to know the other characters too. In fact, it's making me wonder something. Could Michelle be Susie's ex-boyfriend's ex-girlfriend? If Susie didn't know her full name, it's quite plausible. Why don't we hold that thought by jotting it down in our book? It might be a red herring. Or it could be something.

Using Diaries, Emails, Texts and Ads

The above are crucial tools for any viewpoint but they can be particularly helpful if you're writing in the first person because they can help you get into the other characters' minds. Let's imagine that

Susie finds Chris's mobile, which he dropped when he walked past on his way to the lavatory on the plane.

> I picked it up and tried to call him back but he was walking so fast that he didn't hear. I'd just have to hang on to it until he came back. Then curiosity got the better of me. I know I shouldn't have but my index finger was already clicking the Sent Mail.
>
> *'Think I'm onto something.'*
>
> Onto something? What did he mean? Then I saw the address he'd sent it to and froze. The *Daily Globe*? Instantly, it all made sense. Chris Wilson was a journalist!

Great. We've got into Chris's head through his text and, at the same time, we've moved the plot along nicely. The cat is out of the bag. What will Susie do? Will she kick him off the group? Or will she accept his argument that yes, he is a journalist, but that he's here for personal reasons. His 'Think I'm onto something' message to his friend on the paper suggested that he was keen on one of the girls in the party.

Using Viewpoint in Short Stories

Viewpoint in short stories is usually limited to one character or the overall narrator because of space restriction. The first person can be a useful technique when it comes to creating twists. You can fool the reader into thinking that a character is someone else, e.g. a man instead of a woman or a child instead of an adult.

Here's an opening extract from one of my short stories, called 'Five Days to a New Me' (published by *Woman's Weekly*). The 'I' character is not whom you might think (the answer is at the end).

> DAY ONE. That's what it said on the blurb. *'Find a "New You" with our Five Day Transformation Special'*, it promised. Then there were all these 'before' and 'after' photographs of people

who'd been to this health farm and coming out looking – well, not that different actually. Yes, you could see that their skin was glowing and they looked a lot happier, yet I wasn't convinced.

But Sam was. Apparently, it was 'just what I needed' and besides, it would 'do me good' to have a break from the children. So here I am, feeling like a beached whale in this white dressing gown which everyone seems to wear round here instead of proper clothes. It was in my room when I arrived along with a programme of treatments and activities that Sam had booked me into. Mud bath? Meditation? Maximize Your Image consultancy session? What on earth had I let myself in for?

The 'I' character is a stressed house-husband who has been given a spa voucher by his high-flying wife as a Father's Day present.

EXERCISES

- Pick one of the characters on the plane and write a couple of paragraphs from their point of view.
- Do the same with another character.
- Take a third character and write in the first person, bringing in some of the techniques outlined above, e.g. texts/dialogue/imagining.

SUMMING UP

- Viewpoint means 'Whose shoes are you standing in?' or 'Whose eyes are you looking through?'.
- In romantic fiction, viewpoints are normally separated either through a line break (frequently denoted by a line of stars) or a new chapter.
- The first person is also popular in romantic fiction, although it's often more suited to a short story than a

novel. It can be harder to bring in the viewpoint of other characters in a longer piece.

- Viewpoint tends to be limited to one character or the overall narrator in a short story.

EXPERT TIPS

Viewpoint deepens characterization. A first-person narrator is immediate and intimate and if the voice is engaging, the reader will want to come along on the journey. If you prefer the third person, then go for a close third person, where the reader has access to character thoughts. Whatever narrative viewpoint you choose, be consistent. Stay in that viewpoint or you risk losing the reader's empathy as they won't know where to stake their allegiance.

Sophie Duffy

Viewpoint in romantic fiction can be used to develop character and plot, and even to create humour. The key is to *be selective* when deciding through whose eyes a particular scene would work best: the female/male lead, or a secondary character acting as an independent observer?

Once you've selected your viewpoint character, *choose their words carefully* to reflect how they would describe the people involved in the scene and the action that takes place. In romantic fiction, conveying what attracts people to each other – or not, as the case may be – is part of the characterization.

For example:

- What would the viewpoint character report and what would they leave out? When we first meet Mr Darcy in *Pride and Prejudice*, Jane Austen lists his attributes according to local gossip: 'Mr Darcy soon drew the attention of the room by his fine, tall person, handsome features, noble mien, and the report which was in general circulation within five minutes after his entrance, of his having ten thousand a year.' Needless to say, for the matchmaking mothers of Meryton, his reputed wealth is the most important thing about him.

- How would the character describe the scene, in terms of their choice of adjectives, figures of speech and tone of narrative voice? Early in *Pride and Prejudice*, we observe Elizabeth Bennet briefly from Mr Darcy's viewpoint, learning that her face is 'rendered uncommonly intelligent by the beautiful expression of her dark eyes'. This tells us a lot about Darcy: he values intelligence, considers it a rare commodity in women – and, given that he has been watching Elizabeth closely enough to detect the expression in her eyes, is obviously not indifferent to her!
- How reliable or misleading do you want the viewpoint to be? *Pride and Prejudice* is told largely through the eyes of the lively and endearing Elizabeth Bennet, which means that we readily adopt her prejudices and sympathies. When she learns later that her first impressions of Darcy and Wickham were very misleading, we share in her remorse and self-blame.
- Would the scene benefit by being told twice, from differing viewpoints? This is often a technique for building tension or creating humour, by exposing misunderstandings between two characters.

Juliet Archer, author of *Persuade Me* and *The Importance of Being Emma*, modern retellings of Jane Austen novels, www.julietarcher.com

If you're using several different viewpoints in a chapter, for goodness sake help your reader out by separating the scene with those little asterisk thingies! Also, make it abundantly clear whose viewpoint you are in. Use the viewpoint/POV [point of view] character's name in the very first sentence of a new scene so the reader is clear.

Gina Rossi

These days third-person limited is the king, followed by first person, which is closely related. Don't head-hop. True head-hopping isn't frequent change of point of view. It's when there are frequent and unclear points of view so that the reader can't tell whose head he or she is in.

Lynne Connolly

8
HOW TO WRITE ROMANTIC SCENES: ARE YOU RECLINING COMFORTABLY?

I have to be honest. There's a downside to writing romantic fiction. And it's this. People whom you know are going to assume they're party to your sexual fantasies, because that's how they'll probably interpret your romantic scenes.

There's something else too. How on earth do you actually describe in words what happens between your hero and heroine in bed? It's enough to make even the boldest writer feel a little bit uncomfortable.

Don't panic. This chapter is going to help you deal with both issues and also give you some ideas that you might not have thought of before . . .

Step 1: Getting Yourself into the Mood

It's no good trying to write a romantic scene if you're feeling frazzled or uptight. The body actually needs to relax in order to let the imagination do its work. So make yourself your favourite drink; treat yourself to a delicious snack (author Julie Cohen dished out chocolate in her writing class I once attended); spray on some perfume; put on some music; sink into a comfortable chair and close your eyes. Imagine you are about to be seduced by your partner or that yummy actor on television. Let your imagination go and allow yourself to sink into fantasy.

Don't make notes just yet; simply hold that feeling in your mind. What is your body doing? Melting with desire? Seizing up with panic? Contorted with guilt? Feeling foolish? Wishing you had put on some nicer underwear?

Any of the above will do when it comes to romantic scenes. In fact, I always warm to a heroine if she suddenly realizes she's wearing her comfortable baggy knickers from the market!

If that doesn't do it for you, try reading something raunchy or watching the kind of film that sets your pulse racing. Analyse how the writer or scriptwriter shows passion. What do the characters say? What do they do? Where do they do it?

Don't start scribbling your scene yet. Instead, jot down any ideas that come to you during this chill-out time. Your list might look like this:

- subdued lighting;
- office desk;
- car;
- touch of a hand under a dinner party table;
- smell of skin (pine aftershave? Chanel?);
- music;
- taste of each other's mouths.

Now add your own . . .

So far, so good. But true love never flows smoothly – or at least, it shouldn't in a good romantic novel with lots of twists and turns. So what might interrupt this love scene?

- The character's anxiety about performance?
- A physical problem, e.g. scar from mastectomy?
- A sudden noise that stops you at the last minute?
- Forbidden love?

Can you add to this?

Step 2: Introducing Humour

Laughter is a great aphrodisiac. If only more men realized that! It's one of the biggest turn-ons there can be (providing it's not sarcastic laughter) because it makes us feel warm, happy and included.

Not all romantic fiction is funny but, personally, I think it's an important factor. All my books have what one reviewer described as 'a wicked sense of humour'.

So how can you bring humour into a sex scene?

Someone might do something 'wrong'. I have a friend who accidentally kneed her new partner in the groin when she was trying to demonstrate her nubile qualities (which weren't bad for a fifty-something out-of-practice divorcee). Instead of moaning and groaning, her new man made her feel much better by telling her that 'a lot of people pay money for that kind of thing'. Once he was able to breathe again, they ended up having a good old laugh about it. It certainly took the heat out of the situation, so to speak. In fact, it apparently put in a great deal more heat an hour later but we won't go into that right now.

She gave me permission to use that in one of my romantic novel scenes so watch this space! But it was the lesson which was just as valuable. Characters who don't 'perform' smoothly in the bedroom can be great sources of humour; especially if we can identify with the situation ourselves.

Here are some other ways of introducing a laugh into the bedroom:

- eccentric characters;
- inappropriate clothes;
- dialogue;
- a discovery.

Can you add any more?

Step 3: Bringing in Tension

Nervous humour or more serious tension also goes a long way towards making those bedroom scenes more convincing. In *Happy Families*, I describe a scene in which Vanessa, a glamorous fifty-something granny, goes to bed with her new boyfriend for the first time. Here is a short extract:

'Did it hurt?' asked Brian, looking across at her.

They were lying naked on her bed, the gourmet meal for two lying uneaten in the cooker. Earlier that evening, when he'd arrived, it was as though he knew exactly what she was thinking. Wordlessly, he had taken her by the hand and led her to her own bedroom which she had had the foresight to tidy up first.

For the last two hours, they had done nothing but touch. She hadn't realized it could be so erotic.

Now she nodded, watching him draw his finger along the neat scar where her right breast used to be. 'Yes. Scared too. But – and I know this sounds awful – the worst bit was losing my hair. It came back a different colour and the texture was different.'

He nodded, glancing at the line of wigs on her dressing table. The wigs that she alternated every six months. Then he ran his fingers through her short spiky mouse-coloured real hair. 'I like this as well. It's natural. Did you find the lump in the shower?'

She nodded.

'My wife did the same.' He spoke quietly. She hadn't realized it was breast cancer. It had been one of those subjects they'd steered clear of.

'When?' he said, moving his hand to the other breast. For the first time in as long as she could remember, Vanessa felt a quickening below her waist.

'Five years ago. I've got the all-clear now. One of the nurses at the hospital told me that I could do two things. Worry myself to death in case it came back. Or put it behind me and live each day to the full.' She smiled to herself at the thought of that kind woman; one of so many. Say what you wanted about the NHS, there were some amazing people in it. 'I chose to do the latter,' she added.

He nodded, gently turning her to one side so that his naked body spooned hers. She could lie like this for ever, she thought to herself. The great thing about going to bed with someone who was your age was that they didn't have perfect bodies either. But at the same time, she could feel herself sweating with anticipation.

'Is that why you haven't slept with anyone since Harry?'

She whipped round to face him. 'How did you know?'

He smiled down at her, tracing the outline of her face with his thick index finger. 'Instinct.'

She nodded. 'I wasn't ready before and then when I was, I got this.' Forcing herself, she looked down at the scar. It might be neat but it was a constant reminder that she had nearly copped it. Not that anyone would have cared if she had. It had been a weird feeling when she'd been unable to put a name in the Next of Kin box. No point in putting Brigid's.

'I think it's beautiful.'

Beautiful? 'You can't really mean that.'

'I do.' His tongue gently licked her scar. Slowly. Carefully. Exploring her. 'It's a sign of bravery. And a medal to show that you have won.'

Then his mouth came down on hers and his hands began to do things that she had never known possible. 'Headmaster,' she murmured. 'Are you feeling my legs, like you size up a race horse's?'

'Absolutely,' he murmured back. 'And I think we've got a real winner here . . .'

You will see that I deliberately misled the reader in the first line. One assumes that the *'Did it hurt?'* refers to the sex act. In fact, it was a reference to Vanessa's mastectomy.

Here are some other ways to bring tension into the bedroom:

- unexpected arrival;
- phone call;
- inability to perform;
- someone else's name spoken in the heat of the moment.

Now try adding some of your own suggestions.

Step 4: Using Sexual Language

There are no set rules about whether you use an all-out expletive to describe the sex act or whether you are a bit more subtle about it. Personally, I favour the latter although there are times when the plot and the character do, in my view, demand a four-letter word. However, that's up to you. My advice is to write in a way with which you feel comfortable while, at the same time, allowing the novel to work.

However, there's no doubt that language in a love scene is often different from other scenes. Characters might start to call each other endearments that they hadn't used before, like 'babe' or 'darling'. This can do two vital things: it adds to the character and it can add to the plot. I used to know someone who called his wife 'lady'. When she died, he found a new wife and promptly started calling her the same. This didn't sit very easily with his friends and family. In a novel, it might suggest that this was a character who was fickle. Or it might be that the poor man just needed stability. However, it could annoy a character's grown-up children to such an extent that they become distant from him.

If you're stuck for language, a thesaurus is a good option for finding some equivalents. So too are films and television programmes.

Watch your sentence structure too. Most people, when making love, don't have the time or breath to say very much. Less really can be more: a few words or even one can be even more effective.

Which do you think sounds (and feels) better?

> 'That was amazing,' she said, turning to face him in the dark. 'Different, too.'

or

> 'Amazing.' She turned to face him in the dark. 'Very different from five years ago.'

For me, the last example is punchier and more intriguing.

Mind you, post-coital conversation can be a real winner when it comes to character and plot. It's incredible what secrets people come out with when chatting after sex.

Let's get shocking here! What might Susie say if she finds herself going to bed with someone on her first night in Paris?

> 'I've never slept with a stranger before.' She turned away from him in disgust at herself. 'I don't know why I did it.'

That tells us quite a lot about Susie's character. It also pushes the plot. So, too, could the reply.

> *'Je ne comprends pas.'*

So now we know he is French!

Foreign language can be very seductive. However, don't assume that everyone will know what you mean. You might have to include a translation.

Step 5: Doing Your Research

If you're still feeling woefully inadequate in the bedroom department, do some research. Ask your friends if they can tell you about their experiences, providing you promise not to use their real names.

Here are some more tips:

- Watch mildly erotic films – or just good old-fashioned romances.
- Interview 'sexperts'. I have a journalist friend who specializes in features on how to flirt. Sometimes I ask her for advice.
- Use the internet but be careful. Steer clear of sites that might compromise you.

Step 6: Less Can Be More

You don't have to be graphic when describing what goes where in the bedroom. Sometimes, a simple suggestion is enough. Let's go back to Susie's bedroom scene but take it one step back.

'Shall we go to bed?' Susie asked, shocked by her own boldness.

He studied her face for a minute. 'I think we have to.'

Slowly, they rose as if one already and walked through the hotel lobby and up the stairs to room 101.

***

The following morning, Susie woke before the sun was up. Slowly her hand went out and traced the shape of his naked back. Even if it never happened again, she knew she could never go back.

The asterisks stand for the unspoken action: in other words, the love act. It says it all, without going into the nuts and bolts. The scene's effect rests almost entirely on dialogue with a touch of narration. The 'have to' bit suggests desire coupled with the unspoken feeling that they are breaking a rule.

I don't know about you, but I want to read on.

Step 7: How to Cope with Fallout from Friends and Family

Personally speaking, I used to get embarrassed when told that some of my scenes were 'unexpected'. Now I laugh it off and tell people that sex is part of life.

However, if you really think it might cause problems, consider changing your name. A lot of writers do this.

You could also use humour to bat away criticism. If your nearest and dearest don't like what you've written, tell them to enter you for the Bad Sex Award, run by the *Literary Review*.

Let's Get Steamy!

Right, now we're going to get writing. Together, we're going to do the scene where Susie goes to bed with a stranger in Paris. We've already dipped our toes in, so to speak, earlier on when she wakes up the next morning and wonders how she could have done it. We've also tried another angle: just before they go up to the room. But now we're going back a stage before, to describe the seduction. I will try to bring in all the points I've mentioned before about setting, language, humour and so on.

Here goes . . .

It had obviously been a good idea to take them all to a bar on their first night in Paris. Barry had really hit it off with Michelle, the plump girl who was convinced Chris was a journalist. In fact it looked as though she was doing her very own research from the way she was nibbling Barry's ear: even though she'd just been dancing with Chris. The others had paired off too or else slunk away. Susie couldn't help feeling like a teacher in charge of a group of adolescents. It was a fine line between being in charge of them and letting them have fun.

The only person who's not doing that, she thought wistfully, is me. What's James doing right now? Is he back with his old girlfriend? Is he trying to get hold of me? Don't look at your phone to check. Don't . . . Now look! I've dropped it!

'Excuse me. I think this is yours?'

Before she had a chance to pick up her phone, a pair of warm hands was pressing it into hers. Confused, she looked up. And up. Never had she seen anyone so tall before. Or with such brilliant blue eyes which stood out against his flop of dark hair. 'You would like a drink. Yes?'

Without waiting for a reply, he cupped his hand under her elbow and steered her to the bar. Automatically, without him even ordering, the barman placed a bottle in front of them. 'You are a champagne girl, I think.' He poured her a glass and then filled his own before raising it to clink against hers. 'My name is Jean Paul.'

Stunned by the speed of the events in the last five minutes, Susie began to say, 'Mine is . . .'

'Non.' He laid a hand on her arm. 'I do not want to know. It is better that way I think because it adds to the mystery.'

What was she doing here? Part of Susie wanted to jump up and run. But the other part was strangely hooked.

'We will dance, yes?'

Had she really finished her glass so soon? Almost robotically, she found herself getting up and allowing Jean Paul to place his arms around her waist before drawing her closely to him. He smelt of cigars and whisky: a combination which she wouldn't normally have cared for. But the relief of having gathered her flock of Singles – together with all the doubts about James that were crowding into her head – made Susie feel dangerously different.

How long did they dance for? Later, Susie couldn't be sure. It might have been half an hour. Or two. All she knew was that it was like dancing through chocolate; smooth, delicious and undeniably wicked. Not because of what he said but more because of what he didn't say. Not a word or a question about what she did or who she was or who she was with. Simply his touch which trumpeted the word 'Experience' and 'Not to be trusted'.

'We will go now, I think.'

Unsteadily, Susie allowed herself to walk across the room with him. You don't have to do this, she told herself. But she wanted to. The 'good' Susie that had told James to deal with his feelings towards his ex-girlfriend before they went any further, was fed up with being good. She wanted excitement. She wanted what the others in her group were possibly getting right now!

Everyone seemed to know Jean Paul, from the concierge to the girl who showed them to the room on the seventh floor. Seven is my favourite number, she thought irrelevantly, as he began to peel off her dress before they'd even shut the door. This isn't me, she told herself. I don't do this kind of thing. Then she felt his skin on hers. Warm. Getting hotter.

> 'You are so beautiful,' he murmured as he knelt down. Paralysed, she felt him butterfly-kissing her inner thighs. Every muscle in her body wanted him. Now, she wanted to scream. Now.
>
> But just as he straddled her, there was a noise. A distinct Charge of the Light Brigade coming from her handbag. *James.* She could see his name flashing.
>
> 'James,' she murmured.
>
> 'No.' There was a low growl of amusement. 'I told you. My name is Jean Paul.'

Wow! I don't know where all that came from but clearly I've got a few fantasies lurking inside . . . Now it's over to you. What comes next? Try writing the next three or four paragraphs.

EXERCISES

- Think back to a love scene that happened in your life. Write it down as though it was happening to Dilly behind the bar.
- Take a look at your picture file. Select two and imagine what would happen if those characters got together. Write a paragraph about their first kiss.
- Make a 'tea tray' containing perfume; something nice to eat; a picture of a romantic hideaway; and a colourful scarf. Using those 'ingredients', write a three paragraphs about a couple who are trying to make their relationship work again.

Writing Erotic Fiction

I've purposefully left this bit to the last in the chapter because there is a difference between romantic fiction and its erotic cousin. Erotic fiction is much bolder and more graphic both in words and action. It can also include S & M (I used to think this was a brand of sweet until a friend enlightened me!). There's no doubt that *Fifty Shades of Grey* struck a nerve and made the genre more acceptable for both readers and writers. So don't be ashamed of trying it out if you feel this is for you.

EXERCISES

- Write down your innermost fantasies. Don't allow yourself to be inhibited. Imagine someone has told you that you have to do this. You have no choice. Describe what your imaginary partner is doing to you. What are they saying? What are they doing? What kind of words are you both using? What are you thinking and feeling?
- Let's go back to Dilly who works at the airport coffee bar. Imagine she's in bed with a new boyfriend, Tom. Dilly is nervous because it's been several years since her first husband John – even though she still can't stop thinking of him.
- Use the emotions you've gathered from the first part of the exercise to write an erotic scene involving Dilly and Tom.

HELPFUL HINT

Plots in erotic novels aren't usually that different from romantic novels. They normally involve characters looking for love and trying to overcome difficulties on their journey. It's the way you tell their story (language and actions) that makes it different. The characters too make the story stand out: at least one is larger than life.

SUMMING UP

- Love scenes don't have to be explicit.
- Suggestive can be sexy!

- Use smells, colours and memories to pep up your romantic novel sex scenes.
- Bring in humour where appropriate.
- Don't forget tension!
- Do your research if necessary.
- Less can be more.
- Pay particular attention to language.
- Consider changing your name if you're concerned about embarrassing friends and family.
- Erotic fiction means bolder and more graphic scenes.

EXPERT TIPS

As an erotic romance writer, when I'm writing a sex scene, I try to remember three things: language, choreography and purpose. Language is vital to drawing the reader into the scene – one wrong word can completely ruin the atmosphere. A lot of people struggle with heat levels, turning an explicit scene into an anatomy lesson and a low-level scene into a morass of purple prose. It may be awkward to find alternative words for body parts, but refer to a 'bobbing male cylinder' and erotica turns into comedy.

I had no idea how important choreography was until I read a sex scene where someone apparently developed three hands. This was compounded when I wrote my first threesome scene, which required all three characters to be physically involved at all times. While I'm not averse to 'passionate blur' scenes, explicit ones are rather like a dance – I plan out where everyone is, where their hands are, which position they're in and how they have to move. It's easier than suddenly discovering, two days after publication, that your heroine has just done a 360-degree revolve from the waist.

The third point, purpose, applies to every scene but is often forgotten in erotica, when sex can be thrown in purely for the excitement value. In erotic romance, the sex is there to build relationships and develop plot; the purpose informs the emotion of the scene. Is this the heroine's first time in years? Has the hero been dreaming of this for months? Are they trying to get each other out of their system? Is one trying to dominate the other and failing? Focus on the purpose and the scene will work – without it, it will be empty.

Tanith Davenport, author of *What's Her Secret: Photograph* and *Sleepwalker*, www.tanithdavenport.com.

For me, less is more. I don't want to read or write about the mechanics of sex. But I do want to know what the characters are thinking about the possibility, the actuality and the aftermath of that sex. Desire is great for adding tension to your writing. Anticipation. Will they, won't they? Here the use of subtext is a useful tool: what is going on below the surface?

Sophie Duffy

Don't put a sex scene in for its own sake. It should always have the same purpose as any other kind of scene – it's to develop the plot, or the character, or both. And don't forget that you don't have to love what your characters are doing – they do. Don't impose your taste on theirs.

Lynne Connolly

9
HOW TO CREATE ROMANTIC FRICTION

All good stories need a problem. But in romantic fiction, it's even more important. After all, we all know that the course of true love never ran smooth. So if your hero and heroine don't encounter some pretty big hiccups along the way, the chances are that your novel might fall flat. Almost as flat as your heroine's chest, although maybe that belongs to the chapters on characterization!

Nor should you limit the problems to your main characters. Setting up the minor players with some pretty big decisions to make might be just the firework you need to get the plot cracking.

But how to do it? Let's go back to 'Love Is in the Air'. I'm going to take it forward a scene. Our characters have assembled for lunch after that memorable night in the club where Susie got together with a French stranger.

Michelle is making a play for the journalist Chris, although she's not entirely certain yet if he's there for pleasure or for business. He, on the other hand, is more interested in Susie and wants to know where she went last night. In fact, this seems more important than wondering why Rosie (his ex-girlfriend) isn't picking up the phone. To his annoyance, his personal interest is taking over from his need to get a story. Susie, however, is fending off his questions, which makes him certain that she might have spent the night with that Frenchman he spotted in the club.

This particular scene, I feel, needs to be written from his viewpoint. It might go something like this:

> 'Did you have a good time last night?' asked Chris casually, passing the bottle of house red round the table.

Susie's eyes flickered slightly. 'The question is, did you?' She laughed lightly. 'The whole point of this holiday is for you to enjoy yourselves.'

There was a light touch on his arm. Michelle! It was all he could do not to groan out loud.

'We had a great time dancing, didn't we, Chris?'

That little-girl voice really irritated him. How could he have found it attractive last night? If only he hadn't had that extra glass. Perhaps he ought to give up drink entirely. Maybe the features editor might be interested in a piece on abstention instead of a Valentine singles holiday.

Or maybe not. Perhaps he ought to make his excuses and try Rosie again. Maybe she'd have turned her phone back on now. Perhaps he shouldn't have had that silly argument with her. On the other hand, she would keep on nagging him about small things like how to load the dishwasher . . . Such a control freak. Still, as she'd said, it went with her job.

'So where did you go?' he continued, knowing as he did so that he was prying.

'What do you mean?'

Susie's cool eyes turned on him, making him blush.

'I mean, did you find another club? One that's, you know, worth checking out.'

Susie was giving him the sort of look that insinuated all too clearly that he was overstepping the mark. 'I might be in charge of the group but I'm still entitled to some private time,' she said quietly.

Chris felt himself getting really hot under the collar now. 'I'm sorry.' Then he added in a lower voice, 'I just felt worried for you. That's all.'

Her eyes widened. 'Why?'

He'd dug himself into a real hole now. 'You know,' he began to stammer. 'Single woman alone in Paris. That sort of thing. It might not be safe. I mean . . .'

Thank goodness. His pocket was vibrating now, saving him from this awful muddle that his mouth had found itself in. Rosie? No. Dammit.

'Sorry. Just got to get this.'

Grabbing the phone, his hands – slippery from the olives – lost their grip. The handset went skittering onto the floor; right below Michelle's chair. 'I'll get it,' she trilled.

'No, it's all right . . .'

Too late! How dare she? She was actually glancing at the screen. Too late, Chris realized he hadn't put the lock on. 'I think we need to talk,' she said quietly, handing him the handset. 'This is going to cost you a drink.' She thrust out her chest. 'One to one, that is.'

Feeling sick to the core, Chris glanced at the screen. 'Got a story yet?' it demanded. 'Text immediately with update.'

You'll see that most of the tension has been achieved through dialogue that works in tandem with the plot. Chris fancies Susie, although Rosie is still in the picture. We also know a little more about her: she's a control freak, which might be a result of her job. Meanwhile, Michelle has an eye on Chris whose cover is about to be blown. There's only one possible way out – if he gives into Michelle's blackmail. And if he does, he stands to lose any chance with Susie.

I'm not entirely sure why I thought of the sequence of events in that little scene. It just seemed to come, partly because I put myself in the characters' different skins. Many years ago, I was quite upset when a man whom I liked was clearly interested in someone else instead. So there's a little bit of me there. I also think that men can get just as embarrassed as women and end up saying the wrong thing. That's why I made Chris go too far when quizzing Susie.

Hopefully, it will make the reader feel a little sorry for him. This is important because Chris is actually playing a dangerous game.

He's pretending to be part of a group while writing a story about them. That alone might make us dislike him, so I need to include something that makes the reader feel more sympathetic. That's why I've made Cupid's bow hit Chris firmly in the chest, even though he's on the job, so to speak.

Meanwhile, there's another main character whom we've left behind at the airport. Dilly. We need to follow her story and add some tension. I'm going to start by thinking about what a woman like her might feel like as Valentine's Day approaches. We've already worked out that it makes her feel nostalgic because it reminds her of her wedding anniversary. We've also jumped ahead a bit and described what it was like for Dilly to sleep with another man.

Now I want to go back and write the lead-up to this scene. You will see that I'm not doing this in chronological order. Sometimes, when you try to write a scene, the words won't come. Then it can pay to write a few notes to yourself and move on. Afterwards, when you feel more inspired, you can go back and write the scene more fully. This is what we're going to do here when describing how Dilly got together with Tom.

For a start, her job is important. I intentionally gave Dilly a bar job because it means she meets lots of people. So let's suppose that Tom is one of Dilly's regulars: perhaps he's a frequent-flyer businessman. He's known her for a few months (simply chatting over the bar before taking off) but now he's asked her on a date. She's feeling very nervous.

> What should she wear? thought Dilly as she rifled through her wardrobe. Something different from her usual working clothes. So that ruled out trousers. On the other hand, it needed to be something that she could take with her to work and hang up in the back as there wasn't time to go home and change. 'Seven o'clock on the dot,' Tom had said. He'd been very specific about that.

'Maybe he's married,' suggested her friend Pam. 'Married men are always clockwatching.'

No. Dilly knew that wasn't true. It wasn't just that he didn't wear a wedding ring. It was more a gut instinct. She'd made enough mistakes over the years to spot a bad 'un. Tom was a nice man. She'd first noticed that the other month when he'd lent a customer fifty pence because he didn't have enough money. It showed a generous spirit.

You might see that I'm beginning to build up tension here. Tom is nice. At least, Dilly is convinced he is. We're worried that he isn't. But perhaps now is the time to take the tension in a different direction. Let's fast forward. Dilly has finished work and is waiting by the Arrivals board, which is where Tom said he was going to be.

He was late. Dilly cast an eye at the Arrivals board. 'I'll be flying back from Düsseldorf,' he'd said with that casual ease of one who travelled a lot. 'We'll have a meal, shall we?' He'd given her a nice warm crinkly smile. 'Not in the airport. I expect you're fed up with that.' He'd rested his hand briefly on hers. 'I'd like to take you somewhere nice.'

That had been two days ago, just before he'd flown off. The plane from Düsseldorf had landed half an hour ago. Tom only travelled with hand luggage. 'Makes it quicker to get away,' he'd told her. So why wasn't he here?

A cold feeling crawled through her. Maybe he'd changed his mind. Or forgotten. Or maybe . . .

'Would Dilly Evans please come to the information desk?'

It took her a second to realize that this was her name on the Tannoy. Her heart began to beat in her mouth. How often had she heard it requesting someone? It was always bad news. Someone was being contacted because something had happened. And now it was happening to her. I've got a bad feeling about this, Dilly told herself as she threaded her way through the crowds. Something had happened to Tom. She just knew it.

This is a different kind of tension: the sort that comes from the unknown. We want to know what has happened to Tom. We need to see if he's a decent man or not. Why? Because we feel for Dilly. We suspect she's had a rough ride in the past and we want her to be happy.

In other words, I've created this tension through a mixture of character and action. Now, over to you!

EXERCISES

- Write 300 words that follow on from this scene. Mix narrative with dialogue: in other words, include lines that describe what is happening as well as speech. If you're stuck consider the following problems. Can you use any of them in your plot?
    - Sudden illness
    - Mix-up over dates
    - A secret
    - Lost luggage/purse/wallet
    - An argument
    - Someone gets drunk
    - An accident
    - Change of mind
- Make a list of all the things that have gone wrong in your love life – and that of your friends and family. See if you can work these themes into your romantic friction. Here are some examples to kick you off:
    - Infidelity
    - Pressure of family life
    - Pressure of work

- Misunderstanding
- Dithering between two people
- Unable to forget old love

Using Character to Increase Tension

Go back to your folder of characters. Take a look at some of the faces. I've got a picture here of a woman with a very hard face. She looks rather predatory to me. I think she's the type of person who might home-in on someone even though he's married. How might she slot into the plot puzzle? Is there a male equivalent – in other words, a man who is determined to make a married woman fall for him?

How might children fit in with this? Many romantic novels nowadays take in the difficulties (and the pleasures) of extended families. How would a woman, who had always wanted children, cope with the kids from her new man's life? She might try to make them love her only finally to realize that she can never take the place of their mother. But what if circumstances occurred that meant she became their sole carer? (New man dies; mother disappears.) That would cause lots of lovely problems, wouldn't it?

Establishing Misunderstandings to Create Tension

Misunderstandings are constant tension themes in romantic stories. Maybe Dilly got the wrong day, for example. Make a list of all the misunderstandings you've come across in your own love life and that of your friends. Here are some of mine:

- wrong place to meet;
- wrong time;
- getting on wrong train and being late;
- thinking someone meant a date – but it was really just a friendly invitation for a drink;

- assuming someone was being friendly – but was really making a pass;
- someone is older than he/she says – or younger.

Using Sex as a Source of Friction

Look through any problem page and it's plain to see that many sources of friction come from:

- one person wanting sex and the other not;
- one person loving someone but not wanting sex;
- one person feeling a physical lust but not actually liking the object of their desires;
- lack of sex;
- too much sex;
- weird sex.

Now sit down. Close your eyes. And ask yourself some hard-hitting questions.

- What would happen if a woman (or man) fell in love with someone who had a reputation for being a sexual Lothario?
- Is it possible for that person to change?
- And supposing one of your characters was a woman with a seedy background but she turned her life around, met Mr Nice and married him, what would happen if one of his business colleagues was an earlier 'client'?

Interesting . . .

Creating Financial Friction

'What's one of the biggest sources of romantic friction?' I asked my husband. 'Money,' he said promptly. Do you know, I'd forgotten that one! Here are some more themes that would make some cracking romantic fiction plots:

- arguments between a couple about how money is spent;
- one of them spending money secretly;
- one not telling the other how their money is earned;
- gambling.

Using Career Friction

There's nothing like a job to add to the romantic friction in a plot. What would happen if one half of a couple:

- works too hard?
- is work-shy?
- falls for someone in the office?
- is a workaholic?
- is sent somewhere, causing a change of scene or leaving one of the characters behind?

Turning to Food and Drink to Provide Tension

Alcohol is another great source for arguments and tension.

- What if one of your characters is an alcoholic? How could that affect a relationship?
- What if one drinks and the other doesn't?
- What if one is a social drinker and embarrassed the other at a dinner party?
- What if one of your characters blurts out a secret when drunk?

More romantic disharmony in the making comes via diet.

- What if a woman loses weight but her husband doesn't like the new her?
- What if a woman nags a man to lose weight, spoiling their relationship?
- What if a couple meet at weight-reducing programme (her husband made her join; so did his wife)?

More Sources of Romantic Friction

- Clothes ('You're not wearing that, are you?).
- Religion (woman not allowed to marry a man because of different religions/one person converts to new religion and the other doesn't).
- Holidays (one wants to go away; the other doesn't; difference in views when it comes to destinations).

EXERCISE

Pick one or more of the issues above and add it to the 'Love Is in the Air' passages you've already written. Write as much or as little as you want.

SUMMING UP

- Use examples from your own love life or any other stories you've come across to create confusion/misunderstandings/arguments and so on.
- Make sure you change the details.
- Use pictures to give you ideas.
- Create tension through dialogue and plot.
- Include the tension of the unknown as well as arguments.

EXPERT TIPS

Too many people believe that writing 'Romance' means it must be a slushy story about a predictable boy-meets-girl affair. But no, that isn't the case at all. I am a historical writer. My novels are full of dramatic adventure and danger in exotic settings, but they are always driven by a powerful love story that gives motivation to my characters and provides a sharp focus for the reader to identify with.

It is essential for stories to contain elements of conflict – even love stories! So the romance must never run smooth. One of the ways I create tension within a relationship is by erecting barriers between the lovers that they have to overcome. In this way, they are tested and the reader discovers what hidden layers lie beneath the veneer of their character – you have to get under their skin – as well as showing the true strength, or lack of it, of their love for each other.

The kind of barriers I have used in my books are these:

1. She was part of the white colonial world; he was a Chinese communist.

2. She was married, he was not.

3. She was Russian aristocracy; he was a working engineer.

4. He possesses secrets which, if known, could destroy the relationship. This builds towards a powerful climax of confession/revelation near the end of the book.

5. He is her best friend's loved one, so should be off-limits.

Many other problems can raise their heads to form a threat to the bonds of love: past lovers or other men/women who intrude, family demands, misunderstandings, yawning gaps in belief (political and religious), clash of ambition, divisive difficulties with drink or addiction, physical separation . . . The list is endless. Let your imagination run wild.

As I write historicals set in the first half of the twentieth century, I make use of real historical events to separate and challenge the lovers, in the form of war, political riots, Russian prison camps, angry Egyptian dissident groups, etc. But history in any guise can be used to delve deeper into the cracks that open up when a relationship is put under pressure.

Kate Furnivall, author of numerous books including *The Russian Concubine* and *Shadows on the Nile*, www.katefurnivall.com

> To create friction in a story it is important to have the characters externalize their conflicts. Writing is an introspective activity and new writers often create passive-aggressive characters who simmer internally before walking out of tense situations. Don't let them! What we want as readers is to see them verbalizing their differences and fighting their corner – this makes friction exciting and brings energy to the narrative.
>
> Norma Curtis, author of *The Last Place You Look* and *Holy Bones and Ava Jones*, www.normacurtis.com

10
IF LANGUAGE BE THE FOOD OF LOVE, READ ON

'O Romeo, Romeo! Wherefore art thou Romeo?'

It has to be one of the most famous phrases of all time. And not just for the romantic notions behind it. There's also the cadence; the rhythm and the sound. Not to mention that heart-felt plea behind it. But there's something else too.

And that's the actual language that lies at the heart of all romantic fiction.

If we analyse the first paragraph, we might notice:

- the repetition of words;
- the question;
- the archaic language.

We can do exactly the same with a modern piece of dialogue. Let's go back to our 'Love Is in the Air' plot. Susie has taken her group of hopeful romantics to Paris. It's her first job and she's feeling very nervous. So much so that she finds herself drinking too much and ending up in bed with a stranger.

Meanwhile, Chris finds himself increasingly drawn to Susie even though Michelle is after him. Back home, Dilly is left standing at the airport, waiting for her date who hasn't turned up.

Right at the beginning of the plot, if you remember, Susie is getting over a painful breakup from an old boyfriend, James. We don't know much about this but maybe now is the time. It might also be a way of showing how language can be used to strengthen a situation,

I'm going to start a scene where Susie has gone back to her bedroom ostensibly to collect the tickets for a play they are all going to see that night. When she is there, her phone rings. I want to make this a telephone conversation because, that way, we can concentrate on the language rather than too many actions.

Here goes.

'Hello?'

Susie knew it was James because his name had flashed up on the screen but she wasn't going to give him the benefit of the satisfaction.

'It's me.'

She felt sweat trickle down her back. 'Who?'

'Susie-Soo, please don't play games with me.'

She was tempted to retort that that was exactly what James had been doing with her for the last nine months.

'Are you still there, Susie?'

She forced herself to stay silent. What was the point in talking? He would only twist her words. Lawyers were good at that.

'I miss you.' His words, usually so self-contained and confident, came tumbling out in a rush. 'I miss your smell, Susie-Soo. I miss the feel of your hair as I run my fingers through it. I miss the touch of your smooth skin. And I miss the taste of your . . .'

'STOP.' The word flew out of her mouth like an electric shock. 'It's no good, James. I've heard it all before – well actually, I haven't. I'm quite impressed by your flowery language. Maybe you kept that for the others before.'

'What others?'

The hurt in his voice was so realistic that if this conversation had taken place last year, when she'd met him, she might have been convinced. But not any more. 'I've seen the light, James. Besides, I've found someone else.'

'Someone else?' His voice rose like a high-pitched bird. 'But it's only been a week since I last saw you.'

'A lot can happen in a week,' she snapped.

'What's his name? I'll kill the bastard.'

The old Susie would have been thrilled by such a demonstration of passion. But somehow, being with her group for a few days had shown her how important it was to find the real thing. Just look at that couple who had hit it off right at the beginning! They'd done nothing but talk non-stop. When she'd left them at the lunch, she'd noticed them holding hands under the table.

'What's his name?' repeated James furiously down the phone.

'Jean Paul,' she whispered. 'I slept with him last night and it was wonderful.'

'You what?'

His indignation virtually spat its way into her ear.

'Susie? Are you there?

'Is that him I can hear?'

'No. It's Chris.'

'You've got two of them on the go?'

'Why not? You did, didn't you?'

And with that, she put down the phone to see what on earth Chris wanted.

If we analyse the above text, we can see that the language:

- had some flowery bits (when James talked about smelling her hair);
- contained a 'love name' (Susie-Soo);
- had various questions, stressing the significance behind the meaning;
- also used silence;
- used contemporary phrases;
- included swearing. (Note: I personally think that less is more when it comes to bad language, otherwise, you lose the impact.)

However, what might happen if we took another look at the scene with the help of a thesaurus . . .

Referring to a Thesaurus

A thesaurus is a vital tool for any writer. It's amazing what words it can come up with that you might have forgotten or simply never known in the first place. Remember how we used to write down new words as children? I suggest you do the same now as writers. In fact, you could create a Love Dictionary for your romantic novel.

Below, I have changed the text of the scene above, using suggestions from my thesaurus (as well as my own imagination).

'Hi, gorgeous.'

James's name flashed up on the screen but Susie was damned if she was going to make it that easy for him.

'Who's calling?' she asked stiffly, even though every bone in her body was crying out 'Yes, yes.'

'Susie-Soo, don't play games with me.'

She was tempted to retort that that was exactly what James had been doing with her for the last nine months.

'Are you still there? Come on, babe. I know you're sore with me but I can explain.'

There was so much she wanted to say to him! So many questions she needed to ask. Like why he couldn't make up his mind about her. And why, just when she'd decided to erase him from her mind, had he popped up again to muddle her life?

Better to stay silent. Besides, what was the point in talking? He would only twist her words. Lawyers were good at that.

'I miss you.' His words, usually so self-contained and confident, came tumbling out in a rush. 'I miss your smell, my fragrant Susie-Soo. I miss the silky feel of your hair as I run my fingers through your cascading curls. I yearn for the touch of your smooth supple skin. And I would walk to the ends of the earth to taste your . . .'

'STOP.' The word flew out of her mouth like an electric shock. 'It's no good, James. I've heard it all before – well actually, I haven't. I'm quite impressed by your flowery language. You've never treated me to it before. Maybe you've been keeping that for the others.'

'What others?'

The hurt in his voice was so realistic that if this conversation had taken place last year, when she'd met him, she might have been convinced. But not any more. 'You've lost your touch, James. At least as far as I'm concerned. I've found someone else.'

'Someone else?' His voice growled with disbelief. 'But it's only been a week since I last saw you.'

'A lot can happen in a week,' she said, realizing as she said it, how true that was.

'What's his name? I'll murder the bastard. Slice off his ears and a lot more besides.'

The old Susie would have been thrilled by such a demonstration of passion. But somehow, being with her group for a few days had shown her how important it was to find the real thing. Just look at that couple who had hit it off right at the beginning! They'd done nothing but talk non-stop; their eyes firmly on the other. When she'd left them at the lunch, she'd noticed them holding hands under the table. Bet they'd be smooching by now.

'What's this bloke's name?' repeated James furiously down the phone.

'Jean Paul.' His name slipped out without her meaning it to.

'Jean Paul? What kind of poncy name is that? Don't tell me you've fallen for a frog? Thought you'd have more sense than that.'

He was so cocky! So self-assured. 'Actually,' she said challengingly, 'I slept with him last night and it was wonderful.'

'You what?'

His indignation almost hurt her ears so that she had to hold the receiver away.

'Susie! Talk to me.'

'Don't you dare shout at me.'

'I'm sorry – but I'm shocked.'

Join the club, she thought to herself.

Suddenly there was a loud knock on the door.

'Susie? It's me. Chris. Sorry to bother you but there's a bit of an emergency downstairs.'

James's voice was laden with suspicion on the other end of the line. 'Who's that I can hear?'

'Just a friend,' she said hurriedly. 'Chris.'

'Chris? Just a friend? So you've got two of them on the go?'

'Why not? You did, didn't you?'

And with that, she cut James off before he could carry on ranting, before opening the door to see what on earth Chris wanted.

Makes a difference, doesn't it? It's definitely worth going back over scenes to substitute more meaningful words and phrases. (See also Chapter 14 on good writing practice and revision.)

Writing Sex Scenes

If you feel embarrassed writing sex-scene dialogue, don't worry: you're not alone.

One way to tackle it is through finding different words for the sex act itself and also bodily parts. This is where the thesaurus can come in handy again. Here are some examples.

Alternatives for 'sex':

- nooky;
- love making;
- mating;
- seduce;

- go to bed;
- bonk;
- get it on;
- become intimate.

Options for 'sexy':

- alluring;
- seductive;
- desirable;
- beddable;
- fanciable.

Equivalents of 'aroused':

- stirred;
- horny;
- randy;
- raunchy.

If you don't like 'penis', try:

- member;
- manhood;
- thing.

For 'breasts', think:

- bosoms;
- voluptuous chest;
- pert appendages.

Oh dear, I'm blushing! Once you've stopped laughing, I'm sure you can think of some more to add to your own list . . .

EXERCISE

Make a list of erotic words, using the thesaurus, and write a paragraph or two – using as many as possible.

I'm going to do the same, below, to get you going. I'm going to fast forward to a scene in the future when Dilly finally gets together with Tom.

> Gently – yet somehow purposefully at the same time – Tom slid his hand under her lacy T-shirt. Dilly held her breath. It had been so long since anyone had done this that she'd forgotten the thrill of skin on skin.
>
> Especially there.
>
> 'May I?' he whispered.
>
> She nodded, hardly believing she was doing so. Fumbling slightly with her pants (why hadn't she worn something prettier instead of that old navy pair?), he eased them down her legs.
>
> Was she meant to do the same to him? And if she did, would it look too forward? What did modern-day protocol demand? For a minute, Dilly wanted to giggle. Nervous laughter to take away the scary, excited thrill that was zapping through her.
>
> Then she gasped out loud as his full weight bore down on her. 'Am I too heavy?' he murmured.
>
> 'No,' she whispered. Automatically, her hand went out to guide him in. It felt right. Natural to have him inside her.
>
> 'I want you,' she breathed, taken aback by her own daring. 'I want you now.'

Can you carry on? If you're stuck or embarrassed, pretend you are someone else, perhaps a character you have seen on television or at the cinema. Just shut the door and let your hands flow across the keyboard.

Getting Tense

This section is all about getting the right tense in your narration. Sometimes, in a romantic scene, it can be effective to switch from the past tense to the present. It makes it more immediate – and it also shows the reader that something important is happening.

Not everyone will agree. Some writers might argue that this is an artificial ruse which takes the reader out of the zone. Personally, I think there's a place for it in certain plots. Here's what the previous scene might look like. You'll notice that I've introduced it with the past tense.

> Gently – yet somehow purposefully at the same time – Tom slid his hand under her lacy T-shirt. Dilly held her breath. It had been so long since anyone had done this that she'd forgotten the thrill of skin on skin.
>
> Especially there.
>
> It launched her into another world. One in which everything was happening right now. Immediately.
>
> 'May I?' he whispers.
>
> She nods, hardly believing she's doing so. Fumbling slightly with her pants (why hadn't she worn something prettier instead of that old navy pair?), he eases them down her legs.
>
> Was she meant to do the same to him? And if she did, would it look too forward? What did modern-day protocol demand? For a minute, Dilly wants to giggle. Nervous laughter to take away the scary, excited thrill that is zapping through her.
>
> Then she gasps out loud as his full weight bears down on her. 'Am I too heavy?' he murmurs.
>
> 'No,' she whispers. Automatically, her hand reaches out to guide him in. It feels right. Natural to have him inside her.
>
> 'I want you,' she breathes, taken aback by her own daring. 'I want you now.'

Makes a difference, doesn't it?

EXERCISE

Take your own partial sex scene and change some of it to the present tense. See what the effect is.

Making Sex Funny

There's something else we could do, too, to liven up the scene: use humorous dialogue. Sex, as I've said briefly before, goes well with humour. I've hinted at this when Tom is fumbling with Dilly's pants. But what if she gets herself in a bit of a twist?

> She nods, hardly believing she's doing so. Fumbling slightly with her pants (why hadn't she worn something prettier instead of that old navy pair?), he eases them down her legs.
>
> No! They were stuck! Twisted somehow round her knee. He was trying hard to disentangle them but it was making it worse. The elastic was cutting into her leg. 'You're cutting into me,' she gasped.
>
> Reaching down, she tried to pull them off but it made it worse. Somehow – heaven knows how – she'd got both legs caught in one hole.
>
> 'I'll switch the light on,' he said in a voice that revealed all too clearly his embarrassment.
>
> No, she wanted to say. Too late. Now he couldn't just see her all flushed in the face. But he could see the rest of her too. Her flabby tummy with its twenty-year-old stretch marks. Her pubic hair which she hadn't had waxed for years. And those awful pants.
>
> But what was he doing now?
>
> 'Nice granny knickers,' said Tom with a grin, twirling them round in the air with his forefinger. 'I mean it. It's a real turn-off for a man if a girl wears those terrible thongs.'

> Then he began to laugh. A lovely warm laugh which made her join in. 'This is the man for me,' she realized as his weight bore down on her. 'This is the one.'

I think this gives the passage a completely different perspective. It also makes us warm towards the characters.

EXERCISE

Try bringing in humorous dialogue to your own sex scene. The following ideas might help:

- something happens to make one of the characters feel silly;
- one of the characters is jokey;
- the sex scene is interrupted (by children or dogs?).

Mixing Sex with Confrontational Language

It's easy to assume that all romantic scenes are happy. In fact, they are a great way to bring in tension. What if your character:

- isn't able to perform?
- doesn't want sex?
- is forced into sex?
- calls out someone else's name?
- or feels disappointed?

EXERCISE

Make a list of words that might relate to the above. Then write as little or as much as you want about one or two of the characters in 'Love Is in the Air', bringing in one of the above themes.

Spicing Up Sex with a Foreign Accent

There's no doubt about it. A strong foreign accent can do wonders for sexy dialogue. Let's go back to Susie's night of unbridled passion with her Parisian stranger. Would it have had the same effect as an unknown man from London? I don't think so.

Warning!

Foreign accents can seem comic if overdone. Do your research carefully. If that means spending an evening with an Italian, just put it down to research . . .

> **HELPFUL HINT**
>
> If you still feel embarrassed about writing sexy dialogue, try:
>
> - a stiff drink beforehand (providing you don't have to do the school run);
> - imagining you're someone else speaking;
> - pretending that you *have* to do this;
> - brainstorming sexy language ideas with friends.

Using Internal Thought

Using internal thought is particularly useful in romantic fiction. It's a device used to show how people think inside their heads. Simply imagine what they are saying to themselves without actually speaking out loud. You don't need speech marks.

> I've got to give Tom a chance, Dilly told herself as she washed up the last glass of the evening. He'll never be another John but then again, do I want him to be?

It gets into her character, doesn't it?

EXERCISE

Write some internal thoughts from the point of view of Barry, who would like to ask out Michelle in 'Love Is in the Air'. You might drop in clues about why he is as he is. If you find this difficult, pretend you are Barry. Get up and walk round the room. Imagine you are in a hotel, thinking about Michelle and wondering how you can get her to like you. Or do the same thing from Michelle's point of view.

SUMMING UP

- Use your thesaurus.
- Sexy dialogue can be funny/sad/confrontational.
- The language should push the plot along.
- Don't be embarrassed by language: why not call a spade a spade?
- Use dialogue in real life/films, etc. for inspiration.

EXPERT TIPS

Watch out for trying to reveal back-story through dialogue, without having created a suitable dialogue partner. The heroine can plausibly say to a long-lost friend, 'Didn't you hear? My parents disappeared five years ago on the road between Winchester and London.'

She can't say to her brother, 'As you know, our parents were . . .'

Or even, 'Don't you remember that our parents . . .' The other person would surely remember that!

Jo Beverley

Try to have at least a third of your writing as dialogue. It makes the narrative flow, deepens characterization and relationships, sets the tone of the novel. Dialogue should sound natural but to do this you have to prune it. Cut out superfluous words such as 'well' or 'just'. Use appropriate language for your characters. For example, young men don't say 'lovely'. Cut the 'he said/she said' as much as you can. You should be able to tell who is speaking by the language they are using and by their actions.

Sophie Duffy

The one piece of advice I would give to those writing dialogue is to use 'beats', which are movements of characters while speaking, which forward the action.

So, instead of:

'I love you,' he said.

She said, 'No, you mustn't.'

You write:

He touched her hand. 'I love you.'

'No, you mustn't.' She moved away.

Veronica Heley, author of *False Charity*, *Eden Hall* and *Murder at the Altar*, www.veronicaheley.com

Make your hero a human, but not a superhero. Throw in a few flaws with an endearing trait or two to make him more attractive. Avoid clichés. Give him a secret that the heroine longs to discover. Let him stride arrogantly across the page if you will, but show his unsung charitable side as well. Reveal his worth by cranking up the pressure on him when he has to make choices. Never let him take the easy way out unless he has a unique reason for doing so.

Yves Potter, novelist and short-story writer, www.yves-potter.com

11
ESTABLISHING SETTINGS AND USING THE SENSES

Where is your romantic novel taking place? In the bedroom? On the park bench? On the other end of a phone? A five-star hotel in the Maldives? A one-bedroom flat on the wrong side of town? A railway station or on Eurostar?

Wherever it is, the reader needs to be able to picture it. As the writer, it's your job to create that scene. It's also your challenge to magic up the smells and colours and noises that are part of the setting. Exciting!

Creating a 'Settings Folder'

I don't know about you but I'm a great Sunday adventurer. One of my favourite leisure-time activities is to browse through the travel supplements and declare to my nearest and dearest that I've always wanted to ride in the Rockies or take a train from Vancouver to Toronto or visit my cousin in Vanuatu.

But if I can't, there's nothing to stop my characters. In fact, maybe I should have made Susie take her singles group to Paris on Eurostar, instead of on a plane. They could all meet at the champagne bar in St Pancras! Michelle and Barry would be quaffing down a glass of champagne and Dilly would be behind the bar. Naturally I'd have to do some research as I have to confess that I've never been to the bar myself. Fortunately, however, I do happen to have a picture of it, taken from a glossy magazine and stored safely in a large folder marked 'Settings'.

Over the years, I've found this invaluable. We all think we can describe a holiday scene. All we have to do is think back to that summer in Spain or Greece and describe the clammy heat or the mouth-watering ice cream or the line of lounger chairs by the pool. But it's the small details we might forget, like the pink and yellow paper parasol in the cocktail or the view over the bay with the hills behind you, which bring the place alive. That's where pictures can come in so handy. They are right in front of you. You can see how that cloud is unfurling in an S-shape in the sky. You notice the exact shade of the sea (aquamarine instead of simply blue). And you take note, as a writer, of the way the model is sitting very close to the man next to her on the beach. Sometimes people go overboard with affection when they are actually trying to hide something . . . How interesting that the setting can give you ideas for plot too!

Travel ads and brochures are great for your Settings Folder. But so too are postcards and photographs. If you're like me, you probably have lots of photos on your phone or computer. Print them out and add them to your folder.

I'm lucky enough to have travelled to quite a few places, partly through work. (I particularly adore Italy where I am a regular speaker at the Matera Women's Fiction Festival – great for contacts! See Useful Contacts at the end of this book.)

Naturally I take photographs but I also buy postcards and, if I can, a print to remind me of each trip. In my hall, I have a small oil painting from a trip to France with my cousin one summer. Even as I look at it now, I am reminded of the way that those purple flowers tumbled down the dry-stone walls and of that ornate garden arch leading into a private garden. This could be a perfect setting for one of my characters in 'Love Is in the Air'. After all, there's nothing to stop it from belonging to the handsome French stranger (Jean Paul) when he whisks Susie off to his family home just outside Paris at the end of the novel. Then again, Susie might decide to choose someone else. Like Chris . . . That might mean a different setting: London, perhaps, or maybe Milton Keynes. The choice is yours.

Some continental houses can work in different scenes or places. During my last trip to Matera, I bought an Italian print from a street artist. It shows a pretty courtyard square with five-storey houses and beautiful windows with ornate balconies. When I look at it, it reminds me of a place in France I once knew. Simply having it in front of me helps me to recall the way the balustrade curved and the smell of coffee from the shop below. There's nothing like having a picture right in front of you to give you ideas for place. This in turn can lead to new plot twists. Come to think of it, I might transport my singles group to an old-fashioned hotel in Paris. Chris and Susie (or maybe Michelle) might engage in a heated conversation on the balcony and . . . well, almost anything could happen. One of them might fall over or almost fall. Romantic novels can – and should, in my view – have dark elements (see Chapter 4 on plot).

If you visited my study, you would find it lined with bookshelves and also postcards because I always buy one wherever I go (even if it's quite local). I've got the Bonchurch Pond from the Isle of Wight, where I used to spend my childhood summers. There's a wrinkled old woman in traditional Brittany dress, knocking back a glass of absinthe. There's a David Hockney model, sitting in her underwear (from an exhibition I went to). And there's a postcard from Spain, showing a town hall that looks more like a palace. I haven't used all of them yet in my novels or short stories, but I'm certain that one day they will each find a home.

Home brochures can also be great for settings. I have sub-divisions within my folder: travel; kitchens; bedrooms; sitting rooms; gardens. They're perfect for describing the exact shade of quarry tile in your heroine's kitchen or the cover of the duvet on her bed or the type of shower she shares with the hero or the love bench at the bottom of her garden.

HELPFUL HINT

Laminate your pictures to stop them from getting creased. You can buy laminating machines quite cheaply.

Using a Notebook

It's a family tradition that whenever I travel, I keep a diary. But it's no ordinary diary. Although I record what I (or we) did, I concentrate on settings. I take care to describe the colours of the land or the way the hills rise sharply or the crowded airport train.

I also paint a bit so I use a notebook that I can sketch in. Sometimes I take a travel paint sheet with little blobs of paint instead of tubes. Even if you don't think you can draw, you might surprise yourself. My recent sketches from a trip to Vietnam to visit my daughter and son-in-law came in very useful when I was writing my eighth novel.

Alternatively, you could stick photographs or postcards into your travel notebook. This way it acts not just as a portable 'memory pad' but also as a research tool for describing settings in your work.

EXERCISE

Start compiling a Settings Folder. Use:

- photographs;
- postcards;
- magazine/newspaper cuttings;
- travel articles.

Using Your Senses

It's easy to forget, when writing, that setting isn't just a matter of recording what places look like. It's bringing in the senses too.

Sometimes, I will add the following to Post-it notes, which I then stick on certain pictures:

- Smell
- Colour
- Noise
- Taste

- Texture
- What happened there?

It's a good exercise to help you focus on small details that you might otherwise forget. Recently, my husband and I visited Ibiza (we were the only ones at the airport over forty!). It wasn't until I looked at the photographs the other day that I remembered the walk down the cliffs to the bay and the feel under my feet of tree roots that climbed out of the ground like old men's fingers. I wouldn't have thought of that last sentence if it hadn't been for the picture that prompted me. I also remember:

- bending down to smell the lavender bushes;
- the colour of the early morning sun as it rose over the pool;
- the unpunctured silence until everyone else got up (I love being an early riser – you see so much);
- the chatter in the evening bars;
- the taste of the grilled sardines at lunchtime (mouth-watering!);
- the feel of the soft duvet at night, along with pillows to sink into;
- why we were there (that's another story – although it wasn't to go clubbing!).

HELPFUL HINT

- If you find it hard to describe smells, imagine what they reminded you of. Then embellish it with your imagination. For instance:

'His pine aftershave took me straight back to my dad, twenty years ago. It was the last time I saw him.'

or

'The smell of the room reminded me of something. What was it? Of course! Beeswax. Not the type from a spray but the old-fashioned variety which came out in big clumps unless you were careful. That's exactly how I stained my grandmother's carpet and, in so doing, met the man I would marry.'

- Collect perfume samples/aftershave from department stores or magazines. Use them to describe what your heroine or hero smells of.
- Listen to some romantic music and then write whatever comes into your head. Also treat yourself to a naughty 'food' treat like a square of chocolate and do the same. You'll be surprised at how it can change your writing!

EXERCISE

Go back to your Settings Folder. Attach Post-It notes to each picture describing the smells/noises/colours/textures that you might find if you were really there.

Taking a Straw Poll for Settings

Still stuck for settings? Ask your friends and family to describe places with a romantic significance. Here are some of mine:

- the Lake District, where my second husband proposed. I'll never forget the trees by the water that reminded me of Arthur Ransome's drawings;
- a (tasteful) burlesque club where a friend's third husband took her on their first date!
- a favourite pub of mine when I was in my twenties – that then became sullied in my memory for reasons too personal to mention (settings can be dark too);
- a flight to New York where a friend of mine met a stranger and married him.

EXERCISE

Make a list of settings that have been important in your own or your friends' life and describe them. Think about how they might fit into your novel.

Warning!

It's hard to describe a specific place unless you've been there. I had a student who wanted to set her novel in a pole-dancing club. However, she'd never actually visited one. I suggested she did some research. The result? A much more authentic piece of writing – not just because of the character but because of the way she described the actual place.

Putting it into Practice!

Let's go back to 'our' novel, 'Love Is in the Air'. I'm going to imagine that Susie has taken her group on a walk along the Seine. Now I have to confess here that I haven't been to Paris for a couple of years and my memories of the Seine are a little hazy. However, I'm going to 'brainstorm' what I do recall:

- booksellers along the side, selling books from booths;
- families walking;
- river banks;
- restaurants at the side;
- near the Louvre;
- cold;
- rainy;
- buying a delicious cup of hot chocolate from a stall.

That will do for now, but I'm also going to look at some photographs. There's a couple walking past, arm in arm. I remember them because, soon afterwards, she slipped on a stone and almost fell in the river. Come to think of it, a slippery cobbled pavement might come in useful.

Here goes:

Susie tried to hurry along to keep an eye on her group. It wasn't easy, especially with this late afternoon mist which made it difficult to see ahead and cloyed at the back of her throat. Paris was all very well in the sunshine but it was a different animal in the winter where the sun was a pale apricot imitation of its June cousin. Had it really only been six months since she'd been here with James? They'd picnicked by the side of the Seine, she recalled and someone had been playing the violin from one of the houses nearby. The strain had reached them and James began to sing to her. But then his ex had rung him on his mobile and he became cool and distant.

No. She mustn't think about that now. Besides she had a job to do. Where was everyone? Ah, there was Laura, browsing through the bookstall at the side with its array of battered paperbacks. The chap in charge was wearing a French beret and smoking a Gauloises. The smell of the cigarette drifted out towards her, making her want to sneeze.

Meanwhile Barry was trying to chat up Michelle who was more interested in the menu displayed by a small restaurant just before the bridge. That might be a good place for a break later on, thought Susie. It looked rather nice with those picture-frame windows and jolly red and yellow canopy outside. She was just about to inspect the menu prices when she heard a shout.

'Careful,' called out someone.

Oh dear, it looked as though an argument had broken out between Barry (always so argumentative!) and a French jogger. 'Look where you're going,' shouted Barry.

The Frenchman, wearing black Lycra bottoms, was putting both hands on his waist and gabbling rapidly in French. Susie couldn't catch everything he said but it didn't sound friendly. Running up, she tried to sort out the situation.

'I'm sure my colleague didn't mean to be rude,' she started to say in French but then, to her horror, she slipped on one of the wet cobbled stones.

'Help,' she called out, clutching the Frenchman. But his Lycra shorts were too slippery to hang on to. 'I'm falling . . .'

Can you take over? Try to add as much colour, noise, smell and taste as you can.

SUMMING UP

The setting is crucial to the story. It not only helps the reader picture the place but also gives you ideas for the plot.

- Include noise/colour/smell/touch/all senses.
- Use travel magazines/photographs/travel diaries.
- Start a Settings File.
- Talk to friends about settings.

EXPERT TIPS

Smells are crucial to a place. When you walk into a hotel, you might catch the whiff of cigarette smoke or air freshener. Newly washed cotton sheets are another one. I'm also a great fan of Google Earth which will take you to any place in the world. I once had a harbour scene in a place I was writing about and then found there wasn't a harbour there! Luckily I changed it in time.

Catherine Jones, previous chair of the Romantic Novelists' Association; author (as Fiona Field) of *Soldiers' Wives*

Creating a strong sense of time and place involves more than just describing setting. It must be an intrinsic part of the story, woven into the texture of the novel so that it couldn't take place anywhere else. Never write great chunks of unnecessary description that the reader will simply skim over. The secret is in the detail. But provide a good reason for putting in the detail by viewing it through your heroine's eyes, her inner thoughts, actions or dialogue. The emotion and mood of a person is often closely linked with where he or she lives, or was born, or where their ancestors lived. We are what our parents made us but we are also influenced by where we live. Every region or country has its own intrinsic characteristics. Show what effect the psychology of place has upon your heroine. What is her relationship with the place? Build your world, real or imagined, but do it through your characters, one in which they must live and survive.

Freda Lightfoot, author of numerous novels including *Lady of Passion* and *Lakeland Lily*, www.fredalightfoot.co.uk

The best settings for romantic novels are either invisible or integral. By invisible, I mean that it may not matter in which village or town the action takes place, but none of the background details should jar on the reader and pull them out of the story. By integral, I mean that the story would not be the same if written against any other background. A romantic novel set on a cruise ship, for example, will use elements of shipboard life as part of the plot and be very different from one set in a horse-racing stable. In all cases, the most successful novels are ones where the created world has been crafted with just as much care as the love story.

Jan Jones, author of numerous novels including *The Jigsaw Puzzle*, winner of the Joan Hessayon Award 2005, http://jan-jones.blogspot.co.uk

I'm an Italian writer of mostly contemporary romantic comedies. It's a lot of fun writing them. Yes! Romance is a good therapy in my opinion, both for readers and writers. Though my bibliography is still quite short, I always try in my novels to pay a lot of attention to the setting, the secondary characters and the dialogues: I love small villages, weird and funny characters (acting like a whole), witty (as much as I can) dialogues. I think that working on these three points can personalize my writing and make it strongly recognizable by the reader. It's important to make your books stand out. Every story has already been written in the romance genre. You can write about dukes, vampires, sexy detectives or Navy SEALs. But you still need something else, beyond the happy ending, to offer them: your personal style.

To begin with, I work on the setting. I try to imagine it, to design it precisely in my mind. At the moment, I'm working on a small island in the Hebrides. Believe me, just to imagine it, to spot the places where the story will develop, is a lot of fun. In this, Google helps a lot. Setting then helps me create character. I like to think of the community as a character of their own. Once I have established location and community, my characters begin to take form. I draft a hero (my heroes are always dead-stunning, at least for now) and a heroine (usually an Italian woman far from home). I imagine the way they look, think and react to different circumstances, and at the end of this process I work on their story and on the inevitable conflict growing between them.

Viviana Giorgi, author of *Tutta Colpa del Vento* and *Alta Marea a Cape Love*, www.vivianagiorgi.it

12

MAKING ROMANCE FUNNY

Love should make you laugh as well as cry. Otherwise, it can all get too heavy. Besides, as we saw in the chapter on dialogue, humour can be very sexy in a man or a woman.

The funny thing about humour is that the more you try to be funny, the harder it can be. But don't panic! Here are some ideas on how to do it.

Making a List of Funny Things

Make a list of all the funny things that have happened in your love life – and to your friends – such as:

- Dress strap broke during date.
- Telling someone how you feel about them on the phone – only to find that the reception failed a few minutes earlier.
- Borrowing an aunt's mobile phone and sending erotic text messages to her boyfriend (I'm ashamed to admit that my children did this to my sister but, reader, she married him).
- Not recognizing your first love when he comes up to say hello at a party, thirty years on.
- Spilling a glass of wine during the first date.

How could these suggestions or items on your own list fit into our novel 'Love Is in the Air'? Maybe one of the girls in the group turns out to be Chris's very first girlfriend. After all, people change. He might not recognize her. I used a similar device in my new Janey Fraser novel, *After the Honeymoon*, when the woman running a honeymoon hotel recognizes one of the guests as the father of her child . . .

Making Your Characters Funny

Most humour in romantic fiction is either character driven or plot driven. I'm going to start with some tips on how make your characters funny.

Establishing eccentricity

I love characters who are a little off-the-wall. You can do so much with them. They do odd things like:

- wearing clashing colours;
- talking too fast without listening to the other person;
- always fussing;
- thinking they're attractive but they aren't;
- being an interfering parent/sister/friend;
- doing inappropriate things;
- having strange habits;
- slapstick behaviour;
- embarrassing others;
- being very bossy;
- having jobs that make us laugh for some reason, e.g. funeral director/extras in steamy scenes (remember that couple who simulated sex in *Love Actually* while conducting a conversation about the traffic?).

So how could this work with our novel? I bet we could find some odd habits in a group of people. I once knew someone who was only able to make a decision if they tossed a coin first. Perhaps we could bring in a rather nervous, anxious single who does this. Maybe one of the others could befriend her and help her realize, by the end of the week, that she can make her own decisions. This might involve bitter-sweet humour.

I'm going to call her Laura and set the scene on the Metro. Perhaps she and a man called Matt (one of the older singles) have become separated from the others.

'Which way should we go?' asked Laura nervously.

Matt was studying the Metro map. He was older than her, she observed. Very quiet and steady. Completely different from anyone she'd ever dated before. Not of course that she saw him as boyfriend material. He was just nice to be with, that's all.

He touched her elbow gently. For some reason, it sent little shockwaves up her. 'I reckon it's this way.'

Laura felt the old familiar wave of panic rising. She needed to ask the coin in her pocket but she couldn't do that in front of Matt. He might think she was weird. Just like all the other men she'd known in her life. 'I've . . . I've just got to do something.' She turned her back, reaching for the coin. Maybe she could flip it in her hand, without him noticing.

'You don't have to do that, you know.'

'Do what?'

'Flip a coin. You can just make a decision. If it's wrong, it's wrong. But the important thing is that you'll be free.'

Laura heard her voice coming out in a scared squeal. 'You don't know what you're talking about.'

Matt's eyes grew misty. 'I do actually. I used to need a coin too. But then I learned to live without it.'

Laura gave him an odd look. Was he trying to make her feel better like the doctor at the clinic who pretended to sympathize but then wrote bad things down on her notes. 'How did you stop?'

Matt smiled. 'I dropped it by accident. It was when I walking along a street and it just fell down a drain. I didn't have any other coins on me at the time so I took it as a sign.'

Laura wasn't sure she believed him. 'What decision were you trying to make?'

'Whether to cross the road or not.'

She understood that.

'So what did you do?'

'I crossed it.'

Laura held her breath. 'And?'

'And I got knocked over.'

'No!'

'Honestly. I didn't get hurt. Not badly. Just a few scratches.'

'So that proves my point!' she said triumphantly. 'If you'd flicked the coin, it wouldn't have let you.'

Matthew gave another slow smile. 'How do you know?'

'I just do.'

She grabbed the coin determinedly. 'Well I'm going to toss this. If it's heads, I'm going this way. If it's tails, the other.'

As she spoke, there was the sound of a train approaching. Quick! She needed to make up her mind. The coin flew into the air. Catch it, said that voice inside her that wouldn't go away. Catch it.

She tried but it spun and twirled in the air. Hitting the platform with a thud, it flew onto the track.

'Now look what you made me do!' called out Laura. 'Don't laugh. It's not funny.'

Then something really odd happened. The more Matt laughed, the more Laura wanted to laugh. And the more she tried to stop, the harder it became.

The train had stopped by now. Suddenly Laura became aware of a large warm hand taking hers. 'I reckon we ought to go with this,' said Matt steadily. 'Is that all right with you?'

Goodness. I'm not quite sure where that came from. It wasn't hysterically funny by any account. It was more of a soft, sad humour with a positive outlook. But it wouldn't have worked without the characters behaving as they did.

Telling Jokes

I don't know about you but I have two or three friends who stand out because they're always telling jokes. Some of them are truly awful jokes but they still make us laugh.

When you have a large cast of characters, as in 'Love Is in the Air', it's vital to make them stand out from each other. Making them tell jokes is one way of doing it. I've got a feeling that Dilly's new man does this. It would be a way of making her fall in love with him.

EXERCISE

Write a scene where Tom includes jokes in his dialogue.

Misusing Words

This is another way of injecting humour into your romantic fiction. It could work particularly well in Paris, the setting for our 'Love Is in the Air' book. Let's imagine there's a man called Gary who is one of the minor characters. He likes to show off his French. When Laura and Matt meet up with the others, they find them at a table, ordering lunch.

> Gary, as usual, was in full flight, spouting away in French to the waitress. Suddenly, she went bright red and slapped him on the cheek.
>
> 'What did you do that for?' gasped Gary. 'I was only asking if you could bring another bottle of wine.'
>
> 'Actually,' said Matt quietly, 'I think you'll find you asked her if she'd like to do something rather intimate with you.'
>
> 'That's impossible!'
>
> Matt pointed to the small plastic device in Gary's hand. 'Maybe you pressed the wrong button on that "How to Teach Yourself French" app.'

Characters might also misuse words on purpose or they might pronounce them incorrectly. I have a friend who refers to 'lingerie' as 'linger-ee'.

EXERCISE

Try making a list of your own examples of misused or incorrectly pronounced words and then think of a character who might use them. You could choose someone from 'Love Is in the Air' or a story that you're working on yourself.

Introducing Someone Who Plays the Fool

We all know someone who enjoys playing the fool and doesn't mind making an idiot of themselves. The beauty of a character like this is that they are usually very shy deep down. Perhaps they are hiding a secret. I suspect that this applies to Dilly. She's desperate to put the past behind her so she is always laughing and smiling. But behind that bright exterior is heartbreak. She needs help in moving on.

> 'Come on! You don't really mean I'm attractive.' Dilly sucked in her cheeks in an exaggerated fashion. 'Maybe if I was two stone lighter.' She perched on the edge of the bar stool. 'Or if I . . .'
>
> 'Careful,' called out Tom.
>
> Too late. She'd gone flying – straight onto the floor. Exactly what she'd intended. Anything to put an end to a conversation which was becoming far too serious for her liking.

Quite poignant, isn't it? It moves the plot along and it tells us something about Dilly's character. At first, we think she's just taken a tumble. Then we realize she'd actually intended to do that. She's stronger than we first thought and we like her all the more for it.

Using Children to Introduce Humour

Children's humour can also play a part in romantic fiction. I've found that dialogue is the best way to make this work: it puts the reader in the scene.

Let's imagine that a small boy at Arrivals sees Susie and Chris kiss for the first time.

'Look at that man, Mummy! He's trying to eat that woman!'

When my children were younger, I had a pair of guests to stay who had recently become an item. 'You can't put them in the same bedroom,' gasped my daughter. 'They're not married.'

That led to a bit of explaining, I can tell you . . .

Introducing Pets to Get a Laugh

I recently heard of someone who got a new girlfriend. The only problem was that he didn't introduce her to the dog. On their first evening together, the dog jumped up on the bed as usual – only to find a naked girlfriend. Both 'rivals' regarded each other with total horror.

P.S. The girl won.

EXERCISE

Make a list of funny things that children have said about love.

You'll Never Guess What Happened . . .

Some of the best humour in romantic fiction comes from the plot itself. Here are some ways of doing it:

- coincidences;
- mistiming;
- drunkenness – making a character say or do something that they shouldn't;
- misunderstandings;
- an outsider at a party wrongly presumes that one of the guests is married to someone else.

Now let's see how we can weave this idea into our novel. Suppose Susie gets a message from the hotel receptionist to say that her 'friend' is on his way to her room. She thinks it's Jean Paul.

> How embarrassing! What was she going to say? Susie wrapped a towel around her – there was no time to dress after her shower – and opened the door just a crack. 'About last night,' she began. 'I want you to know that I don't normally go to bed with someone without knowing them . . .'
>
> Then she stopped. In front of her was not just one surprised face. But two.
>
> 'James,' she gasped. 'What are you doing here?' Then she took in the other visitor. 'Mum?'

Making the Reader Part of the Scene

Somehow, humorous scenes are never particularly funny when the author recounts them, rather than putting the reader into the scene.

Let's take the following passage.

> Chris was so drunk that he started telling Susie exactly how he felt about her. She wasn't impressed.

This is telling the reader what happened. It's all right, I suppose. It does what it's meant to do in explaining what happened. But there's no emotion. Nor do we feel we are there on the stage with our characters. Instead, we're far back in the theatre; feeling very distant.

However, it all changes if we put in some dialogue.

> 'I shnow we shaven't known each other very shlong,' he began, draping his arm around her shoulders. 'But I shfeel we've known each shother for ever.'
>
> Susie stepped back. 'You're drunk, Chris. Know that? Whoops. Be careful!'

Too late. He'd fallen back into the table, knocking a large bottle of wine all over Michelle. 'It doesn't matter,' she gabbled. 'If Susie's not interested in you, Chris, I am!'

The dialogue works much better, don't you think? It also adds to Michelle's character. She's gone off Barry (why?). Now she is desperate to get together with Chris and doesn't mind showing it. As a reader, we cringe for her: partly because we probably know someone like that. It all helps to engage the reader with our characters.

Integrating Humour into the Structure of the Novel

One of the trademarks in my Janey Fraser books is to have a funny anecdote or saying at the beginning of each chapter. In *Happy Families*, I made up limericks. Here's an example:

> There was a young mum who lived in a shoe –
> Though it felt, at times, just like a zoo.
> There were kids always fighting
> Or kicking and biting.
> Oh what, oh what, should she do?

In *After the Honeymoon*, I had lots of funny facts about honeymoons as well as amusing real-life stories. Here's an example.

> 'We bumped into my old boss at the airport on our way to our honeymoon. I decided not to tell my new husband we used to date.'
>
> Sylvia, about to celebrate her silver wedding

We could do the same with 'Love Is in the Air'. How about starting each chapter with a list of French phrases that might come in handy for a single girl looking for love in Paris? We could begin with some English phrases and then Google them to find the French equivalent. Here are some examples:

Do you come here often? *Venez-vous ici souvent?*
Thanks but no thanks. *Merci mais non merci.*

Not So Funny Ha Ha

Not everyone shares the same sense of humour as you – or me. It's worth bearing that in mind when writing your funny scenes. Ask yourself if your scene might:

- hurt someone;
- be recognized by someone if you've taken it from real life.

EXERCISES

- Take one of the characters in 'Love Is in the Air' and write as much or as little about them. Try to make them funny.
- Write a scene for 'Love Is in the Air' that centres on an amusing plot incident.

SUMMING UP

- Humour comes in all shapes and forms. It's not always laugh-out-loud humour. It can be poignant too.
- Humour usually comes from character or plot or both.
- It's usually more effective to make the reader see the scene through dialogue, rather than just telling them what happened.
- Humour can be very personal. You might think something is funny - but someone else might find it offensive.

EXPERT TIPS

To me, there seem to be two kinds of romantic comedy. One is the slapstick type, where a series of often cringe-making catastrophes of a Bridget Jones nature befall the hapless heroine, and excellent authors in this genre include Sophie Kinsella and Jane Costello. The other kind is where the gentle humour arises from the characters themselves as they deal with what everyday life throws at them.

I write the latter sort and I've never tried to create a funny novel: I just write. You can't force humour into a book if it isn't in you, which is where my typically Lancashire dark sense of humour in adversity comes in: it runs through my books like the letters through a stick of Blackpool rock, an integral part of it.

So I would say to aspiring writers that you should look at the kind of novels you enjoy and find funny before you begin writing your own, and decide which kind suits you best, because if the humour arises naturally, then you could be on to a winner!

Trisha Ashley, author of several novels including *Every Woman for Herself* and *Finding Mr Rochester*, www.trishaashley.com

Humour in a novel (or a short story for that matter) is not a string of one-liners, although we could have a character who delivers them as part of his character. Neither should humour be overly sarcastic unless, of course, it is the baddy issuing the put-downs. If you develop a character who has a funny turn of phrase (I developed a secondary character who tries to use big words but mispronounces them, often to comic effect) then keep up the momentum – don't drop it around chapter six as your novel develops.

Linda Mitchelmore

> It's a fine line. Trying to be screechingly funny on every page is never going to work. One way of getting a chuckle out of your readers is to make your characters human – let them suffer the same everyday disasters we all do, even if they are tall, dark, handsome, even tempered and rich.
>
> Gina Rossi

13
USING TRAGEDY IN YOUR NOVEL

Love hurts. There's no denying that, either in life or fiction. But it can also make you stronger as a person – and it can give teeth to a romantic novel. Many writers call this 'upping the ante'. In other words, adding a really big problem to create extra tension.

How Do You Start?

Tragedy can also come in all shapes and forms. It might be:

- death;
- missing person;
- accident;
- severe illness;
- paralysis.

But it could also be something slightly different such as:

- divorce;
- character running away;
- prison;
- infidelity.

Most writers draw inspiration from their own lives or those of others. Here are some examples to kick you off:

- parent with dementia;
- multiple miscarriages;
- fall down staircase;
- lost while windsurfing;
- suicide;
- family divided when a brother fell in love with his sister-in-law.

Can you add to this list? If you're stuck, turn to the local paper – always a great source for ideas.

Less is more

Obviously you don't want to pile on the tragedy or else you're going to have a misery memoir on your hands. It will also feel unrealistic if you have too many awful things going on. The trick is to pick something that works well with your characters and the plot.

In 'Love Is in the Air', our characters are wandering round Paris in search of love and the occasional tourist site. Do you remember Matt? He's the quiet, steady man who is with Laura. We like him and we have hopes for him, but supposing something happened to Matt? What if he had an asthma attack and dropped down dead, just as he's telling Laura that he has feelings for her?

My first thought is that it would definitely pull the reader up. But I've got a hunch that it might be a bit too much. If someone dies during a group outing like this, it would put a dampener on everything – to put it mildly. It might even result in the group going home.

My feeling is that we should write a scene where Matt has an asthma attack and make the reader think he has died, through Laura's speech.

> 'Quickly, someone! *Au secours*! My friend is dying. He's not breathing any more.'

Then, in the next chapter, we can show him in intensive care in hospital with a devoted Laura at his side.

If you feel this is copping out of it, you could indeed kill Matt off. However, I would suggest this comes towards the end when they are all about to head home anyway. That would take away the problem about what to do with the group who will obviously be too upset to enjoy themselves any more.

Another thought that has just occurred to me (funny how ideas just pop into your head!) is that Matt is terminally ill. This in fact is why he has come on a singles holiday. He wants to have one last fling. But now, too late, he realizes that he has indeed fallen in love. He is now going to have to break Laura's heart, unless he breaks it off with her without telling her why. On the other hand, his death might show Laura that she is lovable. I can just hear her saying, 'Better to have loved and lost than never loved at all.' Matt might also leave her some money which will help her start her own 'Single Again' retreat.

It's certainly food for thought.

Tragic Timing

Tragedy can be a great way to move the plot forward but only if it comes at the right time. If you introduce the reader to a character and encourage them to form a bond, they're going to feel quite cheated if you kill them off in Chapter 2 or 3. The reader will have invested time and energy into that person and suddenly they're no longer there. Unless, of course, you then go back in time and tell the story up to that character's death and then beyond. I rather like plots like that. You know what's going to happen – up to a point – but you want to know what happens afterwards.

Beware of bringing a character to a tragic end before the reader has a chance to get to grips with them. It may not have as much impact. For example, if Matt had a fatal asthma attack at the airport, just before the group sets off, you may well lose the opportunity to create some angst. That's because you haven't allowed your reader enough time to care for him. Therefore the reader won't grieve as much as they would if quiet, caring, well-meaning Matt had been around for most of the novel.

It's also worth bearing the 'surprise' element in mind. When I'm writing romantic fiction, I try to shock the reader every now and then with a piece of bad news or a terrible event. For instance, in *The Au Pair*, one of my Janey Fraser romantic novels, Marie-France is a French girl who has come to England in search of her father.

Her own mother, Collette, had been an au pair twenty years earlier in England and had got pregnant by a 'John Smith'. It turns out, as you'll see, that the real father may have died. I like to think that this took the story to another level and gave it more depth after some funny scenes.

Here's an excerpt:

> Marie-France shot her mother an accusing glare. 'So much for John Smith!' she hissed in French. 'Do you know how much time I wasted?'
>
> 'I lied, cherie.' Her mother shrugged as though this was perfectly acceptable.
>
> Jilly's mother snorted. 'So she still hasn't learned to tell the truth. And before you say things you might regret, Collette, you might recall that my French is pretty good.'
>
> 'And I,' flashed back Maman, 'understand more English than you might think even if I do not speak perfect!'
>
> 'Please, both of you!' cut in Hugh. 'Let me continue. Angela had two sons. The older one, from her first marriage, was called Adam who was a great friend of Jeremy's.'
>
> Was? Instinctively, Marie-France's skin began to prickle.
>
> 'Tragically,' continued Jilly's father, 'Adam died from an asthma attack at twenty-three. He was allergic to all kinds of things.'
>
> 'Mon dieu,' said her mother, quietly crossing herself. Marie-France's head was spinning. Adam was allergic? To all kinds of things? Including dogs, perhaps?
>
> The older man was looking directly at her now. 'When the boys were only sixteen, Collette was babysitting Adam's younger brother in Corrywood. Jeremy was staying with them during the summer holidays and we were due to collect him that night. But when we arrived, we found him and Collette in, let's say, a "compromising position" upstairs.'

'Dad!' Jeremy was puce red.

'Let me continue, son. But it transpired that Collette had also been intimate with Adam too.'

'Non!' Marie-France whipped round to face her mother. She still couldn't get used to the change in her appearance which made all this seem even more surreal as though it was happening to someone else. 'Please tell me this is not true?'

'They were just silly boys, experimenting,' added Angela quickly. She smoothed down her hair nervously. 'I wish now that we hadn't made such a fuss about it. In fact, we wouldn't have done if . . .'

Her voice tailed away but it was too late. 'If my mother hadn't got pregnant with me, you mean! That's what happened, wasn't it?'

Collette nodded slowly.

'A baby?' Jeremy gasped. 'You had a baby?'

'We kept it from you, son,' intercepted Hugh smoothly. 'No point in ruining your life. Or Adam's either.' He sighed. 'At least that's what we thought at the time. Anyway, when this girl wrote to us from France about her pregnancy, she admitted she didn't know which one of you was the father. For all we know, it could have been a third person!'

'Non!' Collette's eyes were flashing. 'I am no slut.'

Jilly's mother snorted. 'Really?'

'We paid her a sum of money every month.' Angela took over in a subdued voice. 'It wasn't easy for us because we weren't as well off as Sheila and Hugh. But the worst bit was that it destroyed our friendship. Sheila said I should have somehow stopped Collette from seducing a pair of teenagers under my roof.'

She threw Hugh a grateful glance. 'Luckily not everyone blamed me.'

Jeremy, pink faced, cut in. 'She didn't seduce us. We . . . we were just as willing.' He looked at Collette now as though seeing her for the first time. 'She was a real stunner and, well, we'd never been that close to a girl like that before.'

Collette pouted. 'So you do not think I am good looking now?'

'Of course but . . .'

'Please!' Jilly made to cover her ears. 'I don't want to hear any more.'

'But you must!' thundered Collette. 'You are all forgetting what happened to me! My parents, they said they would have nothing to do with me. I had to bring up my daughter on my own.' She pointed at Jilly's mother. 'That woman, she returned the pictures I send of you as a baby. Didn't even want to know your name. Not like Angela. She was much more gentille.'

She swayed as though she was going to faint and Marie-France held onto her arm. 'I had to move into a small village where no one else knew me. At first I pretend I am a widow but then the rumours started. After that, many people, they would not talk to me. And their children, they would not play with my daughter.'

She gave Marie-France a scared look. 'I am sorry, cherie. You must be so ashamed of your mother.'

Yes she was! But she was also shocked by the way she had been treated by these people in front of her. 'My mother was barely eighteen!' Marie-France glared round the room. 'Not much more than a child. Yet you thought you could just pay her off like that and get rid of us. Well you can't.'

'Can't we?' Jilly's mother's eyes flashed. 'From what my daughter has told me, you have inherited your mother's morals. Didn't you make a play for some woman's husband? Phillip, wasn't it?'

Marie-France shot Jilly a baleful how-could-you look. Then she realized they hadn't covered the most important point of all. 'But who is it? Who was my father? Was it Adam?'

Silence.

> 'Or is it,' she continued, pointing a finger at Jeremy in his clerical collar and pink face, '*you*?'

There are several clues in this scene, including the reference to dogs. Marie-France herself has an allergy to dogs so she naturally wonders if Adam might have been her father.

You'll also notice that I didn't write a flashback showing Adam's death. That wouldn't have worked here because it would have reduced the impact of the current scene. However, Adam's death did create a certain amount of gravity, which was tempered by Collette's feisty dialogue.

EXERCISE

Choose a 'tragedy' either from the list above or think of another one. Imagine where you might place it in 'Love Is in the Air' or another novel that might be forming in your head.

Revealing Secret Tragedies

I rather like it when a character has a secret tragedy that comes out during the course of a novel. It can explain so-called 'bad' behaviour or 'moodiness'. Let's take Michelle, who won't leave Chris alone. Perhaps, on the final night, she might confide in Chris on why she's so clingy.

> 'You're probably aware that I've been following you around rather a lot,' she said, now sitting on the opposite side of the table instead of trying to sit next to him. 'The truth is that you remind me of someone.'
>
> That old line again! Chris was always being told that when girls tried to chat him up. He shifted uncomfortably in his seat. 'I'm always being told that.'

'No. Honestly. You do.' Her eyes filled with tears. 'His name was Sam.' Her voice took on a dreamy tone. Chris sat forwards, all ears. She was being more honest now, he sensed, than she'd ever been. 'He was sixteen and he rode a motorbike . . .'

You just know what's coming, don't you? Or do we? Over to you now!

EXERCISE

Write the next few paragraphs, describing what happened and then bringing the reader back to the present. Try to make Michelle more sympathetic than she's been before. It's a classic example of a baddy/unpleasant person becoming nicer, once you've added the reasons behind such behaviour.

Using Black Comedy

I love black comedy! It can be deliciously wicked. It makes you want to laugh but at the same time, you know you shouldn't. Here are some real-life examples:

- Fellow parents were caught having sex at a school ball.
- A friend got her new man's 'appendage' stuck in her dress zip (don't even ask).
- A woman sent a wreath to the wrong funeral (the florist's mistake), declaring herself to be the deceased's 'real love'.

Tragi-comedy can reel the reader in. It gives the character permission to behave badly.

EXERCISE

Take one of the black comedy examples above or make up your own. It doesn't have to fit into 'Love Is in the Air', but make sure you include dialogue as well as action.

How to Prevent Romantic Fiction from Getting Too Morbid

Laughter and black humour aren't always enough. Here are some other tactics:

- bring in a contrasting scene soon afterwards;
- focus on an upbeat character;
- combine with humour;
- use upbeat dialogue, even when referring to the tragedy.

Let's try this out with 'Love Is in the Air'. I'm going to put Chris in a sticky situation. Already, we know that he's got a brilliant story for his newspaper: a secret fly-on-the-wall piece about a singles group in Paris. He knows his editor is going to love it and he also knows that this will save his career. The problem is that if he files his copy (journalist-speak for emailing over his article), Susie will never talk to him again. And, to his surprise, he is falling hook, line and sinker for this feisty team leader who also has a vulnerable side.

I think something tragic is called for to bring matters to a head. But at the same time, I need to make sure that it isn't too misery-heavy.

'I don't believe it.' Chris stared at his iPhone screen.

'What?' asked Susie sleepily as she cuddled up to him in bed.

'It's my editor. She's . . . well she's dead. Heart attack apparently. Bet it was stress.' His heart began to race.

Susie raised herself up on her elbows. 'That's awful.'

'Yes. Yes, it is. But at the same time . . .'

He stopped.

Susie took his hand comfortingly but with a puzzled expression on her face. 'At the same time, what?'

'At the same time, it lets me off the hook,' murmured Chris without being able to stop himself.

Susie looked even more confused. 'I don't understand.'

Chris took a deep breath. 'It's no good. I can't go on hiding it any more. Susie. I must come clean with you. I'm not really an ordinary chap, looking for love. I'm a . . .'

Susie moved away. 'You're a journalist,' she said quietly.

'You knew?'

'Michelle saw the sticker in your passport on the way out.'

This time it was Chris's turn to edge away. 'Then why didn't you say something?'

'Because I need the publicity in order to keep my own job.' She looked away blushing. 'And I was hoping you might write a nice piece.'

This was awful! 'But my editor's dead,' Chris winced. 'Poor woman,' he added as an afterthought. 'And Russ – her deputy – was against this idea in the first place. It won't run now. I'm sorry.'

So we have a death. And although it's sad, it's not morbid because we didn't really know the editor. If, however, you're uncomfortable with this, we could just say that Chris's editor was headhunted for another job and left overnight, as often happens in journalism. Either way, it does have long-reaching effects on the story.

EXERCISES

- Look through a magazine or newspaper to find a tragic story. Think how you could modify it to make a tragic scene either in a short story or a novel.
- Make a list of tragic ideas that might fit in with future stories.
- Do the same with black comedies.

SUMMING UP

- Tragedy can give great depth to a romantic novel.
- Lighten the tragedy with humorous scenes either before or after.
- Time it carefully.
- Use it to increase tension in the plot.
- Don't overdo it.
- Secret tragedies can be teased out.
- A tragedy might turn out to be all right after all.

EXPERT TIPS

When writing romantic comedy, you don't have to make everything too light and jolly, especially at first. All fiction needs conflict, and a great many romantic comedies begin as the hero and/or heroine are in a very bad place – are bereaved, have been dumped, have lost their jobs or their homes. If your story is to hook your reader and keep her reading, your hero and heroine will need to face challenges: the bigger the better.

What makes a romantic comedy funny? The characters, both good guys and bad guys, should have lots of witty, wry or smart one-liners which will make your reader smile. So, as you write, set your own inner comedian free. Your hero and heroine should get into situations which in real life might result in tragedy – for example, the heroine could smash into the hero's beloved Aston Martin, or the hero could destroy the heroine's Mini Clubman – but which in romantic comedy could offer them a chance to get to know each other and for the reader to find out how these two people behave in times of crisis. If they behave well, this will get the reader on their side.

It's often been pointed out that comedy and tragedy are closely related, and this is just so true. I once went to a funeral at which a bird blew in through an open window in the church, flew around having hysterics and then messed all over the coffin. The incongruity of the situation – and remember, incongruity is a vital ingredient of comedy – made it difficult for anyone to keep a straight face.

As your characters walk back to happiness, let them make jokes and get into sticky situations, which will encourage your reader to love them. Provided you can give your hero and heroine their happy-ever-after, almost any starting point can be right for a feel-good romantic comedy. Give your characters a basketful of lemons and let's see if they can make lemonade.

Margaret James, author of *The Wedding Diary*,
www.margaretjamesblog.blogspot.co.uk

I tend to bring in tragedy during the heroine's back-story. What difficult event in her past made her do something that led to her current situation? I once killed off a character's husband which, I must admit, put me in a difficult place. How could I describe this woman who was beaten down by grief? In the end, I decided to make her non-functioning. For her, the world stopped because she couldn't cope. Her mother came in to help but eventually she told her daughter that she had to sort herself out. Then I made my character pick herself up and carry on.

Catherine Jones

14
DEVELOPING GOOD WRITING PRACTICE

It's all very well having a great romantic fiction idea and dreaming up some wonderful characters. It's great too, writing sensuous dialogue and getting into different viewpoints. But if you haven't mastered the technique of good writing practice, you might not get very far with your romantic novel. Good writing practice involves all kinds of factors. It's:

- finding the right time to write;
- finding a space where it's comfortable to write;
- choosing the best way to write (longhand or keyboard or voice recognition);
- being a responsible author;
- presenting your work professionally;
- revising your work before sending it off.

Finding the Right Time to Write

When I first started writing, I didn't have the luxury to choose a writing time. My children were little and got up early, which meant I couldn't rise before dawn to scribble a chapter as they were already awake! One in particular took ages to sleep at night, which meant I couldn't write at night either. Instead, I would get up early at weekends and write then.

It wasn't a great recipe for family life. But I still managed to complete a novel in a year. If your own personal routine makes it difficult to find the time to write, consider the following actions:

- cutting something out of your list of regular activities to free time;

- asking a friend to have the children for one day a week;
- making a time-management programme to see if there are any gaps you could use for writing;
- writing while you're on the train/bus to work;
- writing during your lunch hour at work.

Along the way, you may well find that you write better at certain times of the day. My preferred choice has always been the morning. I'm fresher and brighter and the ideas from the night before are still in my head. They tend to flood in when I'm half-asleep so I always have a notepad by my side.

Now my children are older, I have been known to get up at 5.30 or 6 a.m. I write in my dressing gown without the distraction of the phone or the dog barking at the postman. Brilliant! Many writers swear by the early-morning approach. As the writer Dorothea Brande pointed out in her brilliant book, *Becoming a Writer*, an author is in an almost meditative state between getting up and 'doing'. This can create some extraordinary prose.

However, it is possible to teach yourself to write at a different 'optimum' time. When I was a single mother, between marriages, I took on various writing jobs outside the home. At the same time, I was writing a novel. So I had no choice but to write at night. At first, I was exhausted but then I discovered I got a 'second wind'. The situation also had the added benefit of making me write in a slightly different way. My characters became night owls and heard sounds through my ears at midnight that they wouldn't have heard in the morning.

Finding the Right Place to Write

Personally I think that it's comforting to have one writing base but to also 'visit' different writing locations every now and then to glean extra stimulus. I have a study at the top of the house, although for years I used to write at the kitchen table. But I also travel a lot on trains, which is great for giving me character and plot ideas. Funnily enough, although I need complete peace at home when writing, I don't mind a certain amount of chitchat on trains as it can add to my imagination repertoire.

We also moved to the coast a few years ago and I found, to my surprise, that this changed my writing. My settings were no longer landlocked and the sea became a character in its own right. I'm lucky enough to travel for my work (I speak at writing festivals all over the world) and I always take my laptop. It's amazing how writing a scene while sitting on a patio overlooking an olive grove can give you a different voice. So too, can the Docklands railway!

EXERCISE

Using your normal writing place, write a scene involving two characters from 'Love Is in the Air'. Perhaps they're coming to the end of the week now. Maybe they've made a decision about each other. Then take your laptop and move to another room in the house or go out to a café and rewrite the scene. Do the same on a bus or train, and – if you work – at your office desk during the lunch hour.

My bet is that these different venues will give you ideas for plot and character and setting.

Choosing the Best Way to Write

My background is in journalism so I have been writing on a keyboard since I was twenty-one. In fact, I find it difficult to write longhand now. But the other day, as an experiment, I used a proper ink pen to write a page of prose. The effect was extraordinary! I found myself thinking about each word much more carefully. Yes, the pace was slower, but it gave me some different ideas.

Some of my writer friends suffer from repetitive strain injury (RSI) and have turned to voice recognition. They say it's changed their writing style for the better, simply by making their brain work in a different way.

EXERCISE

Take the scene you have just written. Rewrite it using a different method from last time. If you wrote it by hand, try to type it, or vice versa. If possible, experiment with voice recognition.

Backing Up Your Writing

If your computer goes wrong, the first thing that a smart alec will ask is 'Have you backed up?' We know we ought to but it isn't always easy to remember, especially when you're in full flow. Here are some tips that might help:

- Send each day's work to yourself as an email.
- Copy in a friend who can be trusted to keep your work-in-progress in their inbox without reading it.
- Back up every day onto a memory stick.
- There are also 'storage units' online that might be worth considering.

Making Sure You Are an Ethical Author

We discussed earlier in the book the danger of hurting people's feelings. It's horribly easy to do this in any kind of genre but especially in romantic fiction and sex scenes. Husbands, partners and siblings tend to be particularly sensitive and can be 'certain' that they recognize themselves, even when nothing could be further from the truth.

There's no easy answer to this. Most writers have a certain toughness inside that they themselves don't always want to acknowledge. I can't advise you to write the scene and be damned.

I can only point out that the problem exists. However, personally, I think one needs to be true to oneself. That might mean writing what you want but refining it so you don't hurt others' feelings.

It's also very easy to write about real people without realizing. This can be the subconscious creeping in or it might be down to a bad coincidence. I know of one writer who picked a character's name out of a phone book. It was an unusual name but she was certain she didn't know anyone who was called it so she thought she was safe. However, it turned out that she had briefly been introduced to someone with that name at a party. As a result, there were all kinds of problems.

EXERCISE

Go through all your characters' names and descriptions. Is there a chance that they might resemble someone you know? If so, consider changing their sex, appearance, name, job and/or geographical location.

Presenting Your Work

With today's technology, editors expect novels and short stories to be word perfect and neatly typed. I have some writer friends who write by hand and then type up their work or find someone to do it for them. Obviously this is expensive so it might be worth investing in a touch-typing course.

Some writers pay to have their work professionally edited. There are pros and cons to this. If a writer isn't capable of writing in the way that's expected, how is he or she going to cope if the novel is accepted? On the other hand, there are some brilliant writers out there who haven't been taught how to write. And there's no doubt that certain basic writing skills *can* be learned, however old you are.

Most publishers and short-story editors like a clean font such as Times Roman or Arial and a readable point size, such as 12 or 14.

Also make sure that your manuscript is double spaced. Here are some other points to consider.

- Quotation marks: if you're writing a novel, the preferred style is generally single quotation marks. However, most magazine short-story editors prefer double.
- Dashes and hyphens: use sparingly. Don't litter the page with them.
- Paragraphs: generally speaking, each page needs at least two or three. You need a new paragraph when making a new point/moving to a 'gear change' in the plot/every time a character speaks.
- And/But: it's generally acceptable nowadays to start a sentence this way although house styles do vary.
- Chapters: make sure they are numbered correctly and that each new chapter begins on a different page.
- Numbering: your novel/short story should have page numbers. In my version of Word, I find Insert and then look along the bar for the part that says 'Page Number'.
- Identity: if you are sending your short story on paper, put your name and contact details on each page. If emailing (see Chapter 15), put your contact details on the first page. A novel only needs to have the contact details on the first page although it can be wise to include the title on each page.
- Synopsis: a synopsis isn't necessary for a short story (see Chapter 15). However, it's vital for a novel. It can be written in single spacing.

Reading Out Loud

I only learned the value of this a few years ago. Now I wonder how I managed without reading each chapter or short story out loud. It's crucial to do this from the printed page rather than the screen. For some reason, you pick up more mistakes that way. You will also get to 'read' the rhythm after a while. For instance, you'll find yourself catching your breath if a sentence is too long or if the line needs a break in the form of a comma or a full stop.

EXERCISE

Read out one of your passages from a printed-out copy and see what changes you make to it.

Asking Other People's Opinions

It's so hard to know if your novel or short story is any good. After a while, you are so familiar with it that you're beyond self-criticism. This is why many authors ask a friend or relation to read it. That might sound a good idea but I'd advise you to choose that person carefully. Someone too close to you might be critical (in which case you could both end up hurt); too keen to praise (this won't help); or feel threatened (is the hero/heroine too close for comfort?). Writing groups can react in the same way although I do have one very famous writer friend who reads out certain chapters to her group in order to get feedback. Then again, her group contains some very good writers in their own right so they are more likely to give professional, considered opinions.

Appraisal services can also be useful. However, choose one carefully. Ask questions about the tutors. What kind of books do they write? Have they been published? If so, do they specialize in your kind of genre? How many writers have they helped to get published? It's important to ascertain this as you will be paying an average of £200–£500 for a 100,000 word novel.

Revising Your Work

Revision can mean the difference between getting published and not getting published. It's not just a matter of checking there aren't any typos. It's also making sure that you have:

Consistent characters

During the novel, you might well have decided that your character looks different/has a different job or lover. Be prepared, during the revision process, to change some of these elements in the earlier part of the novel. It's normal! In fact, I'd be worried if you didn't.

No plot holes

It's very easy, in the passion of writing, to create a plot that doesn't stand up. Revision gives you the chance to find those holes and repair them.

HELPFUL HINT

This is also a great time to add another twist to your plot. While revising, you might spot a missed opportunity to do something with one of your characters. Remember Chris's ex-girlfriend Rosie whom we only briefly alluded to at the beginning? Maybe we could drop her in at the end by revealing that she heads the employment agency that hired Susie on behalf of Single Again.

There's no reason why Susie would connect Rosie with Chris. And, as there's been an argument, there's no reason why Rosie would have known that Chris had wangled himself a place on the trip. All might be revealed when Chris writes a glowing review of Single Again for his new editor at the paper. Rosie will then see his name. Not only will she be thrilled by the publicity for 'her' client but she will also confess to Susie that she used to know the journalist in question and that she still has feelings for him. Susie would then be in a tricky situation because she's in love with her boss's ex.

But wait a minute! There's a problem with this. We've already decided that Russ, the deputy editor, wasn't keen on the singles story in the first place but had been over-ruled by the editor. Now the latter has gone, the story won't be published. Or will it?

Dilemmas like these are very common when it comes to plotting. In fact, you don't always notice the holes until you start revising. When you do, you might not instantly think of a way out. That's when I'd advise having a break and doing something completely different. At some point, either today or tomorrow or in a few days' time, you will find that a solution comes to you out of the blue.

Suppose, for instance, Russ is moved to the showbiz section of the paper after a reshuffle. To his amazement, Chris finds himself promoted to Features Editor. Then he is free to run the story and, in so doing, finds himself in hot water when Rosie discovers he's having a relationship with Susie. Complicated? Good! Romantic fiction needs to keep your reader guessing.

It's funny how twists like this don't always occur to you when you're writing the main bulk of the novel. It's only when you're going back and seeing the story in its entirety that the scope for extra subplots is revealed.

The revision period is also a good time to go back and drop in clues, which make the later part of the plot more believable. For instance, at the beginning of 'Love Is in the Air', Chris might mention that his ex-girlfriend was rather bossy because she worked in the 'employment business' and was used to telling people what to do.

The correct timeline and structure

Again, we all get carried away. During the revision process, you can make sure that someone doesn't get out of bed twice in one page! Or that a pregnancy takes eleven months . . .

Also make sure that each chapter is roughly the same length (I aim for around 3,000–4,000 words) and that it ends on something that makes the reader want to go on. There should be something eventful happening in each chapter. There also needs to be at least one big problem to be solved plus several little ones to keep readers on their toes. And there needs to be a happy ending that is clear. Few editors like romantic novels to end with a question mark.

While writing, it's essential to make a note of all your character details and plot events in a sturdy notebook. Then, while revising, you can check these details to ensure you've been consistent. You may well have decided to change a character name or you might have misspelt it by mistake. Your notebook could be your saving grace.

Read each chapter out loud from a paper copy and make alterations on the screen as you go along.

SUMMING UP

- Take another look at your writing routine and play around with different writing times and locations.
- Revise thoroughly.
- Consider the pros and cons of showing your work to someone else.
- Make sure your novel or short story is professionally laid out.
- Back it up. You don't want to lose it.

EXPERT TIPS

A professional editor can be an invaluable guide and in time your confidence will grow and the process will become easier. It's about taking time to make it the best book it can be; discovering your inner editor; and then trusting your instincts.

Helen Bryant, director of Cornerstones Literary Consultancy, www.cornerstones.co.uk, co-writer of *Write a Blockbuster and Get it Published*, co-publisher of Three Hares Publishing

Don't send your work out into the world until it's completely polished. Unless you're very experienced, it's not always possible to do this yourself. A new writer doesn't know the way that agents and editors think. The management of viewpoint is a case in question. A consultant can stop people from sailing ahead and making an easily remedied mistake. Much better than carrying on with the same error for the rest of that book – and future ones too!

How should you find a literary consultant? Choose one who advertises in reputable publications such as *Author* magazine or *The Writers' & Artists' Yearbook*. Also find out how much experience the consultant has and his/her background.

Hilary Johnson, director of the Hilary Johnson Authors' Advisory Service, www.hilaryjohnson.com

If you are writing historical romance, never let the history take over. You should know everything about the period yourself and keep descriptions and facts as accurate as possible, but for the reader it should only be a backdrop while the romance takes centre stage. If you're writing general historical fiction, however, where the romance is only incidental or a small part of the story, you can put in a lot more historical detail. Think about who you're aiming at – is it a reader who wants a sweeping romance or a history buff? (It could of course be both, but usually the story will be aimed more at one than the other.)

Christina Courtenay, chairman of the Romantic Novelists' Association, author of *The Secret Kiss of Darkness*

- Try to write every day even if it is only for a short time. This means that you keep writing the story in your head in the twenty-four hours in between.
- Once you have started your novel, write it as quickly as possible. Ideas, words, everyday life, cultural references change all the time and suddenly a perfectly good novel can sound tired.

- Beware of (even small) things which will sound out of date by the time the novel is delivered to the agent, never mind to the bookshop!
- Don't give up the day job. The best novels are often the ones inspired by the world in which the writer lives and works, and written within time constraints.
- When submitting to an agent or publisher, a strong, intriguing title in an email 'Subject' box will catch their eye, e.g. *The Apothecary's Daughter*, Charlotte Betts.
- Never send your short pitch letter as an attachment, always in the body of an email.
- A blurb accompanying the proposal/manuscript shows the recipient that you know how the book would be pitched on the back cover.
- Read, read, read again the type of fiction you admire and wish to emulate, ideally a bestseller. Don't use the idea of 'unintentional osmosis' or concerns about inadvertently 'stealing ideas' as a reason not to read in your genre – you must!
- A real sense of place, be it Oxford, Somerset, the TV world, a family, a home, often gives your novel an extra appeal to both readers and TV producers – *cf* Morse in Oxford. Readers like to read about a familiar world or to escape into an unknown one which potentially fascinates them.
- Try just to tell a good story as though you were talking to a girlfriend over a glass of wine.
- Jilly Cooper manages a cast of characters brilliantly but I suggest writers don't overdo the number of characters in their novel unless they are writing a BIG story, à la Penny Vincenzi. The reader wants to get to know and love (or otherwise) the central characters and also to be able to remember who's who and what they stand for. Going backwards to check something – particularly difficult with a Kindle – is not good.

- Heroes and heroines are flawed; that's why we like them.
- First person or third? There are editors out there who really don't like first-person novel submissions. I have had a senior one refuse to see something when they discovered it was 'I'.
- Authors should avoid writing a novel thinly disguised as their autobiography!
- Don't lose heart at the end – so many fiction submissions we see suggest that the author has slightly given up the ghost by that point!
- In my book, romantic novels require happy, resolved endings.

Heather Holden-Brown, HHB Agency Ltd,
www.hhbagency.com

15
HOW TO GET PUBLISHED

Have you ever read a book and wondered how on earth it got published? I certainly have. Similarly, I've read quite a few manuscripts by talented writers that have been turned down by agents. Sometimes it seems that there's no rhyme or reason when it comes to getting published. But that's not surprising as writing is a subjective game. There are no rules for getting it right or wrong.

There are, however, some great tips on how to maximize your chance of getting published. And that's exactly what this chapter is all about.

Getting Your Short Story Accepted

There's an enormous difference between getting short stories published and hitting the jackpot with your novel. Don't make the mistake that it's 'easier' to get a short story accepted. It's not. In fact, I know many published novelists who can't get the hang of shorter fiction. There is also a different publication route to follow.

The best market for romantic short fiction is the magazine world. There are still some big magazines out there that publish fiction regularly. They need good stories to fill their pages week after week. Here are some examples:

- *Woman's Weekly*
- *My Weekly*
- *People's Friend*
- *Fiction Feast*
- *Yours*

Each magazine has a list of guidelines which they expect contributors to examine carefully before sending in a story. It's worth noting that these change regularly.

Guidelines don't just refer to content: they also tell you how the story should be presented. For instance, *Woman's Weekly* likes double quotation marks instead of single. It's also essential to follow the rules on how to submit your story. Some magazines are happy for you to send in email submissions. Others prefer paper. Certain magazines request an 800 word count while others are more flexible: anything from 900 to 3,000 plus.

The trick, as I said in my chapters on plot and character, is to make your story stand out with warm, irresistible characters. However, if you don't follow the guidelines, even the best stories could fall by the wayside.

Here are some other points to consider before sending off your short story:

- You don't need an agent.
- Your covering letter can be brief. The fiction editor will be more interested in your story than your background although it's worth mentioning that the story was inspired by a certain event or if you've won a writing prize.
- Never send the same story to more than one magazine. It's very bad etiquette.
- You may have to wait three months to hear whether a story has been accepted or not.
- Make a note, in a special notepad, of the stories you have sent; where to; and when. After three months, it's perfectly acceptable to send a gentle email or make a courteous phone call to ask if the magazine received it.
- Consider foreign markets such as fastfiction@pacificmags.com.au. You can resell stories that have been published in the UK, provided your contract allows this. There is often a time period before you can do this.

Short stories can be quite lucrative. You can earn between £80 and £300 per story, depending on the magazine.

If you succeed in getting a story published, pat yourself on the back and then register it with the Authors' Licensing and Collection Society (ALCS). This organization will pay you every time someone photocopies your story. This also applies to journalist articles and novels published abroad. Don't ask me how they do it but it can result in an unexpected handout every now and then – which you must declare in your tax.

You can, of course, publish your own short stories on the internet. See the section on internet publishing below.

Getting Your Novel Published: The Traditional Route

You don't need me to tell you that publishing your own work via the internet (both digitally and in paper format) has become far more acceptable than it has ever been before. I'm going to go into more depth about that later on. However, there is still an overriding feeling that it's more 'professional' to be published by a publisher who has bought the rights to your book.

I'm going to explain how this works now and also give you some tips on how to secure that deal.

Most publishers will only look at a novel if it comes through an agent, although there are some notable exceptions, such as Choc Lit. Finding an agent can be just as tough, if not tougher, than finding a publisher – but it's not impossible! You could start off by going down the traditional route of sending the first three chapters and the synopsis of your novel to an agent listed in *The Writers' & Artists' Yearbook* (which also lists publishers who don't need agents). A synopsis is a one- or two-page summary of your plot, usually told in the present tense in single spacing. It needs to say what happens from beginning to end so is best written after you've finished the novel. Don't confuse it with the 'blurb' that appears on the back of a jacket cover and ends with uncertainty, e.g. 'But what happens after they walk off into the sunset . . .'

You can also 'pick up' an agent through serious networking. Join organizations like the Romantic Novelists' Association which holds regular events with agents and publishers. Sign up for writing festivals such as the Festival of Romance (http://festivalofromance.co.uk) and search online for 'writing festivals'. Look for those which offer one-to-one appointments where you can take part of your manuscript to show an agent or publisher. There's nothing like a face-to-face meeting to sell your wares! And in the last few years, there have been an increasing number of unknown authors who have been signed up in this way. Don't ignore foreign festivals either. I'm a regular speaker at the Women's Matera Fiction Festival in Italy (which takes place at the end of September). It's a great way to meet agents from all over the world, including the United States. Go to talks held by authors as well as classes. I'm proud to say that I put one of my students in touch with an agent who subsequently took her on.

If you do get taken on by an agent, you might be expected to do some work to your novel. However, some agents 'edit' more than others. A good agent will have a wide network of publishing contacts and will then send your novel off electronically (avoiding the problem of dog-eared manuscripts from a few years ago). If you are taken on by a publisher, you may be given a one- or two-book deal. You should also be given an 'advance', which might be anything from £500 to a six-figure sum. However, one agent whom I spoke to put the average advance for a first-time novel as roughly in the area of £3,000 to £15,000.

You will then be given an editor who will send you pages of notes on how to rewrite or clarify certain parts of your novel. After that, it will be copyedited: in other words, a copy editor will go through it with a highly charged toothcomb and point out inconsistencies – even if you think you've ironed those out during revision. Don't be alarmed by this. It's perfectly normal! Then there are the proofs to go through which you, as the writer, will be expected to go through, along with the proofreader. After that, you have to help promote it through social media and interviews. And then, finally, the book is presented to the book trade (booksellers and digital sellers) and you hope that it sells enough for you to get royalties one day.

Sounds exhausting, doesn't it? The outcome is very uncertain too, which is why an increasing number of writers are going down the digital route. However, on the plus side, you have that wonderful kudos of being published by someone who thinks your story is worth paying you for. Another big plus is that you know your novel has been professionally edited – and that you haven't had to pay for it.

When you get your novel published, make sure you register it for Public Lending Right (PLR). Then, every time someone borrows your book from the library, you receive a small sum. This can add up over the years. (See Useful Contacts for details.)

EXPERT TIP

My advice on getting published is to read, read, read. The more romantic fiction you read, the better romantic fiction you'll write and, importantly, the more aware you'll be of the current market. Like any skill, the more you do it, the more you'll learn and improve. So, write as much as you can too. Start with just a few minutes every day, whenever you can, and build from there. When the first draft is complete, edit, and then edit some more. Be brutal and make sure that every word has earned its place, that every chapter is pushing the novel forward. Make every page say 'yes'. When you think your romantic novel is the best it can be, research potential agents, or possibly potential publishers, and make sure you've selected people who would be a good match for you. Pay attention to submission guidelines and adhere to them. Alongside this, start social networking, attend writing events and meet other writers/agents/editors in

> your genre. The RNA [Romantic Novelists' Association] is a great opportunity for this. Remember too that writing is hugely subjective and remain determined. Don't give up. Agents and publishers are on your side. They want to discover brilliant romantic fiction, and without you, the genre can't survive.
>
> Clare Wallace, agent at the Darley Anderson Literary, TV and Film Agency

Getting Your Novel Published: The Self-Publishing Route

An increasing number of romantic novels are now self-published.

Many established publishers trawl through self-published books to look for hidden gems. Author Kerry Fisher is one of several authors who have been offered a traditional deal as the result of being self-published. You can read her story at the end of this chapter.

However, it's important to be aware that there are several self-publishing routes. You can pay a company to help you self-publish although the cost will depend on how much work you want them to do. This might range from physically putting it online; printing it on paper; professional editing; and publicity.

Here's a list of contacts that might be able to help:

- Lulu (www.lulu.com)
- Smashwords (www.smashwords.com)
- Author House (www.authorhouse.co.uk)
- Matador (www.troubador.co.uk/matador.asp)

Warning!

Before parting with any money, check out the company by searching online to see what other clients have said about it.

HELPFUL HINT

There are also several online sites where you can post examples of your work. Publishers have been known to pick up authors from these too. Take a look at www.youwriteon.com.

You could also approach an independent publisher. Most don't give advances but pay royalties. The amount varies. Tried and tested companies include Endeavour Press (www.endeavourpress.com) and Corazon Books (www.greatstorieswithheart.com), which publishes commercial women's fiction and pays competitive monthly royalties on sales. For more organizations, contact the Alliance of Independent Authors (www.allianceindependentauthors.com).

Doing it yourself

You can also publish your own novel or short story without any professional help – although this can be very hard work.

For a print book, take a look at Create Space (www.createspace.com). For e-books, consider Kindle Direct Publishing (www.kdp.amazon.co.uk), Kobo Books (www. kobobooks.com) or Appleibookstore (www.apple.com).

HELPFUL HINT

Harper Collins has a digital arm called Impulse (www.harperimpulseromance.com) which is open to e-book submissions.

Entering Competitions

This is another way to get noticed, both for short stories and novels: look out for magazines that run writing competitions. Certain monthlies such as *Woman & Home* and *Good Housekeeping* have done so in the past and will hopefully continue to do so. I also recommend *Writing Magazine* and *Writers' Forum*, which run regular competitions as well as publishing lists of national events such as the Bridport Prize and the Harry Bowling Prize.

Before my first novel was published, I was lucky enough to win two major national awards as well as being runner-up for the Harry Bowling Prize. This definitely helped my covering letter to an agent.

Remember:

- It's normal to be asked for a competition entry fee.
- Never send the same entry to more than one competition unless you are certain you haven't been placed in the first.
- Read the rules carefully.

How Not to Get Published

Some writers are too scared to finish their novel in case it is not accepted. This fear of failure is very understandable. But don't give in. Better to have dared to do than not to do at all. In fact, that might make a title for a short story or a novel!

So be brave and persevere . . .

EXPERT TIP

Our short stories are always upbeat, coffee-morning type reads with likeable main characters. They are aimed at the 40+ market. Second time around love is a good theme, as is parenting teens and juggling being a busy mum whether single or in a marriage. Stories with pets also do well.

If a debut novelist wanted to be considered, he or she would need to get in touch (fiction@candis.co.uk) or get their agent to do so, give us some background info on themselves and their new book – being able to send a review copy, either hard copy or digital download, is helpful. They will need to have a release date or if released have reviews on Amazon that can be read. Then I'll get back to them if I think they're right for Candis and if we have a suitable slot – I can only commission twelve short stories a year after all!

Debbie Attewell, editor of *Candis* magazine

EXPERT TIPS: HOW I GOT PUBLISHED

Yes, the romantic fiction world is tough. But you can get there. After all, others have succeeded after a long battle. Here's a selection of real-life experiences, starting with my own:

I finally got published (after several near-misses) when Betty Schwartz, who was then head of the slushpile at Hodder, rang me up one day and told me that she was certain I would 'make it' in the future. She gave me the confidence to keep going – and she also put me in touch with an agent who sold my first novel. My success was down to perseverance, luck, contacts and having an idea that caught the imagination of an editor at the right time.

Janey Fraser, AKA Sophie King,
www.janeyfraser.co.uk and www.sophieking.info

Read a lot, write a lot, learn to take criticism but also learn to judge when the criticism is right. Persevere. It could take ten years to get published. This is okay!

Kate Fforde

I like to joke that my writing journey goes from chocolate to Choc Lit since it began when my primary school participated in the Cadbury's essay competition and I won a posh tin of chocolates for my story 'My Life as a Cocoa Bean' (with tragic ending). However, the path to publication was one of false starts, procrastination and giving up too soon. Then my dad died of pancreatic cancer and it hit me that if I didn't take my writing seriously, I could run out of time too.

I'd produced lots of articles, both in a professional capacity in my 'proper job' years and as a freelance writer, but it was only by applying myself to the task in hand that I became a published author. I wrote my first novel, *Turning the Tide*, in seven months, but realized that I had to send out a really professional script for anyone to take it seriously. At that point I contacted Hilary Johnson Authors' Advisory Service. Hilary liked the script and sent it to an agent, who requested 'a bigger, darker novel', so I added more twists and the word count went up to 110,000! It was a really useful experience even though, for various reasons, the agent was unable to represent me.

I'd just finished a third draft – all of the good bits and none of the waffle! – when I read in the book press about a new independent publisher called Choc Lit. I sent them a synopsis that same afternoon and was invited to submit the full manuscript. Choc Lit loved it . . . but asked me to make it 10,000 words shorter and change the beginning and ending! Two weeks later I had produced the Goldilocks version we were all happy with and I was offered a contract. Whoever said published writers are just unpublished writers who kept going was right. I hope my story demonstrates that if you believe in what you're doing, that self-belief will carry you through.

Christine Stovell, author of *Follow a Star* and *Move Over Darling*, www.christinestovell.com

My first deal came through a small press and my personal belief is that it came about, not only because it was a good book, but because it wasn't my first book. Or my second book. It came about because having finished my first book, I took classes and workshops and entered contests for feedback. Thereafter, I wrote and finished every book I started, sending each one to agents and publishers. While I waited I wrote and finished another book. It was my fifth book that was picked up by a small press and then the next book by a larger press. Finally, after several rounds of well-aimed revisions, I was offered a contract by Harlequin Mills and Boon. I would say a good part of the process for me was perseverance. My publishing tip is to enjoy the writing and it will show and to try to do whatever your editor wants, even if it is not exactly the way she/he suggests you do it.

Ann Lethbridge, author of *The Return of the Prodigal Gilvry* and *Falling for the Highland Rogue*, www.annlethbridge.com

I was on the Romantic Novelists' Association's New Writers' Scheme [NWS] for an embarrassingly long time. I wrote seven novels in seven years. All but one of them went to second reads and then on to a top agent, all of whom said complimentary and encouraging things about my writing but who, alas, declined to represent me. All of those seven novels were contemporary. I was determined to get a novel published so I decided to change genre and wrote a historical romance – *To Turn Full Circle*. The NWS organizer suggested I send it directly to Choc Lit as no agent is required to submit to them. This I did and about six months later I was given a contract. *To Turn Full Circle*, the first in a trilogy, was published in June 2012. The sequel, *Emma: There's No Turning Back*, was published in January 2014.

And all those back novels? A chop and a change, adding a viewpoint here, cutting a character there, and they, too, are starting to make it into print.

Holding your book in your hand isn't the end game, it's just the beginning. You should be prepared to be seen and heard to publicize your book. If you have a local, independent, bookseller then go and introduce yourself and ask if you can do a book-signing with them. A short piece in your local newspaper could garner further sales. And it goes, almost without saying, that a writer needs to become Facebook- and Twitter-savvy today.

Oh . . . and one last bit of advice when you've sent off your manuscript . . . don't sit around waiting to hear its fate – get on with the next!'

Linda Mitchelmore

I have always had a passion for reading (mostly historical fiction) and in 1992 I decided to try my hand at short-story and article writing. I joined Brixham Writers' Group and over the next few years was lucky to achieve publishing success in magazines such as: *My Weekly*, *Woman's Weekly*, *Take a Break*, *That's Life*, *Yours* and the *Daily Telegraph*.

I then looked to turn my hand to novel writing. My first, *Megan*, was an historical romance. The inspiration came from my own mother who, at the age of sixteen, left South Wales to work as a kitchen maid in Bristol.

Megan took me four years to write (with three rewrites) and another two years to get published. Going through rejection after rejection (often made worse by such comments as – they liked it very much but . . .) can be a painful process. At this stage it's easy for some writers to lose heart . . . I say don't! If you believe in your characters as I believed in Megan's story, then you have to stick with it.

While *Megan* (three chapters and synopsis) was doing the rounds, I decided to start work on book two, *Rhiannon*. My work in the theatre provided the inspiration.

My writing colleagues often tell me how much they admired my determination to stick with *Megan* and liken me to a terrier with a bone. My reward came in March 2008. I heard from publisher Robert Hale Ltd, he said he wanted to publish it. He also asked for the first option on my next two books. My second book came out in 2010 and my third in 2012. My fourth, *WOMEN OF STRAW*, should be finished shortly. I've been told that to be a successful author, publishers expect a book a year. We'll see!

Carole Llewellyn, author of
For the Love of Catherine and *Rhiannon*

I'd wanted to write historical romance since my teens. I finally had a serious go in my thirties. I sent it out to suitable publishers and it was rejected. I joined a writing group, listened to speakers, founded a critique group and learned. I rewrote my book a few times then sent it out – and it was bought.

The publisher was a small one and the editor had time to do a thorough editing job, which took me to a whole new level. Getting published is rarely speedy or easy, and why should it be? Any skill takes time. Our first efforts are rarely worth seeing in print, even though we're all sure that our first finished novel is a work of brilliance which will bring publishing to its knees.

Jo Beverley

I went through the usual route of trying to find an agent but got fed up after four years. So I self-published and got an agent and a publisher on the same day! Below is some of my advice on how to write romantic fiction:

1) Watch how people in love – or not – act. Look beyond the clichés of rocking up with red roses, ripping each other's clothes off in the hallway or the opposite, rowing endlessly. If you watch couples in cafés, in the street, at dinner parties, love is often very subtle. Build a picture of a relationship with tiny details. Does he catch her eye across the table when someone else is spouting nonsense or does he talk over her? Does he remind her to take her gloves/tell her to park under the light in the station car park? Does she roll her eyes when someone mentions how hard her husband works? Touch his shoulder as she squeezes past? Squirt de-icer on his windscreen when she does her own? Kick his shoes out of the way in the porch? There are hundreds of telling details that show the state of a relationship other than the obvious ones.

2) First person lends itself very well to romantic comedy. It's brilliant for exposing the internal dialogue your characters have when they first meet a potential partner. It also shows the difference between their hopes and the eventual compromise.

3) To write a convincing love story, the protagonists need to be carrying baggage from their previous relationships. You don't have to tell the reader precisely what went on before. However, your characters will be more believable if you know that your protagonist feels the need to cut short her phone conversations with her friends because her ex hated her spending time gossiping. Or that she hates being the first to arrive in a restaurant because her husband was always half an hour late.

Kerry Fisher, author of *The School Gate Survival Guide*, www.kerryfisherauthor.com

I worked for many years as a journalist on newspapers and women's magazines and I think this helped when it came to finding a publisher. Publishers know that journalists are used to writing fast and to length and to knowing their market inside out. We're also accustomed to having our work critiqued by editors, and to pitching ideas which is useful when it comes to publicity.

Being a writer already, I imagined that the transition to books would be fairly straightforward. I did find, however, that it took a while to let go and allow myself what seemed like the luxury of description. In journalism, of course, everything is pared down. When I started writing my first novel I think my prose was a little staccato, but I soon loosened up.

Emma Burstall, author of three novels, *Gym and Slimline*, *Never Close Your Eyes* and *The Darling Girls*

I learned how to write by failing. I wrote several manuscripts, all of which were rejected many times. I did get discouraged, but by then I was addicted to writing and I couldn't have stopped for anything. Eventually I noticed that my rejections were getting better – there would be specific feedback from an editor or an agent, or I would get a request for my next novel, even though this one wasn't quite right. I felt that I was learning and getting better with every book that I wrote, and with every rejection, I would send out another submission.

As an unpublished author, I joined the Romantic Novelists' Association (RNA) in the UK and Romance Writers of America (RWA), and they gave me my first boosts toward publication. The RNA's New Writers' Scheme gave me valuable feedback on my early manuscripts. With that in mind, I entered the RWA's Golden Heart, which is the biggest contest in the world for unpublished romance writers, and I ended up being shortlisted with my fourth completed manuscript. This helped me catch the eye of both an editor and an agent, and after three years of constant writing and many rejections, I ended up signing with an agent and being offered my first publishing deal within a month or two of being shortlisted for the Golden Heart. Writers' organizations like these can be great networking opportunities for unpublished authors and you can learn a lot from more experienced members.

Julie Cohen, author of numerous books including *Dear Thing* and *The Summer of Living Dangerously*, www.julie-cohen.com

Competing for the Janey Fraser Prize

This is your chance to get published! In this book, you and I have already started writing a romantic novel about a group of singles on a week's trip to Paris. But there's no reason why it couldn't make a short story too. I'm now going to set you a challenge!

Send me the first chapter of 'Love Is in the Air' (maximum of 3,500 words) or a short story drawn from the 'Love Is in the Air' plot (between 800 and 2,000 words) by the end of May 2015. I will publish the winner and two runners up on my website. I will also pass the top three entries to an agent.

HELPFUL HINT

Begin by drawing a tree diagram of the plot as described in 'Using Mindmaps for Planning' in Chapter 4.

I suggest doing a 'story so far'. Here's a brief résumé of some of the scenes we've written followed by some 'questions to self'. This is a good way of triggering other ideas. You might want to put these scenes in a different order or even change them altogether. You will see that I often have the phrase 'Note to self'. This is to remind myself that certain areas need looking at.

The story so far

Susie has just started a new job as a group leader in charge of a singles trip in Paris. She is worried about her widowed mother and she's also trying to get over a failed relationship with James, partly because he still had feelings for his ex-girlfriend. One of the women in her group (Michelle) is sure that Chris, who was late for the trip, is really a journalist. Susie hasn't confronted him yet because she hopes that he might give them good publicity.

One night, drowning her sorrows at the bar, she finds herself falling for a good-looking Frenchman who continues to pursue her all week. So too does Chris. Then her boyfriend from home turns up.

Questions to self: Who does she choose (if any)? Who is the baddy in disguise? What role does her mother play? What if her ex-boyfriend's former girlfriend is part of the group without her knowing? Could there be a big drama that binds the group together?

Chris, a journalist, is on a final warning at work. He's messed up several jobs because he's been too kind to the people he's interviewed. Now he's decided he's got to be tougher to please his editor who has sent him to Paris to 'get a story'. He is also getting over a relationship with a girl called Rosie. Chris overhears his name being called by a singles group leader. It's not him but he decides to masquerade as the missing member of the group. Then he finds himself attracted to the leader and feels bad about writing an exposé on her group.

Questions to self: What happens when the real missing person turns up in Paris, exposing Chris as a fraudster? What happens when his editor dies suddenly of a heart attack – does that let Chris off the hook? What is Chris's own background and how does Rosie, a former girlfriend, fit in? What is he going to do when Michelle blackmails him? His character needs more of a problem than just job issues. Perhaps he's also a single dad – a fact that doesn't come out until halfway through?

Dilly has been working at the airport bar for years. She loves her job because there are always new faces. It's also so busy that it distracts her from thinking. The novel starts on a difficult day – it's an anniversary although the reader doesn't know the details immediately. Then Dilly starts talking to a customer who asks her out. They arrange a date for when he returns from a business trip. But he doesn't arrive.

Questions to self: Why not (plane delayed/something more serious)? He eventually turns up and they end up in bed. But there is a problem (Dilly finds it hard to have a relationship again?). How does she resolve this?

Subplots

What is Michelle's agenda? Do we understand, by the end, why she behaves badly? Is she really James's ex? If so, the two of them will come face-to-face when James comes to Paris to find Susie. Maybe they will get together again; they sound as if they deserve each other.

What is Barry's background? Could he end up with Michelle if the option above doesn't work out or does he have another role?

How does Susie's widowed mother fit in? Does she have a subplot?

What about the missing person who missed his flight at the beginning? What is his story?

Short-story writers

If you want to write a short story instead, you might take one of these threads. Perhaps you could follow Dilly: maybe she had a reputation for helping strangers in distress such as people who have just had to leave loved ones. Then one day, someone helps *her*. Or maybe you could take Chris who is always eavesdropping on conversations. Then he hears something about himself . . .

Or – and this is my favourite – Susie might discover that her ex-boyfriend's ex-girlfriend is indeed Michelle on the trip. However, Michelle is unaware of the connection. She confides in Susie about her failed relationships over the years and makes Susie feel rather sorry for her. Maybe (long shot here) they become friends.

Guidelines

Make sure that:

- the characters are warm and recognizable from each other;
- there are clues suggesting (rightly or wrongly) that someone is a baddy;
- at least one big event happens in the chapter – if it's a short story, there needs to be a 'gear change' in the plot every four or five paragraphs;
- if it's a novel, the chapter ends on a note that makes the reader want to turn the page;
- if it's a short story, it needs to end with a twist and also a sense of warmth – there shouldn't be any open-end conclusions as the readers need to know what finally happens;
- there's plenty of dialogue;
- you 'show' scenes rather than telling them – do this through dialogue, putting the reader in the action rather than saying it happened;

- your language is powerful – instead of 'He kissed her', try, 'He ran his fingers through her hair and then slowly, very slowly, his lips moved down on hers';
- you're clear about viewpoint;
- you've brought in setting/colour/noises/smells/tastes;
- your manuscript is double-spaced in Arial, using 14 point.

Good luck! Please email your entries to janeyfraser@gmail.com by the end of May 2015.

USEFUL CONTACTS

Organizations

Authors' Licensing and Collecting Society (ALCS), www.alcs.co.uk

Public Lending Right, www.plr.uk.com

Romantic Novelists' Association, www.rna-uk.org

Festivals

Chipping Norton Literary Festival, www.chiplitfest.com

Festival of Romance, www.festivalofromance.co.uk

Festival of Writing, www.writersworkshop.co.uk

Matera Women's Fiction Festival, Italy, www.womensfictionfestival.com/en

Winchester Writers Conference, www.writersconference.co.uk

Agencies, Publishers and Consultancies

Author House, publishing services for authors, www.authorhouse.co.uk

Authors Online, self-publishing service, www.authorsonline.co.uk

Book Tango, e-book self-publishing service, www.booktango.com

Booksie, free social publishing site, www.booksie.com

Completely Novel, self-publishing service, www.completelynovel.com/self-publishing/how-to-self-publish

Corazon Books, independent publisher, www.greatstorieswith heart.com

Cornerstones, literary consultancy, www.cornerstones.co.uk

CreateSpace, an Amazon company, self-publishing service, www.createspace.com

Endeavour Press, independent digital publisher, www.endeavourpress.com
FastPrint Publishing, self-publishing service, www.fast-print.net
Hilary Johnson Authors' Advisory Service, literary consultancy, www.hilaryjohnson.com
Issu, hub for links to publishing services, www.issu.com
Lulu, self-publishing service, www.lulu.com
Vook, self-publishing and sales tracking services, www.vook.com
Wikipedia electronic publishing guide, www.en.wikipedia.org/wiki/Electronic_publishing

INDEX